"The story of Harley SwiftDeer as told by Bill Wahlberg speaks of the honesty of friendship. 'I would never betray you,' Wahlberg says to his friend in the beginning of the book. And he doesn't, nor does SwiftDeer betray himself in his own searing self-analysis when revealing his life as a marine in Vietnam, a half-breed Cherokee struggling to find his past, and a practitioner of cures. He is all of these, and his search for truth, which becomes our own, is primal, personal, joyful, and sorrowful."

—Gerald Hausman, author of
Meditations With the Navajo and *Turtle Island Alphabet*

"This book is the story of the spirit of Grandmother Spotted Fawn. Her spirit struggles to guide her grandson, Harley SwiftDeer, through the pain, hate, and violence of today to seek peace. I am sure Grandmother Spotted Fawn tried to arouse in SwiftDeer the awareness of his effect on the people, plants, animals, and rocks around him. When SwiftDeer finally achieves this, it is too late for him to affect the lives of his own family. The spirit's guidance is difficult without personal contact, but she gets help from two 'grandfathers' whom she never meets."

—William C. Smith, Red Bear; principal chief of
the Southeastern Cherokee Confederacy, Inc.

STAR WARRIOR

STAR WARRIOR
THE STORY
OF SWIFTDEER

BILL WAHLBERG

FOREWORD BY
FRANCIS HUXLEY

BEAR & COMPANY
PUBLISHING
SANTA FE, NEW MEXICO

LIBRARY OF CONGRESS CATALOGING-IN-PUBLICATION DATA

Wahlberg, Bill, 1929–
    Star Warrior : the story of SwiftDeer / by Bill Wahlberg :
foreword by Francis Huxley.
    p. cm.
    ISBN 1-879181-07-X
    1. Reagan, Harley SwiftDeer. 2. Shamans—United States—
Biography. 3. Indians of North America—Mixed descent—
Biography.
I. Title.
BF1598.R43W34 1993
299' .7' 092—dc20
[B]   93-3038
                                                                            CIP

Bear & Company, Inc.
Santa Fe, NM 87504-2860

Cover portrait illustration &
frontispiece illustration:
Kathy Sarquist © 1993
Cover design & snake illustration: Marilyn Hager
Interior design: Marilyn Hager
Author photo: Judy Wahlberg
Photos: Courtesy of Harley SwiftDeer Reagan
Editing: Brandt Morgan
Typography: Marilyn Hager

Printed in the United States of America by R.R. Donnelley

1 3 5 7 9 8 6 4 2

With love and appreciation
to my father,
Edgar Malcolm Wahlberg,
1899-1990.

This one's for you, Dad,
dear warrior, dreamer,
father, and friend.
Thanks for holding that space so well
between me and the universe.

❦❦❦ CONTENTS ❦❦❦

Appreciation xi
Foreword by Francis Huxley xiii
Preface by Bill Wahlberg xix
Introduction by Harley SwiftDeer xxv

Prologue: Sundance in Vietnam 3

PART 1: Grandmother Spotted Fawn
First Vision 11
Grandmother Spotted Fawn 15
My Birth 16
Two-Hearted People 19
God's Little Surgeons 29
Smokey 35
Superboy 39
Death of a Tarantula 41
The Rabid Dog 44
Candy Spots and the Bloodgate 46
Second Bloodgate 49

PART 2: Adolescence
Flying 53
Texas Half-Breed Cowboy 63
A Traditional Sexual Initiation 67
My Sexual Initiation 70
First Date 73
False Pregnancy 75
After High School 76

PART 3: War
Vietnam War 81
First Combat 83
Bronze Star 85
Vietnamese Child 87
Mr. Ed Parker and Martial Arts 88

Grandfather Two Bears 93
Grandfather Ding Poan 97
The Last Battle 101
The Final Wound 103

PART 4: The Reagans
Family 115
My Father, Jeff Reagan 116
The Years after Vietnam 126

PART 5: Grandfather Two Bears
Finding Grandfather Two Bears 135
Two Bears and the Graves 144
A Hard Lesson 148
Leukemia 152
The End of a Marriage 156
Excommunication 159
Dance of the Snake 167
Fighting for the Children 172
Raped 177
Bonding Ceremonies 180
Ding Poan's Cigarettes 186
The Cave of the Dead 189
Grandfather Two Bears' Family 198

PART 6: Healing
The Battle of Bloody Heart 203
My Five Sons 213
The Women in My Life 218
The Vietnam Memorial 221

Epilogue: Controversy with Traditionalists 227

Appendix A: The Secret Lodges 239
Appendix B: Genital Sense of Self 244
Appendix C: Chuluaqui Quodoushka: Spiritual Sexuality 249
Appendix D: Heart Pleasuring 254
About the Author 259

❧❧❧ APPRECIATION ❧❧❧

Star Warrior is a reality today because of the continual encouragement, patience, and excitement of my dearest companion: my wife, Judy. You also sundanced, vision quested, were buried in the earth, and faced peril in the desert as together we followed a wonderful vision. Precious and rich years! I love you forever.

I have deep appreciation for the solid support of my family members: my son James Wahlberg, for your brilliant creative contribution; my son Stephen Wahlberg, for your logical and accurate assessments; and my son Lawrence Wahlberg, for your consistent, infectious enthusiasm.

I appreciate my mother, Eunice: you are an amazing role model. Since you wrote a book at age ninety, I was inspired to write at sixty. I thank my sister Lois, for your proofreading and insightful observations. I am grateful to my sister Leah, for your excitement. I thank my eleven-year-old grandson, Jason, because if the chapter about SwiftDeer's sexual initiation was interesting enough for you to read, it must be OK. I give thanks to my aunt and uncle Verna and James Hedlun, for your research and support.

I am grateful for the input from Dr. Robert and Lolly Lurie; Bob, you gave important suggestions about the sexuality chapter. I thank Debbie Fishman, for your open heart: when you read a chapter and cried, I felt good. I appreciate the enthusiastic support of John and David Fishman.

I am also grateful to the people of the Rainbow Bridge Community. You applauded, laughed, and critiqued while I read; you helped me believe the book could be a reality. Hal Milton, your brilliance kept us going when the hill got steep. Thanks, Diane Battung, for your encouragement. David Cooper and Lobo—your computer wizardry kept the "Warrior" on the screen.

And heartfelt gratitude to the Bear & Company family: Barbara Hand Clow, for your brilliant intuition and support; Barbara Doern Drew, for your laserlike precision and pure clarity; Brandt Morgan, your brilliance made this a better book; Marilyn Hager, your beauty

XIISTAR WARRIOR

on so many pages brings happiness to the Warrior; thanks, Hanna Fields, for your important fine-tuning; and Jerry Chasen, for your orderly assault on loose ends in the Bear's lair.

❄❄❄ FOREWORD ❄❄❄

As you will feel as you read this book, Harley SwiftDeer is a remarkably open human being who makes no bones about the kind of man he is and what he has done in his life. In a word, he's approachable, which is not the word that would immediately come to mind when visiting a Native American medicine man of the old school, such as Rolling Thunder, one of SwiftDeer's mentors. I know this because I have had the good fortune to meet with both of them.

When I went to see Rolling Thunder in the company of some friends, we were told that he would lodge and feed us for three days, but that in return we would have to observe the traditional protocol for such a visit. On the first day he would talk to us while we sat quiet; on the second day we could put in a word here and there; and on the third he would ask what had brought us, and we could speak as we wished.

Those three days with Rolling Thunder were a privilege, and it was certainly no hardship to sit quiet for two days while he told us about himself and his work. Indeed, the formality surrounding him was not only a mark of respect that I willingly paid to this remarkable man, but an initiation into Cherokee tradition, where a medicine man puts himself on display so that his visitor may know what to expect from him.

My few encounters with SwiftDeer have been equally satisfying, though in a quite different way. Not for him a three-day visit, with traditional protocol—he welcomes you in, lights up a clove cigarette, and, a can of Dr. Pepper in hand, gets you going in no time. Yes, he will also tell you stories about himself and tantalizing things about what he's gotten up to in the past, but it's all informal and you can always come in with what you want to say. This is because SwiftDeer is not only of Cherokee but also of Irish-American descent; he is at once a medicine man and a Texas half-breed cowboy, not to mention the founder of numerous Deer Tribe Metis Medicine Society lodges around the world. He belongs, you might think, to another tradition entirely, where protocol is of little importance.

But once you start reading this book, you will be in the position of one who spends the first of three days with a traditional medicine man, having to bottle up any questions you may have. Here SwiftDeer gives his credentials as a medicine man of our days, starting with his earliest years and his first vision, telling us what it was like to have a rough father and a Cherokee grandmother and then to live through terrible days in Vietnam and in a military hospital. Then he gives an account of his prowess in the martial arts, of the failure of his first marriage, and of what this did to the lives of his children. He follows with the details of his apprenticeship to the Navajo medicine man Tom Wilson and of some of the ceremonies that put him on the road to become the eighteenth dreamer's *nagual* on the Eighteenth Feathered Winged Serpent Wheel at the thirteenth gateway.

At the end of the book, SwiftDeer forestalls a number of questions that may have been stirring in your mind by speaking about the nature of secret lodges and of spiritual sexuality. By that time you will find that there are only two questions worth asking SwiftDeer. The first is, why should we believe that he is the eighteenth dreamer's *nagual* of Turtle Island, and the second is, just what does that mean anyhow?

The best way to find out the answer to both questions is to walk the same road that SwiftDeer has traveled, with him as guide. For as the Cherokee marriage song has it, "Underneath the blanket all things are laid bare"; or, if you prefer an English proverb, "The proof of the pudding is in the eating." In a word, it is as though the third day of a visit to a traditional medicine man has dawned, and he asks what has brought you to see him: to find out for yourself or to ask questions?

But this last is but the second-best way, which SwiftDeer thinks little of, and I mention it only because he brings up the issue toward the end of the book. There he talks about the criticisms that he, along with Carlos Castaneda, has received from anthropologists and so-called scholars, which challenge the source of the teachings and raise questions about his credibility, after which he recounts a small conversation I once had with him on this very point. So because I once raised the issue with him, and yet have been given the honor to write a foreword to his book, the reader may find it useful if I add my two bits' worth to what he has to say on this score.

Our conversation took place a few days after we had met at the Ojai Foundation, during what by all accounts was the most memorable workshop that Joan Halifax, the director of the foundation, put on in that wonderful place. As I have said, SwiftDeer does not stand on ceremony, so I voiced my doubts to him directly. I have been a practicing anthropologist in my time and have been grateful for the experience even while knowing the limitations of the profession. Since professional ethics have their place in anthropology as much as in the practice of shamanism, I thought it good to say that certain things he claimed were part of Cherokee tradition in fact came from other traditions.

So, he shot back, what did I know about the things that took place in Cherokee kivas? He had me there: I knew nothing. And yet, I persisted, the art of making crystal skulls surely comes out of Mexico, not North America? More to the point, I told him (as he courteously remembers me saying) that I thought his teachings powerfully interesting. Why then queer the pitch by making such difficult claims?

His answer to this, which he here retells, is perfectly candid: The tradition he speaks of is in the keeping of the Twisted Hairs Council of Elders, which has its origin in the planets around the star Sirius. "If you do not believe in the fifth dimension or a dreamscape," he says, "you will have a problem with the history of my people. If you do not believe human beings are descended from the stars, you may have a problem with the history of many cultures"—the Christian one, for example.

That is well said, especially since it comes from the eighteenth dreamer's *nagual*, who has brought many people to appreciate its lively truth at first hand. The tradition that comes down to us by way of dreaming is indeed ancient, so ancient that we cannot imagine a time when it was a new experience. To use a technical term, the Dreamtime tradition is necessarily a syncretic one, and its practitioners make use of each other's knowledge to further the cause the tradition serves.

None of this should surprise us since our own traditions are constantly growing in this manner. No one has ever thought the worse of John Dee, the Elizabethan magician, for using an obsidian mirror from Mexico to scry with rather than the traditional crystal ball or bowl of ink. This mirror, which may well have been the chief divinatory instrument of the Aztec god Tezcatlipoca, or Smoking Mirror, is now to be seen in a corner of the British Museum, a powerful medicine object now relegated to the status of a minor curiosity. Swift-Deer, I am sure, could make better use of it, as he has done with the Sirian connection.

I don't doubt that Sirius, which is perhaps the most noticeable star in the night sky, has its place in Cherokee tradition, as it does in so many others. I do know, however, that ever since the French anthropologist Marcel Griaule published an account of the cosmology of the Dogon of West Africa, the extraordinary details about the Sirian system it contains have become a lively topic of discussion among academics and have entered the thought of channelers and New Agers around the world. So, if readers want to know why the Twisted Hairs Council of Elders has its home in the planets that circle Sirius, they will find that what the Dogon say is not only of great interest in itself but goes a long way to confirm, in its own style, what SwiftDeer has to say about humanity's descent from the stars and Sirius in particular.

Then there is Castaneda, who has provided us with a useful terminology for various shamanic moments. From him we have learned to speak of unordinary reality, of spiritual fibers, of attachment points, of the *nagual* and the *tonal*, which themselves come from Meso-American tradition, and so on, all of which have been picked up as much by Westerners as by Native American medicine men, SwiftDeer among them. These vivid phrases do but pinpoint matters that we all know of in other, often obscurer words, and we should be duly grateful that we can now all understand each other with Castaneda's help.

The harshest criticism that SwiftDeer has received, however, comes from traditional Native Americans, who accuse him of breaking protocol not only by giving the medicine teachings to those who are not full bloods, but by allowing women on their moon to take part in ceremonial activities. He understands this criticism well and sympathizes deeply: whites, as he says, have taken everything possible from Native Americans in ruthless and unscrupulous ways, and they continue to do so.

Yet it is, SwiftDeer says, his sacred dream to share the medicine teachings with the *metis*, or "Rainbow people," even though he realizes that in this sense he brings death to the old ways. There is little that those of us who benefit from this painful decision can do about it except to make sure that we do not bring shame on any of those who follow the traditional path, whether this be the old path or the one leading from it with new dreams into new ways. My friend Bill Wahlberg, who in this book has skillfully put together what Swift-Deer told him in the hours before dawn when dreaming and waking go hand in hand, says of him that his ability to be himself is one of his greatest strengths, that while he is a light to others he makes no claim to personal enlightenment, and that he does not pretend to be other than he is. Which is to say that he's a dreamer's *nagual*, whom I must now invite you to meet on his own terms.

Francis Huxley
London, England
February 1993

Francis Huxley is an anthropologist and an eminent member of the distinguished Huxley family, noted in the Western world for its scientific and literary contributions. He is the author of The Eye: The Seer and the Seen *and* The Dragon: Nature of Spirit, Spirit of Nature.

⋙ PREFACE ⋘

This is Harley SwiftDeer's story as shared in the times we were together in many places in the world. It was told to me mostly in the hours before dawn, for that is *his* time—the time when the changes take place. *Star Warrior* is the personal account of SwiftDeer's struggle through heartbreak and darkness to the light, to personal integration and power. It is told through associations and vignettes in the manner of the old storytellers.

Initially, the book was written in third-person narration. In time, it found its way to first person, its present form, though it did not always come to me that way. *Star Warrior* portrays SwiftDeer's odyssey from chaos and near madness following the Vietnam War to the Native American roots of his people—to the warmth and stability of his childhood memories with his Cherokee grandmother, Spotted Fawn.

The stories describe the intensity of young adulthood through war and initiation, devastation and heartbreak, leading to Swift-Deer's apprenticeship in sorcery with the Navajo elder Grandfather Two Bears. With Two Bears, SwiftDeer began his quest for the greatness he felt within himself. *Star Warrior* describes the experiences, teachers, and ceremonies that inspired and shaped his path.

The year I met SwiftDeer, my life was much too complicated to consider writing a book about a man as dynamic and complex as he is. However, once I knew him, I seemed to have little choice. In November of 1982, my wife, Judy, and I joined a "medicine journey" to the southeast of Mexico, sponsored by Joan Halifax and the Ojai Foundation of California. I learned that Harley SwiftDeer Reagan, a half-breed Native American shaman with a Ph.D. in psychology, would be our teacher.

Who is SwiftDeer? we wondered. We made inquiries and learned that one of our acquaintances, Ms. Judy Bayens, had previously traveled with Joan Halifax and SwiftDeer, hiking in the Grand Canyon.

"Who is SwiftDeer?" we asked Ms. Bayens.

"I'm not sure," she said.

Ms. Bayens is characteristically more articulate in her responses, so my wife asked again. "What can you tell us about SwiftDeer?"

"Well," she said, "I am pretty sure that one night down in the canyon he turned into a crow."

Astounded by her answer, I pressed for further explanation. "What do you mean, he turned into a crow?" I hoped she would give a symbolic, metaphoric, or figurative explanation.

"Just that," she said. "He turned into a goddamn crow and hopped through the campsite. Then he flew away."

In January of 1983, we flew to Villa Hermosa, Mexico, to meet Joan and SwiftDeer; his two wives, NightBird and ShyDeer; and the rest of the entourage. We traveled together for fourteen intensive days in the Land of the Maya.

In addition to numerous well-known ruins, Joan led us to un-excavated sites that only she, with her unbounded passion for adventure, could have discovered. "Follow me!" she called, as she wriggled head first into a narrow passageway leading to a hidden Mayan temple. We did. I loved Joan Halifax immediately! Her charm and energy were irresistible!

When Joan slowed down, SwiftDeer took charge. He explained he was a shield carrier, a "Twisted Hair." He said he was looking for a "missing shield of knowledge" thought to be held by a local Mayan shaman.

SwiftDeer taught from what he called "one of the twelve shields of knowledge of the ancient elders, the Twisted Hairs of Turtle Island." He explained that in the ancient legends of the early people of Mexico, a Twisted Hair was one who wandered, seeking knowledge from many cultures. Twisted Hairs then integrated the truths of many cultures to record what were called the twelve shields of knowledge of the ancient ones.

Near the journey's end we rested at Uxmal, the magnificent Mayan ruins south of Mérida in the Yucatán. I rose early to see the sun hit the highest temple at Uxmal, the Pyramid of the Magician. At its base I observed SwiftDeer also contemplating the pyramid. I watched him as sunlight spilled magically over him. Then, dream-like, I walked directly to him. Sensing my presence, he turned as I approached.

"SwiftDeer," I said.

"Yes, Bill?"

"SwiftDeer," I said unaccountably, "I love you and will never betray you."

He looked at me quietly for a few moments. "Thank you, Bill." He put his arms around me.

Parting from SwiftDeer, I joined Judy where she waited under a large ceiba tree. I described my encounter with SwiftDeer. It is uncharacteristic of me to talk this way with anyone. I had no thought of approaching him and had no words on my mind until I spoke. SwiftDeer appeared to understand precisely what I meant, though I had known him for only two weeks and there had been no previous context for betrayal between us.

Next day the journey ended, and Judy and I returned to Michigan. One week later I dreamed of SwiftDeer for seven consecutive nights. Each dream ended with a clear and sonorous voice saying, "Write SwiftDeer's story."

I phoned SwiftDeer in California. "It seems I am to write your story."

"Yes," he said. He did not sound surprised. "When I come to Michigan next May we can begin."

Unnerved, I replaced the phone in its holder. I closed the door to my study, cedared the room, and prayed to my spirit guides, known to me as "lover gods." "What is happening?" I asked.

A clear voice answered immediately. "A man is nothing without a dream he believes in."

In the years since the Ojai medicine journey in the Yucatán, I have traveled with SwiftDeer in Europe, Mexico, Guatemala, Jamaica, and the Southwest of the United States. I have sundanced, vision quested, fasted, and been buried in the earth overnight. I have learned the blessings of sweet grass. I have prayed in hundreds of sweatlodge ceremonies. I have begun to comprehend the power of the Sacred Pipe.

In the fall of 1987, I developed a lump on my upper right arm, and from the center of a sweatlodge ceremony I experienced Swift-Deer as shaman and healer. It was a powerful and memorable experience. During the "third door" of the healing ceremony, two canoes appeared in the sweatlodge. One was dark, the other light.

"These are your spirit journey canoes, Bill," said SwiftDeer. "You must choose one before you leave the lodge."

I contemplated both and chose the light canoe. To this day I do not know how SwiftDeer knew I had seen the canoes. I asked him once. "SwiftDeer, how did you know about canoes in the lodge?"

"I was watching for them, Bill," he said and smiled.

SwiftDeer is adamant that we are on the planet for two main reasons: the quest for knowledge and the search for pleasure. Often, he says, these are the same.

His search for knowledge is unending. SwiftDeer "walks his talk." I have often heard him say to his audiences, "Don't believe what I'm teaching you. Find out for yourself—then *know*—rather than believe. Don't believe anything . . . *know*! SwiftDeer finds out for himself and urges others to do the same. He teaches others to trust and believe in their personal greatness, and he gives them tools for developing the best in themselves.

SwiftDeer also works tirelessly against the powers of sexual repression in our culture. He teaches sexuality as a source of pleasure and creativity. His *chuluaqui quodoushka* teachings challenge sexual repression and fear.

SwiftDeer is not a guru. His ability to be himself is one of his greatest strengths; he does not pretend to be other than he is. While he is a light for others, he makes no claims of personal enlightenment.

In 1985, SwiftDeer founded the Deer Tribe Metis Medicine Society: A Shamanic Lodge for Ceremonial Medicine. In 1989, he formed the Rainbow Powers Center, which is now located in Scottsdale, Arizona. As the "eighteenth nagual and spiritual leader of the Feathered Winged Serpent Wheel," SwiftDeer is a world advocate for personal and planetary healing. He brings people together. When he leaves, people are united by his teachings. He helps the people find a dream together, and he leaves them practical and precious tools to help them stay united with each other in a dream for a better planet.

As of 1993, Deer Tribe Metis Medicine Society lodges were found in numerous states in the United States, Canada, several European countries, Australia, and New Zealand. SwiftDeer's message, called the "Sweet Medicine Sundance Teachings," provides shamanic tools and awareness for healing the self and the worlds of Grandmother Earth, reestablishing the balance of male and female power, and guiding people to personal freedom.

SwiftDeer's odyssey stands as an inspiration for the human spirit. It offers a healing for Vietnam veterans and provides hope for all people who are alienated from themselves, their families, and the culture in which they live. Once SwiftDeer was enveloped by darkness. He faced it courageously and entered that darkness. Today he stands in the light. He is the killer become healer.

Bill Wahlberg, 1993

⚛⚛⚛ INTRODUCTION ⚛⚛⚛

I wanted my Sundance in Vietnam told first here because it symbolizes for me what the book is about. In a sense, it's what my whole
life is about. At the time I danced in the jungle with my two buddies,
Raoul Guzman and Bub Deer in Water, I was near crazy. The values I
had been raised by were shattered, and there was nothing in their
place except destruction, survival, and taking care of the wounded.
The dance cleansed me and set my heart and mind straight, and I
was never the same over there again. It opened my eyes and spirit so
I could see Grandfather Ding Poan for who he was, and it prepared
me for my apprenticeship with the Navajo medicine man Grandfather Two Bears when I came home. The Sundance in Vietnam was
the start of my return to the roots of my people on my mother's side,
the Cherokee, though I did not know it at the time.

I am proud to be a half-breed—as proud of my Irish roots as I am
of my Cherokee roots. As a shaman, I find magic in both sides of my
ancestry, though today my Native American roots guide my life as a
shaman.

My family lived originally in South Carolina. The family name in
my Native American lineage is Raper, a prominent Cherokee name.
B.B. Raper was my mother's grandfather. He survived the Trail of
Tears. Like nearly all the Cherokee, my relatives were forced west
during the devastating and tragic purge of Indian people by President Andrew Jackson in the 1850s. They went mainly to Oklahoma,
but the records show that one group came to Texas and was befriend-
ed by the president of the Republic of Texas, Sam Houston, who was
married to a Cherokee woman. Later this group was also expelled
from Texas.

My relatives returned to Texas in the twenties and settled near
Lubbock, where I was born. Records show that around the time of
Andrew Jackson, the Pin Society of the Cherokee people sent splinter
groups whose purpose was to escape the purge of the people and
preserve the Cherokee medicine to the hills of Oklahoma and
Mexico. I believe that my grandmother Spotted Fawn was associated

with these people, though I cannot prove it. Because of her knowledge of native medicine she must have been instructed by powerful medicine people.

Stories included in this book show the influence of Grandmother Spotted Fawn, for in her special way she remains my most impacting teacher. She taught me to study my surroundings. She showed me power beyond ordinary understanding in the way she did things. From her I learned the medicine of animals, birds, fish, and insects. Grandmother also introduced me to the sexual powers of the Chuluaqui Quodoushka and other teachings of traditional Cherokee sexuality, which today are the matrix of much of my work. Memories of Grandmother guided me to my second great Native American teacher, Grandfather Two Bears.

I've tried to show in this book who and what impacted me, what formed and shaped me. I've had more than my share of life's bumps and hurts, thrills and inspiration. If all my experiences and pain and bullshit can help someone else, then this book is good medicine.

Ho!

SwiftDeer, 1993

STAR WARRIOR

⊰⊱⊰ PROLOGUE ⊰⊱⊰
SUNDANCE
IN VIETNAM

I have never told this story before today. It is about courage and beauty in Vietnam. It is one of the few memories that gives meaning to my experience there. It's been something private between Raoul Guzman, Bub Deer in Water, and me. Perhaps it is important to tell the story now. It never asked to be told before. I know in my heart that Raoul Guzman and men I knew like him made survival and sanity possible during the horror of Vietnam.

Raoul Guzman was three-fourths Lakota Sioux and the rest Mexican. He and Bub Deer in Water, a full-blood Navajo, and I were three close marines. We stayed within shouting distance of each other at all times, on duty and off. It wasn't planned that way; that's just how it was. We stayed apart from the other men as often as we could. We'd been together in 'Nam a long time and had seen too many buddies go home dead or hurt. We didn't want to lose each other.

We were resting, filthy and exhausted, waiting for the end of a long fire fight we'd been in. It seemed the fire fights there were always either short or long, with nothing in between. Raoul and I shared a smoke. Bub was on our flank. Raoul looked at me and spoke in his steady way with a voice I hear yet for its simple fullness.

"Swift, I dreamt my death in the night. Death sang to me."

I looked at him, shocked. "What! . . . What's that talk?" I understood what the talk was. Raoul was a good Lakota. I knew what he was saying.

"I heard my death song last night, Swift. I dreamt it, and I want to get ready."

I thought, No, goddammit, I don't want to hear this!

"I want to get my purification from all this shit here in 'Nam and

3

all the stuff my people have been through for 150 years, Swift." He hesitated. "I'm asking you and Bub to stand by me."

I was compelled to hear him out. In our outfit men often knew when they were going "home." When they felt it or dreamed it, they'd sit down and write a letter or instruct a buddy about personal effects. Then in the next fight or the next second, or sometimes by accident, they'd get it, and another green bag would be flown out . . . Vietnam.

So I knew what was coming down with Raoul. He meant to sundance to get ready, and he wanted me and Bub to see him through it. I didn't know how to sundance then—had never seen one—but we agreed to help. He said he'd tell us what he needed.

The first problem Raoul faced was when to do the ceremony. We hadn't had a clean break from fighting for weeks. The second was getting permission. He needed time—at least three days, pre-ferably four—to be away from the outfit, which at the time seemed impossible.

Then in one day all the external obstacles disappeared. In the morning both sides broke off contact. That afternoon Raoul found a veteran chaplain who was willing to help him. By late afternoon we had transport and brief R and R papers. We drove out of the combat zone as quickly as possible. I know now that the Great Spirit choreographed the events of those days.

Raoul found a place that suited him. We cleared a little area in the jungle and sat down together. Raoul passed smokes and described his ceremony. We listened as he talked about the Lakota Sundance in his slow, calm way, unfolding the plan and explaining what he wanted from us. His Camel cigarettes were butts, and the sun was behind the tree line when our questions were answered. The jungle was still, and so were we.

Raoul said he'd make a flesh sacrifice and we could do the same. Then we'd build our sweatlodge to purify with him. After that, we'd help him pierce his chest muscles and attach him to the tree at the center of the clearing. He wanted us to stand by him and pray as he danced.

Raoul stated his intent: "This ceremony will bring credit to my ancestors. It will speak to them. It is my way to align with the true way—to honor those who love me and have passed before me. When my people at home hear I danced, they'll know I was of one heart with them when I crossed over to the spirit world. Their pain will be less."

I wonder how they'll know? I thought.

"When I dance they'll feel it," he said.

Raoul asked if we were willing to do what he requested. "Will you sit by me and pray while I dance?"

Bub and I were looking at each other. I'm sure Bub's thinking had been coming to the same place as mine. There was no other warrior way it could happen.

"Raoul," I said. "Bub and me are going to pierce with you."

He studied us without comment for several moments. "Good," he grunted. "We pierce at sunup. We have much to do."

An hour before dawn we prayed together in the darkness of our jungle sweatlodge. I have been in thousands of sweats since Raoul splashed water on the rocks that night. I have witnessed amazing, magickal, and miraculous events in sweatlodge ceremonies. Yet no sweatlodge or healing ceremony is as clear in my memory as that first one, that precious coming together in the Vietnam jungle with two of the finest men I would ever know.

Earlier in the night we gathered our ceremonial items. We found turkey feathers, twine, blankets, whistles, paint, and the small bones Raoul said we needed. Raoul pierced a can and filled it with stones, and he had a rattle.

When I look back, I know the ceremony began for me when Bub and I looked at each other, knowing we were going to dance with Raoul. It gave me an understanding of the saying "A ceremony has begun when a man thinks of picking up a rattle." Today, when I think of all the things we borrowed from the United States Marine Corps for our ceremony, I'm smiling. There were no smiles that night.

Everything we collected—the saplings for our lodge, the USMC whistles and blankets, and cornmeal from the base kitchen—was gathered in a sacred way. Raoul said our ceremonial things must be invited to join us. That was his way. He insisted it must be done this way. "Ask a sapling if it wants to join us," he instructed. If it chooses not to be in our ceremony, leave it and ask another."

Once we started, I noticed the naturalness of events, though I was surprised when the first tree spirit spoke to me. It took me back to my childhood and my grandmother Spotted Fawn.

After making a clearing, we lit torches to the Four Directions and waited for Raoul to explain what was next. He was studying the moon, a thin, brilliant slice of silver in the dark purple sky. Raoul turned to us, "We can take flesh sacrifice now," he said. "Then we build the lodge. When it's finished we'll stand watch and pray until we fire the rocks."

Raoul took a razor and a needle from his kit. "You slide the point of the needle in like this," he said. "Lift the skin up and slice it off at an angle. Then save it."

He showed us how to use the point of the needle to lift the flesh, which was then cut away with the razor. Raoul asked that forty pieces of skin be cut from his arm. "Start at the bottom and work up," he said. "Slice the skin at an angle."

As the blood flowed, I understood the importance of starting at the lower end of the arm. I was surprised at the amount of blood. I cut twenty pieces while Bub held the light. Then Bub cut another twenty. It was easier with practice, but the arm got slick and the cutting area became scarce. Each piece of flesh was saved and wrapped in cloth. Raoul made no sound till we finished.

"Good," he said, looking at me. "Now I'll cut you. How many pieces shall I cut, Swift?"

I looked at Bub. "Er, . . . seven," I said. It wasn't much compared to Raoul. But I was thinking it had been *his* dream, not mine, and, truthfully, seven seemed like a lot. All my life, including now, I am troubled by needles. Sometimes I even pass out. I assumed Raoul was thinking I wouldn't amount to much as a Lakota.

He smiled. "Good, Swift. One for Wakan Tanka. One each for Grandfather and Grandmother, and an offering to the Four Directions." He cut seven pieces and it hurt like hell! He also took seven from Bub.

Then we built our lodge, covered it with USMC blankets, dug the fire pit, and laid our wood. Raoul placed the entrance to the east. We sat quietly in the darkness. Now and then one of us spoke to the others or offered a prayer. My silent prayer was that Raoul's dream was wrong.

In the early morning he fired the rocks. When they were glowing and red hot, we put them in the fire pit, crawled in, and dropped the door flap. We sat in blackness lit by glowing stones.

"Wakan Tanka, Great Spirit, Tunkashila!" Raoul said. "We are three marines coming to purify from all this shit here so we can sundance in a good way. I ask you to be with us and help us dance in a strong way with good spirit. I am dancing with two good men here, Great Spirit, and I give thanks for their friendship."

He poured water on the rocks. Blue lights danced in the darkness. The smell of the hot stones, the stone people singing as the water splashed, that first surprising rush of steam, the ancestors' presence, the chanting and praying—all this is with me always. I've never felt closer to the Great Spirit. The two hours we shared together in the dark was a gift from Raoul to last a lifetime.

Though I did not know it then, the experience turned me toward the path of my people.

Raoul raised the flap as the sky turned pink. It was the first day of my life . . . my first sunrise. I was completely dissociated from the war—the killing, destruction, and waste. I was clean.

Raoul motioned for Bub and me to leave the lodge. He poured more water on the rocks, joined us, and closed the flap. "The ancestors like to sweat without two-leggeds sometimes. Now we sundance."

Raoul pierced me, pushing a sharp bone through the meat of my pectoral muscles on both sides of my chest till both ends of the bone were visible. He did the same for Bub. Then he handed a bone to each of us, asking to be pierced in the same way. The bone I shoved into Raoul's chest was sharp and slid easily. Bub had a tougher time getting the bone through Raoul's muscle.

Though Raoul hurt, he said nothing. When Bub had finished with him, Raoul tied twine to the bone protruding from our flesh and secured us to the tree. We did the same for him. Raoul put his whistle in his mouth and blew it as he pulled his lines taut. Wearing skirts made from USMC blankets, we danced for three days.

I tore loose on the second day. Bub had pulled free the first night. Raoul danced through the third day before tearing away. Bub and I never left his side. That was the way it should have been. We rested on the third night, and the next day we rejoined the unit.

On our first mission after the dance, Raoul was killed instantly as he left the helicopter. He went down without a sound. It was unbelievable. One second we were talking, and then he was gone. He was our only casualty; no one else was even wounded or fired upon. One round of sniper fire came from somewhere we never knew. Raoul had followed Bub and me off the Huey and simply dropped. I didn't hear the shot and wouldn't believe he was hit until I opened his shirt. He took it directly through the heart and was dead as I pulled him into my arms.

Bub and I never spoke of Raoul or our dance together. I felt I couldn't and still do my job there. Three years ago a voice inside asked me to find Raoul at the Vietnam Memorial in Washington, D.C., and say the words that had been frozen in my heart for twenty-two years.

PART 1

GRANDMOTHER
SPOTTED FAWN

FIRST VISION

> A man who has a vision is not able to use the power
> of it until he has performed his vision on Earth for
> the people to see.　　—Black Elk

My first vision came to me at age eight. The never-ending farm chores invented for me that day were finished, so before my daddy could make up something else for me to work at, I grabbed my fishing pole and ran out back across the field. Cat fishing at Fossle Creek was my favorite thing to do in life. Lying on my back under an enormous oak, I looked up at the ropes my cousins and I had hung to swing over the creek. I sighed. It was a truly fine place for our hideout. Best of all, it offered a deep catfish hole.

I was as content as a boy could be. My cane pole rested on a forked stick. My hook was baited and positioned near the bottom of the fishing hole. It was one of those fine, hot Texas days that naturally cause dozing. My eyes closed and I slipped away, drifting into the world between wakefulness and sleep.

Though aware I was dozing, I could still hear the water gurgling near my feet as it splashed over the rocks before turning toward the other bank. I saw our great oak rising majestically above, and sunlight flashed on the water. I felt a gentle breeze and heard the faint buzzing of bees. A dragonfly landed briefly on the end of my pole, then darted away. Gradually I drifted farther into the dream.

Then my awareness shifted. I watched astonished as a semitransparent form emerged from my belly. It wound around itself and grew larger. Then it separated from me and drifted to the ground and became a large mule deer with enormous antlers. The deer stood at the edge of the stream in front of me, close enough to be touched. It glanced across the stream to the far side, then turned back and looked directly at me.

Gazing into the deer's eyes, I felt immensely strong and powerful. I felt that if I tried, I could leap across the fishing hole. The deer turned away and waded into the stream.

Up the hill on the far side of the stream, two bears suddenly emerged from the heavy forest. One was black, the other brown. They paused, sniffing the air, then ambled down the slope and splashed into the water across from the deer. As the bears waded into deeper water, the deer stepped tentatively toward them.

From somewhere above the three animals, I watched my vision unfold. I saw myself dozing under the great tree, my cane pole waiting. At the same time, I watched the bears and the deer in Fossle Creek. I realized with excitement that I was watching my own dream! It was the first time I had experienced such a thing.

The bears plunged deeper into the water. When it reached their belly fur, they rose up together, splashing water in all directions. As the bears reached full height, they merged and became one bear—a huge grizzly! The grizzly continued across the creek.

I glanced at the sleeping boy, wondering if he sensed the mammoth bear. He slept peacefully and was oblivious of the events I watched so intensely.

When the grizzly and the deer reached midstream they stopped, reaching noses forward tentatively, touching.

I wonder if the bear will kill that deer now, I thought.

As their noses touched, Poof!—the grizzly became a white-haired Indian elder wearing a blue velveteen shirt, a green headband, and a turquoise necklace. I recognized him as Navajo. His eyes were piercing, scary, and memorably bright.

At the moment the grizzly became a Navajo Indian, the buck transformed into a younger man I recognized as myself at a later age. The man's hair was curly and peppered with gray. I could not discern his age for sure, but I knew he was myself. My awareness shifted again. As I watched myself dreaming under the oak tree, I became the man in front of the old Indian.

The Navajo looked at me with an intensity I had never before experienced. Then he spoke. "Nice day for fishing."

"Grandfather?" I asked.

"It's me."

"Grandfather, it *is* you."

"I said that," answered the old man.

I reached for him. He took my hand. "Grandfather, is it time for me to go with you?" I asked.

"No."

"Why not, Grandfather?"

The old man glanced at me where I slept as a boy on the bank. "You aren't ready," he said, looking back to me as I stood in the water.

"How will I know when I am?" I asked.

"When you are done killing your brothers and are ready to heal them, your heart will speak to you. When that happens, I'll send for you." The old man's voice was soft. His words were alive and vibrant.

"Grandfather, how will I find you?"

The old man released my hand. "A man under a star will bring you to me."

I opened my mouth to respond, but before I could make a sound the old Indian faded and disappeared.

"Grandfather!" I called. As my voice faded on the water, I was again with the mule deer at midstream in Fossle Creek. The deer stood motionless, staring at the space where the old man had disappeared. Then it turned and waded toward me as I dozed on the bank of the fishing hole. Reaching me, it stopped. It studied me for several seconds. The deer then became a misty cloud and reentered my belly.

I stirred, stretched, rubbed my eyes, and sat up awake. At that moment, a catfish hit my line with a tremendous yank. Before I could land the fish, which turned out to be my first gar of the summer, I was drenched—part covered with fish blood and the rest mud and water. Holding my fish high, I shrieked in bursts of triumph and joy.

As I walked home I thought only of the pleasure I would see on my daddy's face when he saw my gar. Pleasing my Daddy was one of the most important things in my life, though it didn't seem to happen often. I ran most of the distance to the farmhouse.

When I stepped on the wooden porch of my grandmother's home and saw the long shadow my body cast in the late afternoon sun, I remembered my vision at the creek. I shivered. I didn't know what had caused the shiver, but I knew that as soon as I was alone with Grandmother Spotted Fawn I'd ask her about my dream that had been so real. I knew she could tell me.

Daddy was pleased with my fish, and Mother cooked it for our evening meal.

That night as I said my prayers, I thought about my grandmother. I realized that her hair had been gray forever. Then I thought of something else: how strange that I live with my grandmother and I've never seen her sleep.

GRANDMOTHER
SPOTTED FAWN

My mother's mother, Grandmother Spotted Fawn Raper, a full-blood Cherokee, was the most influential teacher of my childhood, perhaps of my life. I stayed close with her until I left for the Marine Corps.

Grandmother remained an enigma to everyone who knew her nearly all her life—except to me. For me she was simply my wonderful grandmother. Even my mother, her daughter Ida, did not understand Grandmother's ways. She was a unique personality. Grandmother kept mainly to herself. In later years she seldom spoke. When she did, everyone got quiet.

Grandmother gave me an understanding of the expression "You dance in my heart!" I still meet with Grandmother in my dreams.

Recently I asked Jeff Gray, a friend who grew up in my home town, if he'd ever met Grandmother Spotted Fawn. "SwiftDeer," he said, "I met your old grandmother once at a Thanksgiving dinner in Lubbock long after you left. She was an ancient Indian lady, with piercing eyes and wrinkles. All the devoted Christian women of Lubbock seemed scared as hell of her, and there were rumors of her being a witch. Everyone stayed clear of her, and nobody crossed her. They tended to whisper behind her back. I remember thinking, What a strange woman this is. I, of course, also kept my distance. She died shortly after that."

I have tried to show Grandmother Spotted Fawn's importance in my life in the stories that follow. If every child had a grandmother like her, the planet would be richer.

MY BIRTH

I found my grandmother alone on the porch in the late afternoon. She was busy with one of her favorite pastimes. Grandmother made floor rugs from worn nylons that other ladies discarded. She took the toe and top of a nylon stocking and rolled them into each other. Using yarn of a similar color, she'd stitch the opening, wrap it through, and braid the loose ends.

Grandmother then gathered nylon hose of different colors—browns, whites, reds, and yellows—bunched them, and, starting at the center, looped them like a snake and stitched them. In this way she made beautiful colored, round nylon-hose rugs. My favorite rug was as large as the big room in the house. I was quick to see that my grandmother could create beauty from other people's castaways.

Though the old woman did not acknowledge my presence, I knew she was watching me. "Grandmother?"

"What is it, Little Grandson?" she answered.

"Grandmother, I had a dream at Fossle Creek the day I caught the gar."

The old woman listened as I described my vision at the creek. I told it fully, becoming the bear or the deer or the old Indian for emphasis. Then I waited quietly.

Grandmother was again looping nylon into her rug. When she spoke, her voice was warm and vibrant. "That's a fine medicine dream, Little Grandson," she said. "It's a spirit dream connected to the day you were born."

Excitement filled me. "Will you tell it, Grandmother?" I asked.

I listened spellbound while Grandmother described the events of my birth. I had never heard the story before.

"You came with thunder and lightning, Little Grandson. For three days and three nights the sky poured hard on us like the Great Spirit wanted the land clean for your coming. The roads were swamped and running mud. Your mother had been waiting for you for three weeks. She was restless and impatient.

"At the peak of the storm, this little house shook and rattled almost sideways from all the thunder crashing. Lightning flashes lit the land like special magic. Right then you decided to join us. Your momma called for your daddy. 'Hurry, Jeff,' she cried. 'Hurry, the baby's coming!'"

I was transfixed, seeing it in my mind as the old woman talked. "Your daddy was home on leave from the military. He rushed through the house gathering things for your mama to take to the hospital. He was mighty nervous! When she was ready, he bundled her into the old pickup, and away they went into the night, tires spinning in the mud.

"They never made it. The truck slipped off the road at one of the bad places and was finished. Your daddy helped your mama out of the pickup and carried her through the storm a mile and a half back here to the house, splashing in mud and knee-deep water most of the way. Your mama was just fifteen years of age and hanging on as tight to your daddy as she could. She was scared as she could be and very brave."

"Wow!" I said out loud.

"I heard your daddy shouting over the storm. 'Help!' he called. The fear in his voice pierced the storm. When the lightning flashed, I saw him struggling up the slope. By the time he banged through the door, I had laid out what we needed. Your daddy's face was pale and his breath fast. 'Truck's in the ditch!' he said. 'We got to birth the child ourselves!'"

"Were you scared, Grandmother?" I asked.

The old woman looked at me. "I asked your daddy to lay your mother on the bed. I explained that it wouldn't be the first time a baby was born with his daddy's help, and that seemed to calm him."

"That was good, Grandmother."

"Your mama labored hard through the night birthing you. Your daddy and I did what we could. The firstborn is often hardest for a woman.

"Near sunrise you were born. The two of you had fourteen hours of hard work. Your mama was worn out from her part in getting you here, and I expect you were tuckered, too. Right after she saw you were safe and a strong, healthy boy, she held you close, kissed you, and fell asleep."

It's a good story, I thought.

"The storm lifted, showing the sun lighting the skyline. I covered you warm, and we went to the porch for your first look. It was 6:41 a.m., a good June morning. I carried you down to the edge of the swollen creek, where I lifted you up to Grandfather Sky. Then I offered you to Grandmother Earth. I did the same to the Four Directions. I unwrapped you and lowered you into the cold running stream. The moment you touched the water, it was clear the Great Spirit had given you good lungs. You yelped so loud I can hear it today if I try."

"Ha, ha!" I laughed.

"When you yelled, a mule deer drinking from the opposite side twenty feet upstream jerked its head and looked at us. It held steady, watching you. The buck had about eighteen points—it was a big one. As it stood at the edge of the stream, it snorted. At that moment its spirit jumped out, crossed the stream, and entered you, Little Grandson, right here in your tummy. When that happened, you stopped screaming, even though I still held you over the water. The buck then splashed into the stream, crossed in front of us, leaped over a log, and disappeared into the forest.

"That was the sign I was looking for, Little Grandson. Lifting you high, I announced that you were Unhua Oskenonton Anikawi, which in our people's words means "The Deer That Runs Swiftly Through the Forest Carrying the Magic."

I sat breathless at the old woman's side, half in a dream.

"Grandmother," I asked finally, "Why did you put me in that cold water?"

She looked at me, smiling. "I put you in the stream, Little Grandson, because that storm water carried the power of thunder and lightning, gifts to strengthen you for manhood. You will be a fire carrier. Also," she added gently, "you needed the water for your own healing."

"Thank you, Grandmother."

I put my arms around the old woman, holding her close. I loved the way she smelled . . . like tobacco and out-of-doors and other things I could not make words for.

TWO-HEARTED
PEOPLE

I have mainly good memories of schools I've attended in my life, though the first year was tougher than I would have asked for. We were living in Portales, New Mexico, when the big day arrived for me to start school. I'd been excited for weeks. I lay in darkness listening for sounds from the rest of the house. Nothing. Even the crickets were silent. How can everyone sleep when it's my first day of school? I wondered.

I put my feet on the cold floor. In the darkness I reached for my new school clothes and touched the soft plaid of the shirt to my face. The cold metal buttons on my new coveralls caused me to shiver. I pushed my arms into the new shirt and lay back on the bed. When I opened my eyes again, sunlight filled the room and Grandmother sat on the bed. Her smile was warm as the sun.

"Funny-looking pajamas, child." She laughed as she tugged the new plaid shirt off my arms. "We don't want to get the shirt wet when you wash up for breakfast. Oatmeal is ready."

She helped me out of bed and guided me toward the bathroom. I looked at myself in the wall mirror. I wondered who had put my new shirt on me in the night.

The old Indian boarding school at Portales had been integrated with non-Indian children for three years the morning Ida Reagan left me at the first-grade classroom. It was a good day for my mother. She was proud of me and excited about having extra time for herself.

I watched her walk away, then stepped into my first day of school. My legs trembled. I leaned against the wall to steady them and surveyed the room. Several other children had arrived before me. Except for voices at the front where the teacher talked with a parent, the room was unnaturally quiet. A wall clock ticked ominously.

I noticed my two new friends, Manuel and Gilbert, in the back of the classroom. They waved, beckoning to me. I joined them and felt happy.

"Hey, what's happening, Gil?" I asked.

Gilbert whispered, lifting one finger. "Shh, not too loud. The teacher don't want no noise."

"She don't like us," added Manuel.

More children arrived. Some sat, others stood with their parents. I was so excited I could barely sit. When the last parent left the room, the teacher closed her class book and stood.

She is tall, I thought.

The teacher faced the classroom, studying us. She'd been at the school many years, her brown hair turning gray. Hard lines in her face sent subtle warnings as she looked fiercely at each of us. My body tensed as her eyes found me.

"Good morning, children," she said. "I am Miss Farther." She paused to let us feel the significance of her announcement. "I am your teacher this year. I am pleased to welcome you to your first year of school. Except for our Gilbert here. It is his *second* year." Big teeth filled her face as she smiled. "Gilbert didn't pass to the second grade last time, so he is with us another year."

She paused, and her voice softened. "It's not really his fault. He's a good child. His deportment is satisfactory; he's just slow. Gilbert will be trying his best to read this year. If he does, he'll be smarter than his parents. Neither of them read. Isn't that right, Gilbert?" Miss Farther glared at Gilbert.

I sensed that Gil was the teacher's special joke. Her smile was fake. Some of the other children giggled. Gilbert shifted nervously in his seat.

"Now, children," she said, "I will assign permanent seats for the year. First we'll fill the back of the room. When I call your name, go quickly to the desk I indicate, understand?"

Miss Farther read from her class book: "Danny Arroyo, sit here. Ann Chavez, this one. Manuel Dominguez, sit next to Ann. Quickly now, move! We have many things to do today. Time wasted is sinful!"

She called the students by name until more than half were seated. I stood in the back near a desk I had been asked to vacate.

"Good," said Miss Farther. "Now, the rest of you children find seats in the front of the room. Pick any you like. Be sure to leave one row empty between yourselves and the children presently seated. Move fast. Time passes!"

From my place in the back I hesitated, confused.

"Harley Reagan," the woman said, "your place is here, up front. Choose a desk here, child. At Portales Elementary School progress is best made with certain children sitting in the back of the room as you see them now. You belong up here." Her words had a sharp edge as she guided me to a desk in the second row. "Here, little Harley, I have a fine place for you!"

I sat down, sensing something different here. The desk top was smooth and freshly varnished. I opened a drawer, examining it. My fingers touched the unscarred desk top. This one is better than those in the back, I realized. It's newer.

Miss Farther's voice droned on, explaining, describing, demonstrating, pointing to areas of the room. Something else pushed into my thoughts. All the kids in the back of the room have black hair, I realized. Everyone up here has different hair colors—brown and blond and red. I glanced at my friends in the back of the room.

"Children, we will have two recess periods each day—at least those of you with good citizenship will have two. One recess comes in the morning. Our second recess will be in the after——" She stopped abruptly. "Harley, dear, whatever are you doing out of your seat?"

I halted as though surprised to find myself on my feet. "Uh, ma'am," I muttered faintly, "I've decided to sit with my friends in the back." I slid into an empty desk near Manuel.

The wind the teacher made as she rushed at me touched me before she arrived herself. Then she had me. She yanked me clear of the back row and carried me to my second-row desk. My feet barely touched the floor en route! *Bam!* Into my seat! I sat stunned, feeling pain from fingernail slashes in my upper arm. Blood seeped through my shirt.

Miss Farther spoke from the front of the room. "You see, children," she paused, catching her breath, "here at Portales our tradition is proud. We understand who we are and where we belong. It's easier for everyone that way. Knowing these things, we avoid conflict and live in peace."

She was smiling again, her voice gentle and caring. "One of the obligations we do have in the historic state of New Mexico is helping people understand our magnificent heritage. Everyone has a place, according to his upbringing. All of us at Portales Elementary are here to help you with this lesson. Later, when you are grown and married with your own little first graders, you will thank us for the clarity we have given certain problems and differences between . . . *Harley! Where in God's name are you going?*"

I paused on my way to the back of the classroom. "I'm sorry, ma'am, but I should be with my friends."

I turned, took half a step to the back, and the woman landed on me. I fell into a desk. Miss Farther grabbed my ear and twisted. She dragged me to the front of the room. My ear had a scary roaring and hurt bad. Miss Farther twisted my arm, forcing my palm up. She lifted her desk ruler.

Whack! the ruler landed hard. I tried not to cry. *Whack!*

"So, little Harley Reagan," said Miss Farther, "you want special lessons your first day of school? You've got them! You want to be my little pet project, eh?"

She twisted harder, her nails cutting. She raised her arm to strike, then paused. I looked at the woman, wondering why she was waiting. Then I knew: she wanted me to cry. She was waiting for me to cry. Something deep in my gut moved and settled quietly, like steel walls coming together. I had never felt it before, but I knew the walls would hold the tears and I would not cry.

Whack! The ruler came down hard across the palm of my hand. Red welts emerged. *Whack! Whack!*

My body trembled. My eyes teared, but I made no sound. I tried to support the beaten hand with my good one. Miss Farther lifted the ruler again, paused, and looked around as if confused; she hesitated, then shoved me roughly at my seat. I bounced to the floor.

Miss Farther glared at me, her breath shallow and rapid. "Get into the seat!" she hissed.

I pulled myself up. Miss Farther returned to her desk. "Now, then"—the woman's eyes darted crazily back and forth—"I think we have clarified seating questions in my classroom!"

I looked straight ahead. My hurt hand rested limply in my lap.

The teacher found tissues, removed her glasses, and wiped them. She blew her nose and dropped the tissue in a wastebasket. From her purse she extracted a small mirror and carefully adjusted her hair. Her eye movement regained normalcy. Muttering to herself, she filed her fingernails ritualistically with a small emery board. I left my seat and walked slowly to the back of the room.

"*I don't believe this!*" The woman had me before I sat. She dragged me out of the classroom and down the hall to the principal's office.

Mr. Krantz turned in his swivel chair as we entered his office. "What do we have here, Miss Farther?"

The man studied me as my teacher described the events of the morning.

"And that is what happened, Russell. In twenty-eight years of classroom teaching, I have never seen a child as sassy and belliger-ent!" Her voice cracked. "He is dangerous . . . a subversive! He is a monster! A degenerate! Everything I have planned for those inno-cent, dear children their first day of school has been disrupted! This child is determined to make a fool of me, and you, and the proud tradition of Portales Elementary!" Her face was white. She slid her glasses up her sweaty nose. She paused, breathing hard.

"I've got the picture," the man said calmly. "Leave him with me, Miss Farther, and wait in the hall. This child obviously needs help to appreciate your efforts in making his school life good. We'll spend some time together—get acquainted."

When the principal closed the door behind Miss Farther, I saw that he was much bigger than my daddy. His body filled the office. "Young Reagan," he said. "We have some simple, basic hu-man being rules here at Portales, and I intend for you to learn them immediately."

The biggest cigar I had ever seen appeared in the man's hand. Mr. Krantz struck a match on the edge of his thumbnail and disappeared behind a cloud of cigar smoke. From behind the cloud he blew smoke at me. I gasped and choked. My eyes burned.

"I consider your daddy, Jeff Reagan, a good man, a respected member of the human race," he continued. "Though he has only recently come to New Mexico, his people have been in the Southwest for years. He is a white man of good Irish blood, and so are you. Do you understand me, son?"

I remained mute.

"Through what some might call misfortune you are part Indian—a half-breed. Lucky for you, you don't show it, and your mama is trying her best to be a good Christian woman. It is not her fault she is Indian, and she is doing her best to overcome it. It isn't that Indians themselves are bad. They just think different than whites. And it isn't out of the memory of some people here when Indians were burning, stealing, raping, and scalping. Now, that behavior is not civilized."

I thought about my grandmother, and the steel walls in my gut came together again. I felt calm and knew I was not afraid. I felt my grandmother's arms around me.

"Boy," the big man said, "it's lesson time for you! Today you learn the civilized ways of white people with a little ass whipping to sharpen your memory. Bend over and grab your ankles."

He lifted a paddle from his desk drawer and hit me. When I did not respond, he hit me harder. The third time he struck, I fell hard to the floor. He replaced his paddle and sat in his large chair. He was sweating, breathing hard, and seemed very excited. "Are you learning, boy?"

I pulled myself to my feet slowly. A smile started somewhere deep inside me. Don't smile, I thought, but I knew I couldn't hold it back. The smile moved through, reaching my mouth. I grinned at the big man, looking into his face. With astonishment I heard myself speak. "Thank you, sir."

The principal stared at me in disbelief. He pushed himself half up from his chair, stopped and sat again. He wiped sweat from his forehead.

"What the . . . ?" he muttered. Then his voice rose, "Get out of here, Injun! Get, while you're able to walk!" He shouted at my teacher waiting in the hall, "Take the insect to his room!"

I followed Miss Farther through the corridor to the first-grade classroom. When she pointed to my seat in the second row, I walked directly to the empty desk beside Manuel in the back. Miss Farther gaped at me. I sat in the back, eyes averted. The teacher walked slowly to her own desk and sat.

"Children," she said after several moments, "we will continue our school activities now. After a thorough discussion, your principal, Mr. Krantz, and I have decided to allow Harley to sit in the back, if that is his wish." She said no more to me.

At midmorning we were excused for recess. As my classmates ran to the playground, I held back, keeping to myself. I hurt. My body ached. My ear was still ringing. Cuts on my arm hurt the most. The slashes festered. My fingers didn't move right. I thought to myself, The bottoms of my feet are the only place I don't hurt.

I found a deserted swing set on the playground behind the school. Among the broken swings, I found one that held together. I sat down carefully. I loved to swing. I'd learned to swing when I was three; it was one of my favorite things. I leaned back, and the wooden seat moved forward. Soon I was soaring as far out as the swing would go, legs kicking and arms pulling. With each swing I felt better. I was alone and free. My face relaxed in a smile.

"Hey, pussy!" a voice called from below. "You, first grader, are you a pussy?"

Startled, I looked down as I swung by. An older boy pointed at me.

"Hey, are you deaf?" the boy shouted. "What you got between your legs? Only girls get on these swings!"

Confused, I slowed my flight. I glanced quickly around.

He's talking to me, I realized. Doesn't he know the difference between boys and girls? Then I understood. The older boy wanted to fight and was talking bad about girls to scare me. Grandmother had told me not to talk bad about girls. I felt scared, then a wave of anger filled me.

"Hey, you stupid first-grade pussy!" yelled the fourth grader. "Are you deaf and dumb and stupid? I said get out of that little girl's swing and show me what you got between your legs, or I'll get a stick and knock you down from there!"

I pumped the swing harder, my anger building. At the highest point I released and sailed through the air. I landed on my feet in front of the other boy, scattering dirt over him. Startled, he stepped back. Then, encouraged by his size, he held his ground. We faced each other, fists raised.

The big boy spoke. "Here's the little pussy girl ready for a sex lesson." He cocked a fist behind his right ear. "Now pull down those coveralls, and we'll see what's between your legs!" He stepped forward, grabbing at me.

Remembering what my daddy told me about fighting big guys, I kicked as hard as I could where his legs came together. He howled, staggering back. He clutched his groin and crouched in pain. "I'll get you for this, you little son of a bitch!" he croaked. His face then exploded in red, purple, and white flashes. I hit him as fast and hard as I could. I leaned back and swung at his nose. *Smack!* He fell to his knees, blood gushing on his shirt.

Responding to his cries, two sixth-grade safety patrollers took me to Mr. Krantz's office. "Fighting is not tolerated at Portales Elementary," he said. "It is not a civilized activity; therefore, you will be punished." He paddled me again and sent me to Miss Farther's classroom.

At my desk I thought, I wonder who protects first graders?

During the lunch hour I remained in the classroom. When we were excused for afternoon recess, I went outside. I again avoided my classmates. I found the old merry-go-round, warped and weathered. When I pushed it, a brown-and-white dog looked up from under the platform. I reached to pet it. "You OK under there, little fellow?" I asked. The dog licked my hand, tail wagging.

Suddenly a larger boy stepped up and kicked the dog in the face. Staggering to its feet, the dog yelped in pain. "Get moving, you stupid bitch!" the boy shouted, laughing. "Get your lazy ass moving so we can run the merry-go-round!"

Astonished, I stood up on the machine. "Why did you kick Sweet Medicine?"

"Sweet Medicine, ha!" the boy sneered. "This here is nothing but a flea-bitten, mongrel bitch bag-of-bones dog! Get moving, bitch!" He aimed another kick at the dog, sending it yelping across the yard.

I leaped on the larger boy's back. Surprised by my weight, he staggered and fell. We rolled in the gravel. Then I was on his chest pounding his face and head. "Take it back!" I sobbed. "Take it back!"

I was taken again to the principal's office. "This is the first time I ever expelled anyone from first grade," said Mr. Krantz, shaking his head. "Send the breed home. He's loco—head's on crooked. His father will have to come in and account for him if this little rat's going to school here."

I walked home. When I could see my house I sat down. My new shirt was torn, my coveralls filthy. Our family dog trotted forward to meet me. "Hi, Pal," I said.

Pal sat beside me, lifted one paw, then licked my face. I wrapped my arms around him and let loose inside. Minutes later, strong hands helped me to my feet. Grandmother led me to the porch rocker. There she held me till I stopped sobbing. I told her my story.

"Why did it happen that way, Grandmother?" I asked.

"Little Grandson," she responded, "do you remember the rainbow blankets you helped me make?"

"I do, Grandmother."

"Those blankets are like people," she said. "They come in all sizes and colors. The way we understand people is by their hearts. They have either one heart or two. The ones with two hearts say one thing and do another. They can't find the real difference between right and wrong from one day to the next. They seem to have a hard time." She looked at me. "Are my words clear?"

"I think so, Grandmother."

"Two-hearted people are hard to understand," she said.

"But how do I know the one-hearted people, Grandmother?"

"Little Grandchild," said the old woman. "The one-hearteds have one heart for all things in life. There is peace in their hearts. Your daddy and mother are this kind. Today at school you saw the other kind." Grandmother looked at me. "How is your heart now, Little Grandson?" she asked.

I felt my heart and the old woman's heart beating together where she held me. "Grandmother, what will I do if the bigger boys try to hurt me again? Mr. Krantz says there are rules."

The old woman looked deep into my eyes. "Little Grandson, you are a warrior. You must always fight the wrongs you see in any way you can. Your way to fight won't always be the same as the others."

We were quiet with each other.

"Grandmother?" I asked.

"Yes?"

"Grandmother, will school always be so hard?"

She looked at me for several moments. "You, Little Grandson," she said, "have the heart of a great chief. But since you are only six years old, we will go inside and have a piece of chocolate cake."

GOD'S
LITTLE SURGEONS

In my heart, my grandmother was the nicest, bravest, smartest, and most mysterious of all the people in the world—including Daddy, I supposed. I had never seen my grandmother asleep or even resting. When she looked to be dozing or napping, it turned out she was studying me or waiting for something to happen. And it usually did!

She was the littlest grown-up I knew, though mainly I didn't consider her the same as other grown-up people. She was simply my grandmother, and there was no one like her. She was smaller than my mother. I saw that when the two women were together. Yet when I considered her, she was bigger than anyone else. She was a full-blood Cherokee Indian and a medicine woman. Her hair fell all the way down her back.

"Why do you make your hair so long, Grandmother?" I asked one morning.

"The Great Spirit chose it that way for my hair, Little Grandson," she answered. "It was so for my mother's hair before me. If I cut it short like your mama's, I might be too weak to rise from bed in the morning." She looked at me, eyes laughing.

"Do you understand?" She said no more.

At the time, I could not have explained the meaning of her words to another person. Yet inside I felt content. She gave me a calmness.

I had seen her angry only once, and I'd seen her cry just one time. The healing for Edwin was what brought her feelings up. It started the morning the banker from Lubbock came to the house with his twenty-three-year-old son asking Grandmother Spotted Fawn to heal his son's deafness. He came in his big Chrysler car and new gray suit, apologizing for having rejected Grandmother's loan request for a new well pump two weeks previous. "Not reliable," read the note from the bank.

With his hat in hand, the banker stood in front of Grandmother trying to say it differently. Grandmother sat quietly in her rocker, her patching on her lap.

"Mrs. Raper, ma'am," he began, "I do so appreciate your giving time to talk to me and Edwin." He hesitated, looking for acknowledgment from Grandmother. There was none.

"Mrs. Raper, I regret the misunderstanding given your loan request earlier. I'm sure it was a natural and understandable error—perhaps by one of our new bank clerks. I have come to you personally at your home here today to correct the misunderstanding."

Grandmother continued her patching.

"Er, Mrs. Raper, ma'am, I . . . I've brought my son Edwin along today to see you." The man pulled his son closer. "He can't hear our words, poor child. He's become stone deaf and doesn't hear a thing. It's a true tragedy!"

His hands were fooling with his hat, bending the brim. "Mrs. Raper . . . er, Grandmother Raper . . . uh, Grandmother Spotted Fawn, ma'am, me and Mrs. Fredrick have done everything we can to improve Edwin's hearing. We've been to the East. The best specialist doctors have concluded Edwin will never hear again. They say his ears are irreparable. No hope, they told us." The banker paused. "It is a painful thing for me and his mother to bear."

Grandmother rocked slowly. She acknowledged the presence of neither the father nor the son.

The man continued: "Mrs. Raper, the town people tell me you have strong medicine." My Grandmother did not respond.

"They tell me you have the strongest medicine hereabouts," he said. Still no response. "With your permission, Grandmother Raper, I have brought you these gifts."

The man placed a beautifully woven brown-and-yellow blanket at the old woman's feet. On the blanket he lay tobacco. From his pocket he pulled an old wooden carving and offered it to her.

Her hands remained folded in her lap, motionless. He put the carving beside the tobacco.

I knew from her face that Grandmother was thinking deep. Outwardly, she acknowledged nothing.

"Grandmother Raper," the man said. "If you heal my son Edwin,

I will personally give you the five thousand dollars requested from the loan department."

Grandmother's face changed. Her black eyes flashed and her breath pulled! She stood slowly, coming up straight. She fixed her eyes on the banker. I sensed the man shriveling under her eyes.

"No money for what I do!" she hissed.

The banker's face sagged at the sound of Grandmother's voice. Though her tone was barely audible, it went in deep. I was glad she spoke to the banker and not to me.

"Mr. Fredrick," she continued in a louder voice. "Your request is not possible! Anyone with a thinking mind knows only the Great Spirit heals our problems. Two-leggeds do not!"

The energy from her eyes seemed to hold the banker on his feet.

"Are my words understood?" she asked.

"Uh . . . yes, ma'am, Mrs. Raper," he said faintly. Sweat gathered on his forehead. "I'm sorry, ma'am. I didn't mean————"

"However," she interrupted, "since you did know to bring medicine gifts in the old way, I'll see to helping the Great Spirit with your son's problem."

Her voice had turned soft, eyes twinkling. She glanced briefly at the wood carving. Then she motioned Edwin onto a stool. When he was seated, she placed her hands gently over his ears. She held them there for several minutes, her eyes closed.

Is she asleep? I wondered. Is she looking at his ears with her hands?

After what seemed a very long time, the old woman opened her eyes and looked directly at me. I wondered if I'd been dozing.

"Little Grandson," she said. "Put on your rain gear! Run down to the walnut grove and bring me six of Grandmother Earth's little surgeons."

"Little surgeons?" I asked.

"Maggots, child. From inside the walnuts."

I ran to the walnut grove, wading, splashing, and sloshing through water and mud caused by the heavy rains. Under trees rotting in the dampness, I soon found black walnuts. From inside the walnuts I selected six fat maggots. I took two extra in case any died as I returned. Hurrying back, I presented them to my grandmother.

She took the maggots from me and carefully smudged the little worms with sage and cedar, fanning the smoking herb mixture over each of them. Then she placed the maggots in a small jar and put them aside.

Next, she cedared Edwin. He coughed and sneezed, and I saw that Edwin was not used to smudge. As she sang an ancient song in Cherokee, Grandmother placed drops of herb oil into Edwin's ears from a tiny blue bottle taken from her bag. Then she pushed three maggots into each ear, one after the other. When the ears were stuffed with the maggots, she packed cotton on top. She then covered the cotton with tape, sealing the ears tightly. She helped the young man stand up and led him to his father.

"Come back here with Edwin in exactly forty-eight hours, not a minute less," said Grandmother.

"Yes, ma'am, Mrs. Raper," muttered the banker. He glanced at his watch, then looked again at Grandmother. He reached for Edwin's arm and seemed to miss. Then he found the boy's arm, and as they walked on the gravel path toward the Chrysler he appeared to lean on his son for support.

Forty-eight hours later the banker and his son returned. "I'm here as you requested, ma'am," he said. "It is the hour I left from two days ago."

The rains had stopped, but the land still held water. Grandmother sat Edwin on the stool as before, undid the tape, and gently pulled it away. Next she removed the cotton packing. Then she took tweezers and, counting loudly, lifted three maggots from each ear. "One . . . two . . . three. Good." She placed them in a jar.

Then she took up her gourd and shook it, humming and rocking. She burned cedar in a large shell while she sang, shaking her gourd at Edwin's ears. The banker watched intently, his face gray.

Grandmother took an eagle-bone whistle from her bag and blew high, piercing screeches at the base of Edwin's head. She moved up the head, shaking the gourd, blowing a shrill whistle through the eagle bone as she moved it in circular sweeps around one ear and then the other. When she had worked herself around to Edwin's face she paused, looking into his eyes. "If you feel pain, tell me," she said.

Edwin nodded. He must have read her lips, I thought.

Grandmother blew the whistle directly into each ear several times. After one piercing screech, Edwin seemed to rise from the stool. Grandmother then blasted different sounds directly into both ears, some loud, some soft.

Edwin's eyes opened wide. "I can hear it, Daddy." His voice was high and squeaky. "I hear the whistle! I got *sound*, Daddy!" He stared wild-eyed at his daddy, his hands fluttering. His mouth opened wide, and breaths came in fast puffs.

The banker stepped forward and grabbed his son, pulling him off the stool. "My son, oh . . . " His words came out as sobs. The son and father held each other tight. That was when I saw my grandmother crying for the first and only time. I couldn't see her clearly because my own eyes were filled with tears.

Grandmother then cedared Edwin and her medicine things again. When she finished, the fan and cedar went into her medicine bag, along with the old carving the banker had given her.

The banker looked at Grandmother, his arms still around Edwin. "Mrs. Raper," he said, wiping at his eyes and nose, "I don't know how you did it . . . this miracle. I'm going to give the loan money you asked for." His voice was husky. "I'll give you more, whatever you name."

Edwin listened like it was the first day of his life.

Grandmother looked at the banker. "No," she said quietly. "But here is what you can do." She pointed to the maggots taken from Edwin's ears. "These are the healers of your son's ears. They are the Great Spirit's little surgeons. They can work in ways humans with the finest knives can't. Their work today is finished. You can return them to the woods. Would you like to do that?" she asked.

"I would," he answered.

"Grandson will lead you."

I led the banker through the mud to the walnut grove on the south forty. There, between the puddles and fallen nuts, the man bent down and carefully placed the maggots among the walnuts. Then, with no thought for his expensive suit, he sank to his knees and opened his heart in thankfulness and prayer to the maggots, then to Grandmother, to God and the Lord Jesus Christ, and to everyone else he could think of who might have helped his son.

Then he asked Lord Jesus how he could balance his debt for what was given to him this day.

I turned away to give the banker privacy. He was on his knees for a long time. When I brought him back to the house, he seemed a different person. Wiping mud from his hands, he found Grandmother in her rocker and went again to his knees. He took her tiny hands in his. If she minded, it didn't show.

He looked at her for a long time, quiet. He cried again." God bless you, Grandmother Raper," he said. "I am deeply grateful that you shared your knowledge with Edwin and me." Then he told her if she would reapply for the loan it would come through different.

"Is it because of the healing?" she asked.

"No, Grandmother Raper," the man said calmly. "It is because I see I was wrong the way I did before."

"Then I will apply," said the old woman.

The banker walked with Edwin to the Chrysler, his arm around his son. Neither seemed to care that they were covered with mud as they drove away.

Grandmother picked up her patching. I sat by her on the edge of the porch.

"Grandmother, can Edwin hear now?"

Grandmother looked at me and smiled. "He can hear that his Daddy cares for him," she said.

I thought about that. My grandmother was right about her long hair, I decided. She is a true medicine woman!

SMOKEY

It was Grandmother's way to teach me about life and myself, utilizing each important incident that came to us. When my pony, Smokey, disappeared, Grandmother was there to help me understand.

The third night that Smokey did not return from the pasture I was awakened by a nightmare. I sat up suddenly in bed, drenched in sweat. The nightmare hovered over me, clinging like a huge cobweb, suffocating me. In my dream, buzzards had attacked Smokey. Dozens of huge, black vultures dove at my small horse, tearing strips of flesh from his back and neck. The pony reared desperately, kicking and screaming, trying futilely to escape the deadly attack. For a moment I thought the horse would escape. Then the buzzards swooped in, and Smokey went down.

"No!" I screamed, waking myself. I shivered in the predawn darkness, trying to clear my head of cobwebs. My pony had never stayed away even one night before. Adding to my worry was knowing that Smokey had a fever when I saw him last, just before the storm blew in two days previous.

I found my clothes and slipped out of the house. As the sky took light, I was in the field. I dreaded what I might find, but I had to know. Smokey and I had been together always.

Soon after I entered the woods, I lost my sense of time. I could have been walking for hours. I covered the many acres of the farm purposefully, looking under every bush and stone and shrub large enough to hide my horse, but I found no trace of Smokey. At the second pasture, I took off my shoes and waded into the pond. I felt the bottom of the shallow water with my hands, fanning wide sweeps. Wading deeper, I did the same with my toes, touching and feeling for Smokey. When I reached the far shore, I sat heavily.

"Good, he's not here," I said out loud. "Maybe Smokey's OK. Maybe the Ortiz family found him and took him in."

When the sun was high, my legs were heavy. Steps slowed. Only one section of land remained to be covered. Entering it, my heart pounded.

"Please, *please*, Jesus! Make Smokey OK. He's gotta be OK."

I thought of the day Daddy gave Smokey to me. "Take good care of him, Son. You and this little critter will grow up together," he had said. Smokey was the best birthday present of my life.

Halfway across the third pasture I saw him. On the far side of the field where the hill sloped to the stream, I saw my horse. Smokey lay quietly on his side. He was much too still. I shouted to him as I ran the distance between us. "Smokey, I'm here! I'm coming! It's me!"

I faltered as I approached the horse. "Smokey, get up! Please!" I dropped to my knees and pulled him to me. I cradled his head in my lap, hugging and holding as tight as a boy can hold his best friend, sobbing, feeling my heart was broken.

In the early afternoon Grandmother Spotted Fawn found me with Smokey. She approached so quietly I didn't notice. A soft rain fell. She knelt and put her arms around me.

I lifted my head. Her eyes were soft. "Smokey's dead, Grandmother."

She sat with me in silence, gently stroking my head. "Are you warm enough, child?"

"He died, Grandmother. I tried to get him up, but he's stiff. I couldn't help him. I should have found him sooner."

"You are shivering. Let me warm you, Little Grandson."

She gathered her big coat around me, pulling me in. I released my horse slowly and turned to Grandmother's warmth.

"You mustn't blame yourself, child," she said. She held me until she felt me calm.

"Why did Smokey die, Grandmother?"

"Are you warm?" she said.

"I am, Grandmother."

The old woman let go of me and knelt beside the horse.

"Come over here, Little Grandson."

I held back, my eyes averted.

"I said look here!"

I knew from her tone that I should obey, but I resisted.

Grandmother reached for me. Taking my upper arm gently, she turned me. I heard, more than felt, the slap land between my shoulder blades. I blinked rapidly, teared, then opened wide-eyed. Grandmother's knife was in her hand. The knife flashed once in the sun before she plunged it into Smokey's belly.

"Uhh," she grunted. "There!"

She pulled the knife the length of the horse's belly and lifted it clear. Guts slid out, as though pushed from inside, slippery and sliding toward me. I gagged and jumped back, repulsed by the smell. Then I hesitated, fascinated.

"Look close here, Little Grandchild," said the old woman. "Tell me what you see. Look here into these guts." Grandmother pointed to the entrails.

I saw only Smokey's insides spread on the grass from the cut Grandmother had made with the knife. Then I noticed movement in the guts. Smokey's innards seemed to wiggle and breathe.

"Look Grandmother!" I gasped. "Is Smokey alive?"

The guts were breathing. Then I recognized the maggots. The horse's insides were filled with dozens of wiggling maggots! I knew them as God's little surgeons, but I did not understand them inside Smokey.

I looked at the old woman. "Grandmother, are the maggots trying to help Smokey?"

"Little Grandson," she said. "Your horse is giving life to these little worms. These fly worms are feeding from this part of Smokey. Your pony is their food. His death gives them life. The maggots here are alive because Smokey has given away to them."

I sat motionless beside the old woman. "How did he give away, Grandmother?"

"Little Grandson," she said, "there isn't any really true death. Smokey still lives in these little worms chewing on him. Later, most of these maggots will hatch into flies. A few will be eaten by frogs in this little stream. Smokey will then be in the frogs and jump around in them." The old woman smiled. "Maybe some of the flies will fly as far as Fossle Creek and be gobbled by fish. Then, if you're lucky, you'll catch one of those fish and take it home to your mama, who will cook it for your daddy and all of us. In that way we'll have

Smokey inside us, Little Grandson. He'll nourish us. Do you understand my words?"

I thought about my Grandmother's words.

"This is the way it always is. As time passes, buzzards and other
creatures will come to this meadow and strip Smokey clean. Then he
will live inside the buzzards. When they fly high, so will Smokey."

The old woman paused, watching me. Turkey buzzards soared
above us, lifting and gliding with the wind.

"Even the grass here in this meadow will get life from your
horse. You see, child, in time Smokey will return to Grandmother
Earth. It is Smokey's giveaway to this grass. The grass will be nourished by Smokey. Then when Smokey's mother and brothers and
sisters come to eat the grass, they will also eat Smokey. He will be
inside them, and he will help them stay strong."

She reached for me, taking my hand. "Can you see these things I
am saying, child? Do you understand what I am telling you?"

I could not answer, though inside myself I felt better. As I walked
home with Grandmother in the grayness of the late afternoon, I
thought, I wonder if Grandmother is going to have maggots inside
her when she dies. I was afraid to ask.

SUPERBOY

When I was eight years old, I wore round, steel-rimmed glasses I would soon outgrow. Because I had collected more Superman comic books than anyone in town, my friends and relatives teased me, called me Superboy, and asked for super acts of strength from me. I took my image to heart and secretly wished my parents and cousins would respectfully acknowledge my relationship to Clark Kent and Superman. I knew for sure that when I grew up I would be a newspaper reporter.

When my Aunt Sophie presented me with a red, blue and yellow Superboy costume with full cape and red "S" embroidered on its chest, the family seemed surprised by my reluctance to put on the new outfit.

"I made it myself, Harley," said Aunt Sophie. "Put it on, child. Fly away and save Metropolis—or Fort Worth! If you can't do that, at least save your daddy's farm!"

"Yeah, Superboy. Go rescue Lois Lane," added my mother. "She's in trouble and needs your help."

"Zoom off faster than a speeding bullet!" shouted Daddy. "Maybe I can use the boy myself when I go deer hunting," he added.

I hugged the costume tightly to my chest. "No, thanks," I stammered.

Grandmother watched silently.

"C'mon, Son. Put it on for your Aunt Sophie, or I'm gonna have my feelings hurt. You won't have me crying now, will you, child?" Aunt Sophie pulled a hankie from her purse and pretended to sniffle.

"Can't," I muttered. "Not the right time."

"Christ sake, Harley," said Daddy. "Put the damn thing on."

I hesitated, stepped back, then ran to my room and shut the door.

"What's into him?" growled Daddy. "The kid never seems to respond normal. I'll get him out here."

"Leave him be, Jeff," Mother said. "Sophie understands. Maybe he'll put it on in his room."

Minutes later I returned to the parlor without the Superboy costume. Sensing Aunt Sophie's disappointment, I put my arms around her. "Thanks, Aunt Sophie. I love the present you made me. It's the best, and so are you! It's just not the right time to wear it."

"It's OK, child," she said. I hope you enjoy it later."

When company was gone and I was alone in my room, I put on the outfit Aunt Sophie had made me. I pulled my regular clothes over the costume and waited.

Suddenly I was alert! With x-ray vision I stared at my bedroom wall. I stood abruptly and pulled at my outer clothing, flinging shirt and coveralls aside. I removed my glasses, lifted a bedroom window, jumped out and dashed across the yard, my cape billowing behind. When I reached the water tower, I leaped on the lower rungs and climbed steadily to the top. At the highest part of the tower, I hesitated briefly, looked at something in the distance, extended my arms and dove into space.

What saved me was my mother glancing out the kitchen window as I ran across the yard—that and the natural speed of Daddy sprinting in terror to save his son's life. Daddy and I came together at ground level, and my fall was cushioned. . . .

As we left the hospital my mother spoke, "What on Earth were you doing up there, honey?"

"I thought I could fly," I answered thinly.

"Seems there could have been an easier way to find out, child," she said.

"A hawk was after one of our chicks."

"Couldn't you just have told your daddy to get his rifle?"

"I meant to fly over and save it," I said. "I didn't want the hawk to have to die."

"Oh," she said, and let it go.

DEATH OF A TARANTULA

All of my early teachings about death came from Grandmother. My father had far more than his share of it in World War II, but he mentioned none of his experiences. Grandmother viewed natural death as a ceremony. She called it a "ceremony of life."

My first experience with the ceremony happened during one of the long walks I often took with Grandmother. I have been able to see the aura of living organisms for as long as I can remember. For many years, because Grandmother also saw auras, I thought everyone did.

I was stretched out on the slope of a meadow where we stopped to relax. Grandmother stood near me. I felt the heavy meadow grass crunch under my belly. Stretched flat, I studied the movement Grandmother pointed to on the slope below.

"Look carefully," Grandmother said. "Mind everything you see. I'll ask you to tell it back later."

I grunted acknowledgment, my eyes on the anthill below. The biggest tarantula I'd ever seen crouched near the crest of the anthill, waiting. Suddenly, hundreds of Texas red ants rushed at the tarantula from secret ambush sites. From all sides they swarmed over the spider, rushing up its legs, stinging and biting.

The ants hung on tenaciously as the tarantula kicked frantically, spinning and turning. More ants attacked. The huge spider crouched, then leaped several feet straight up, flinging ants in all directions. When the spider landed, more ants attacked. The ground was alive with thousands of swarming red ants.

Stunned by the ferocity of the attack, the tarantula turned one way, then another, seeking escape. A tremor shook its body. One leg gave way, then a second. The huge spider struggled to regain balance. Its body tilted precariously. The tarantula shuddered again and slipped, then regained its footing. More warrior ants attacked.

"Look close," Grandmother said.

He could have got away if he'd jumped when they first came at him, I thought. (I kept a small tarantula in a jar at home and considered myself an expert.)

"What do you see?" asked Grandmother.

I saw only the ants and the tarantula. Then I noticed something else. "I see a light, Grandmother. There are colored lights around the tarantula. What makes them?"

"You see the spider's light, Little Grandson," said the old woman. "Look carefully. What is happening to the colors?"

I studied the conflict, spellbound. "Grandmother, look!" I exclaimed. "The lights are shining into the ants. It's a war, and the ants are taking the tarantula's light!"

The spider's long legs trembled violently.

"It's not a war like you are thinking, Little Grandson. The spider is giving its life to the ants. The color you see is the spider's life energy, its essence." The old woman paused, watching the struggle. "The ants know the spider is giving away to them, child. They are taking the spider's gift inside them. The light of the tarantula will make the ant clan strong."

I sat quietly, absorbing Grandmother's words.

"Look again!" she said. "Watch closely for the ceremony."

The tarantula's front legs collapsed. It lurched and fell. Its body pitched forward and rolled to the left. Hairy legs moved slowly in and out. The ants took charge. They tugged the spider till they had it where it was supposed to be.

I wonder if the ants have chiefs, I thought. Some of the ants were positioned apart from the tarantula, alert for other activity. "Those must be the scouts."

Warrior ants continued to sting the dying tarantula. Other ants dragged it to a preferred location. A purple glow surrounded the spider. Then a bright light flashed, and the ants close by lit up. The glow from the tarantula faded and disappeared.

"Wow!" I exclaimed. "Did you see that, Grandmother?"

"Yes," she smiled.

"Grandmother, what was that?"

"Ceremony, Little Grandchild. That was the ceremony. The tarantula gave its light to the ants. It happens this way when the Great Spirit's children cross over to the spirit world." The old woman pointed toward the dead spider. The ants systematically took it apart. "The spider's death gives life to the ants. The flash you saw is the Great Spirit's ceremony of life. It is a celebration."

The old woman pulled me to my feet. "Come, we go home now."

"Grandmother, did Smokey flash like that when he died?"

"Yes, child, only the flash was much bigger."

"Did Smokey flash into the things around him?"

"Yes, Little Grandson," she said. "It is always this way."

As we walked across the field toward the house, I felt a deep fullness, and then I thought of something else. "Grandmother, I wish I had been close when Smokey died so he could have flashed into me."

THE RABID DOG

It was a wonder to me that my grandmother understood all animals, tame or wild. Grandmother Spotted Fawn and animals had a language between them, a communication for understanding and knowing. Grandmother and animals knew each other's intent.

Our cat, Sarah, was a good example. If Grandmother was in the house, Sarah didn't jump on the dining room table. But if Grandmother was not close by, it was Sarah's favorite thing to do, even though my mother chased after the cat, shouting and banging at her with the broom. There were times when I watched Sarah studying Grandmother, waiting. After a time, Grandmother would look down at Sarah as though sending a signal. The cat would then leap on Grandmother's lap, or run to the kitchen to be fed, or scratch at the door to the outside. I called it animal magick.

I was with Grandmother on the porch when a neighbor phoned, asking for help with a rabid dog. "Come along, Little Grandson," she said. "It's the Garcia's dog gone sick. Its brain isn't working right anymore. We'll go see."

I danced in place, excited for an adventure with Grandmother. "What's wrong with Garcia's dog, Grandmother?"

"Its brain can't think right, Little Grandson. We'll take a look."

Grandmother and I walked together on the dusty road toward the Garcia residence. The old woman carried a single shot .22-caliber rifle. I skipped along beside.

"Are we going to shoot the dog, Grandmother?" I asked.

"Only if it tells us we have to," she replied, not looking at me.

"Can we help the dog?"

"Well," said the old woman, "we can help the dog choose its death."

"Why did we bring the gun, Grandmother?"

"Because," she replied, her eyes on something beyond me, "the dog may be past choosing its own death."

"Grandmother, what if it only gets wounded?"

"Hush, Little Grandson," she said. "We'll have time later."

A group of people had collected in the Garcia yard. They were gathered around an old abandoned Buick, keeping well back from the wreck. Their faces showed fear and concern. The people had managed to trick the rabid dog into the Buick and trap it there. They had not known what to do next, and that is apparently why Grandmother had been called.

I could not see what worried the people, though I felt something bad in the air. There was a thrashing in the old car, a scary snarling, and the dog threw itself heavily into the windshield. *Crash!* Then quiet. The car window was cracked and beginning to give way. Clearly it was not going to hold the big dog inside much longer. A green foam smeared the glass where the dog had impacted it. Its snarling was different than any I had ever heard, as if the dog's foot was in a steel trap, though I knew it wasn't.

Grandmother handed me the rifle. "Hold this gun behind you," she said. "I don't want to give this old dog extra worry."

"OK, Grandmother."

I hid the rifle behind my back and watched her walk forward.

As she reached the wreck, the dog leaped again. *Smash!* The sound of breaking glass merged with frantic snarling. The dog charged the window again. Shreds of glass fell to the ground. The window would disintegrate any second.

I saw the dog crouch, readying itself for another rush. It panted furiously. Green foam spilled from its mouth. I readied myself to run.

Grandmother's face was right there next to the glass as the dog leaped. The animal seemed to slow in midair. It hit the window, fell back, then got up to stare at Grandmother. The dog eased back slowly, lay down on the car seat, and was still.

Grandmother opened the car door and spoke in Cherokee. Then she walked toward me, ignoring the people crowding around the Buick. "Let's go home, Little Grandson," she said.

There were so many things I wanted to ask Grandmother: Did that dog know you, Grandmother? Where did that cry come from? Grandmother, were you scared? What made the dog die? What did you say to it at the end? As usual, though, when I felt the magick from Grandmother I was mute. She took the rifle from me, and we walked home.

CANDY SPOTS
AND THE BLOODGATE

Some Native American medicine people have an ability to heal wounds that is beyond scientific explanation. My people called it the "bloodgate." Apparently, it was called this because the medicine person was able to stop the flow of massive bleeding, just as though a gate had been placed in the path of free-flowing blood. Two experiences with Grandmother showed me her gift of the bloodgate.

I lay in my bedroom darkness, stimulated by the events of the day. People are scared of Grandmother, I thought. They don't know what to make of her. Even Daddy is fidgety when Grandmother's eyes shine a certain way. I pondered the ancient woman who was so precious in my life. I bet it's the bloodgate making them scared. The bloodgate is too much magick for them, I decided.

I felt the mystery of the bloodgate and shivered. I snuggled deeper into my blankets. Today was the second time I'd seen it. The first was five days previous, when the stallion Candy Spots got hurt.

I'd stuffed my pockets with carrots and gone to the field to feed Candy Spots, my daddy's favorite Appaloosa. I adored the horse, but the only time the stallion let me close was when I had carrots. If I brought carrots, Candy Spots liked me. When I entered the horse pasture, I was startled to hear the stallion screaming in pain.

Men shouted, "*Mantente firme, caballo grande!*—Steady there! Whoa!"

I approached the men. Wild-eyed, the horse reared up. Candy Spots had gone crazy! Blood splashed on the ground.

"*Busca ayuda!* Help!" shouted one of the men.

My carrots scattered as I ran for the only person I knew who could help. "Grandmother!" I screamed frantically as I reached the yard. "Hurry! Candy Spots is dying! Grandmother—come!"

From her place on the porch, the old woman saw me coming. She dropped the green beans she was breaking for supper and followed.

When she heard the horse's screams, she lifted her skirts and sprinted past me.

Three farm workers struggled to free Candy Spots from entanglement in the barbed wire. The horse thrashed frantically. Each desperate lunge for freedom ripped more flesh. Blood gushed from deep slashes in its forelock and neck.

Suddenly one of the men went down. "Manuel!" shouted Grandmother. "Lie still!" Another quickly pulled him clear.

"Grandmother!" I cried, "help Candy Spots!" The horse whinnied and shrieked, thrashing deeper into the wire.

Grandmother said something to the men in Spanish, and they moved back. The old woman edged into the cloud of dust.

"*Señora abuelita*, be careful, *por favor!*"

Grandmother stepped into the whirl of dust, nimbly dodging the thrashing hooves. I held my breath. She looks so little, I thought. I watched her, spellbound. She seemed to be dancing with Candy Spots!

Unraveled wire was looped around the horse. Terrified, he lunged wildly. Grandmother ducked under the horse's neck and, with two fingers in her mouth, blew a long shrill whistle. Candy Spots continued to struggle against the wire, but now he watched Grandmother.

She whistled and shouted Cherokee words I did not understand. When she lifted her hands again, the stallion slowed his thrashing. The wildness in his eyes subsided. Finally only his head moved slowly back and forth, his eyes on Grandmother.

"Hand me the cutters," she said to the men.

The old woman stared at Candy Spots's eyes as she cut the wire. How can she see where she's cutting? I wondered. The workers watched, motionless.

When the horse was clear of the wire, the old woman stepped in close. Stretching on tiptoes, she touched the stallion's head. Candy Spots leaned down, his eyes wide and deep, filled with the old woman. She whispered in his ear. I heard her singing. Then she passed both hands over the deep gashes, touching the cuts on the stallion. The horse stopped bleeding. It was like turning off a faucet.

Blood streaming from deep slashes slowed and stopped. The men took off their hats and crossed themselves.

"Take away the rest of the wire," she said.

I picked up one of the discarded carrots and approached the horse.

"Here, Candy Spots," I said, "I brought you a carrot."

Candy Spots breathed deeply, his eyes on Grandmother. He ignored the carrot.

"He might like a carrot tomorrow, Little Grandson."

"It was a rattler that caused it," Grandmother told me later. "The wire was left carelessly yesterday when the men were fixing the fence. The horse shied when the snake attacked and stepped into the barbed wire, causing it to spring up around him. Scared and hurt, the stallion didn't know his way out. Poor old horse. His panic is what caused the damage." Her voice calmed me. "Horses have never found good ways to adjust to unnatural things like barbed wire."

When I came back next day with my pockets full of carrots, Candy Spots was carrot friendly as usual. His wounds were healing.

THE SECOND BLOODGATE

I saw the bloodgate a second time the morning a field worker was hurt. The man was plowing to prepare the field for planting and had somehow fallen under the machine. It had sliced his arm in half between the wrist and elbow. Other men were able to slow the blood using a shirt. They carried the sobbing man to the house, where Grandmother was working on a quilt.

"*Señora abuela!*" someone shouted. "*Por favor! Tenemos prisa!*"

She heard the commotion and met the men at the porch. "Set him down here, quick!" she ordered.

The old woman studied the man's face, then slowly unwrapped the bloody bandage from his arm. As it came loose, blood splashed on the wooden porch, causing me to jump back. Grandmother pressed the arm above the cut and began her song. She sang louder till her voice was a high shriek, then it faded out. The bleeding slowed and stopped—the blood stopped clean where it had been pouring out. Grandmother then released the arm.

"Did you bring the cut-off part with you?" she asked.

When the men explained they had not, Grandmother appeared upset, as if she expected they would have known to bring the severed hand when they came for help.

After the men were gone I helped my Grandmother scrub blood from the porch planks. "Did you want them to bring the hand that was cut off, Grandmother?" I asked.

"Little Grandson," said the old woman, "did the Great Spirit intend the man to have two hands?"

Later, from the darkness of my bedroom, I realized that Grandmother had run faster than I when we rushed to save Candy Spots, and I'd won *all* my school races. I have a strange and wonderful grandmother, I thought, as I drifted off to sleep on a cloud of warm contentment.

PART 2

ADOLESCENCE

FLYING

At age fourteen, my best friends were my two cousins, Buddy and Travis Raper. We were double cousins and inseparable. Our parents called us the Three Musketeers. Neighbors called us Mark Twain's Gang. I was obviously our Tom Sawyer.

One afternoon after we'd seen the movie Wings, we discussed the thrills of flying. We agreed we'd be pilots one day and have our own planes. I suggested we build a personal fighter plane right now.

"That's a fun idea," said Buddy.

"Yeah, great! Let's do it!" echoed Travis.

"It will be a three-seater," I said calmly, my eyes on a puff of cumulus cloud in the sky. "And when she's finished, we'll climb aboard, kick over the prop, and fly up into the wild blue yonder." I gestured up and away.

My cousins eyed me closely. "Oh, God," said Buddy. "Here we go again, Travis. He's got that 'I'm serious about this' tone."

"Harley, you don't mean fly it off the ground, do you?" asked Travis. He must have hoped he wouldn't hear the answer he knew was coming.

"I'm serious about this, man. I feel it so deep, I must be born to fly. Just like the Wright Brothers. The three of us have got to fly. Those brothers had courage—and vision and spirit. They flew when nobody else had before." I was into it, my body beginning to sway. I paused, looking at my cousins. "I don't see anything they got on us three, men. The Three Musketeers are going to build an awesome three seater and fly it!"

Buddy and Travis sat mute. Slowly they turned to each other, alarm showing in their faces.

"Harley, you . . . uh, seen a doctor lately?" asked Buddy.

Travis paled. It appeared that he might cry if he relaxed.

The next day, as I studied my disassembled soapbox derby racer, Buddy and Travis were with me. Parts of the racer were scattered throughout the garage. I contemplated the chassis of my little racer. "Travis, hand me that wrench," I said.

"This one?"

"Naw, that one's too little. Give me the big one there with the red handle. The big one's better for this job. This bolt's rusted in."

I took the wrench from Travis, adjusted its jaws to the size of the nut to be loosened and handed the wrench to Buddy.

"This will be a tough one for you, Buddy, but with your strength I think you can do it. The wheel of this racer is what we need for our plane. This work is invaluable."

Buddy took the wrench, engaged it deeply and leaned into it. "Good, Buddy. Pour it on," I encouraged. "I think you're getting it."

"God, this is a tough one," grunted Buddy. "How long since you oiled these wheels?" Sweat rolled down his forehead.

"I haven't raced for a while," I answered. "I think it's moving, Buddy. Travis, run and get a can of oil to squirt on this, eh?"

"Uhh! Ouch! Shit!" cried Buddy.

"What happened, Buddy?"

"Nothing. Shit. I just skinned my knuckles when it slipped. Shit!"

"Try it again, Buddy."

"I think I got it now, Swift."

"Yeah, it's moving, Buddy. Go for it!'

"There, that does it," grunted Buddy. "It's clear."

"Good! Really great job, Buddy. Travis, forget the oil. Get some axle grease instead."

I lifted the wheel clear and carefully handed it to Buddy.

"Here, Buddy. Grease it with the other two and put them together. These wheels have to roll smooth and easy. It's your job to make sure they do. I'll see you guys later."

"Where are you going?" asked Buddy.

"We got to have a prop, don't we? I've a hunch there's one for our flying machine out at the airport."

A few minutes later I pedaled my bike on the road to the airport, located two miles outside the city limits. When I reached a runway that was no longer used, I turned toward the largest of three hangars, swung off my bike, and approached a mechanic I knew from other visits.

"Hey, Mr. Freebs," I called, "got any extra propellers around here you want to get rid of?"

Three hours later I pedaled carefully back to town. Tied tightly to the handlebars of my bike was a damaged airplane propeller. On the runway behind me, seven freshly washed airplanes sparkled immaculately in the Texas sun.

I pedaled my bike directly to my Uncle Harry's house. Once there, I untied the propeller from my bike and leaned it against the house. I waited patiently for the arrival of my favorite uncle. Uncle Harry was a master carpenter and often worked overtime.

When Uncle Harry arrived, he greeted me warmly. "Hey, look who's here! How's my favorite troublemaker?"

"All right, Uncle Harry—good."

"What can I do you out of today?" asked Uncle Harry.

I showed him the propeller. "Can we size it down, Uncle Harry?" I asked.

"I was just hoping someone would bring me a propeller to play with this weekend, son," said Uncle Harry. "The wife wanted the bedroom painted, and you know how I love to paint a bedroom!" He laughed.

We worked on the old propeller through the weekend. We scraped, planed, sanded, glued, and varnished till my hands ached. We worked as one on the project. I loved working with my uncle. With him I felt strong like a man. When our work was finished, we had a new propeller, smaller than the original but beautiful.

"What do you think of it, Harley?" asked my uncle.

"It's perfect!" I shouted, leaping in the air. "It's a masterpiece! Uncle Harry, you're a genius! You're the greatest carpenter on the planet. Even Jesus couldn't have done better!" I hugged my uncle. "Thanks, Uncle Harry! I've gotta show Buddy and Travis!"

I grabbed the propeller, tied it to my bike, and pedaled down the road.

Riding away from the house, I heard Uncle Harry laughing. "He's got me ranked up there higher than Jesus Christ!"

Early the next morning, I was with my cousins at the railroad yards talking to Mr. Robinson, the old warehouse caretaker. He listened cheerfully as we described the construction of our three-seater airplane.

"Mr. Robinson," I said, "we're looking for a big bolt for the front end."

"It's to make the prop spin," added Buddy.

"We have a real prop!" added Travis.

"Swift says we can really fly it!" said Buddy.

When we finished describing our plane, Robinson spoke. His eyes twinkled. "So, y'all are the 'Right' Cousins?" The old man smiled. "Well, I'll tell you what. Y'all seem pretty right to me. I think y'all may just make it with this airplane machine of yours."

Mr. Robinson blew his nose on a large red handkerchief.

"Here's what we'll do to help get this plane of yours off the ground," he said. "I got something in back of these tall weeds that could help." He pointed to the back of the building. "It's in that trash machinery there. There's an eye bolt rusting with that junk that might work. You find it, take it."

We rushed to the back of the building and found the bolt under a rusting train axle and dragged it free. It measured over a foot in length. A steel ring was attached to one of its ends.

"It's exactly what we're looking for, Mr. Robinson!" I exclaimed.

"Good, then it's y'all's. Got no use here," said the old man.

We took the bolt and headed home, carrying it in turns.

"Just don't fly too high, now, d'ya hear? And don't forget parachutes!" Old Robinson waved and we signaled thumbs up.

"What does he mean, 'parachutes,' Swift?" asked Travis.

"Don't worry about it, Trav," I said. "He's just kidding."

Back at my house we went to work. Guided by my supervision, Buddy and Travis sawed, pounded, and bolted four two-by-eight timbers together, drilled a shaft hole, mounted the bolt with washers, and attached the propeller. Next we bolted four two-by-twos together and secured a hook to the far end. In between we placed peach crates and fashioned three seats.

We bolted on wings cut from old plywood sheets, screwed in struts, built a tail from scraps, and nailed it on. Then we bolted the soap-box derby racer wheels to the bottom of the fuselage. We strung inner tubes between the hook at the rear and the propeller shaft at the front. Hours later we painted the plane red and black.

"Those are power colors," I told them. "Baron Manfred von Richthofen knew that when he flew with the Flying Circus in World War I."

"Who the hell is the Baron?" asked Buddy.

"World War I ace," I replied.

Finally, we fell back exhausted.

"You've been a great work crew," I encouraged. "Look at her."

"Can't—too tired," said Buddy.

"Just look at her . . . God," I said. "She's just waiting to lift her nose to the sun."

Buddy and Travis sat up.

"It really is beautiful," said Buddy. "We did it. We really did it! Do you think it needs a little more red paint?"

"It's fantastic!" echoed Travis. "It's all ours!"

"I think it'll do the job," I said slowly. I focused on something behind Buddy and Travis. "And now it's time for us to shift from work crew to flight crew," I added.

"Yeah, let's climb in and try her out," said Travis, stepping forward.

"Hold it, Trav," I said, raising my arm. "Not here. This is not our flight runway. We don't take off from here."

The two boys looked at me. "Well, then, where do we take off from?" asked Buddy.

I lifted my right hand purposefully, index finger extended. I pointed to a spot high behind Buddy and Travis. "I think right about there would be OK, men," I said thoughtfully. "Yes, for certain, right there would be perfect!"

Buddy and Travis turned, following the direction my finger pointed. Their eyes settled unmistakably on the highest point of the enormous red barn on the Reagan property.

"Oh, my God!" gasped Travis. "He doesn't mean it!"

"He's gone mad!" muttered Buddy.

"True, nervous I am, and nervous I have been," I responded. "But why do you say that I am mad? Ha-ha-ha-ha-he-he!" I cackled insanely.

"Jesus, Swift, what's that all about?" asked Travis.

"He's reciting Edgar Allan Poe again," said Buddy.

"Now then, men," I continued, "two things need attention before we take this flight." I grinned at them. "Which, by the way, I guarantee will be successful and will probably make all three of us famous and written up in huge print in tomorrow's headlines!"

Buddy and Travis stared at me.

"The first thing," I said, "we take an oath of secrecy and honor right now that none of you, er, *us*, will mention a word to anyone about our flight, which is scheduled for tomorrow. This flight is classified and top secret!" I spoke in my most convincing and compelling voice. "We've got to agree that if any one of us talks about this top-priority secret mission—utters even a single word or even breathes a thought out loud—that person, that *traitor*, will be banished from the Three Musketeers for life and forever! Is this clear to everyone? There must be no leak!"

I looked directly at Travis, my youngest cousin. "Is this understood?" I demanded, glaring.

"Er, yes, I promise," stuttered Travis.

"You promise what?" pressed Buddy.

"I mean . . . uh, yes, what . . . uh, you said. Like you said. None of us will tell about the flight tomorrow. Especially me," he added thinly.

"Good, he's got it," I said. "Now, the second thing we must do is get some cash together to buy flying helmets and goggles from over at the surplus store."

"Goggles? What do we need those for?" asked Travis.

"God, Travis," I said, "don't be stupid. Did you ever see an ace fly without goggles? Did the Wright Brothers? Did Eddy Rickenbacker? Travis, do you know *anything* about flying?"

"Jesus, Travis," added Buddy.

We worked in the hay field the next morning to earn our spending money. At mid-afternoon we met at the airplane holding used helmets and goggles.

"Travis, what kind of goggles are those?" I asked.

"I couldn't find the right kind," said Travis. He hid his goggles behind his back, looking like he would cry. "Maybe I shouldn't go."

"What are they?" asked Buddy.

"They're welder goggles," replied Travis, holding them up for inspection. "Maybe I should stay home."

"They're OK, Trav. They're fine," I told him. "They show you have a creative mind. And more important, they show us you really want to fly."

I turned toward the plane. "Now, men, let's ready our plane for takeoff!"

"Yeah, man, let's do it!" said Buddy.

We hooked the inner tubes in place. Using ropes and the hay pulley, we pushed, dragged, and hauled the plane to the highest point on the barn roof. We attached its tail to a lightning rod, aiming the front of the plane down the steep slant of the roof. We were breathing hard and soaked with sweat.

"Now then," I told them, "let's wind up this prop. We'll make it tighter than a prop has ever been wound, 'cause we got a sky waiting for us up there!"

We wound the prop, twisting the tire tubes tight. When the tubes were as tight as Travis and Buddy could manage, I leaned into the prop as hard as I could and twisted them twice more.

"Excellent, men!" We were puffing hard. "That should be good enough to fly us to Perrin Air Force Base. Latch them!"

Buddy and Travis latched the tubes, holding them taut.

"Excellent, men. Now we are ready. Pull your helmets on and get into your seats. We're about to be airborne."

Travis sat on the roof motionless, frozen in place. "Wha——, wha——, what if the plane doesn't fly, Harley?"

"We ain't gonna crash, Travis," I said. "Put on your helmet so you look right. Get those goggles on to protect you from the wind velocity, and I'll tell you the flight plan."

Travis did as he was told.

I pointed to the field beyond the hay we'd stacked earlier that morning, nearly one hundred yards away.

"See that far field?" I said. "That's our landing area. That field's plowed and softer than a baby's butt. We are going to fly over the ditch below us here, glide over the hay, and come down light as a feather for a perfect three-point landing in the field."

Travis looked at me strange, and I wondered if he heard fear in my voice.

"OK," I said, "buckle your helmet, Travis, and get into your seat. I'll unlatch the prop here in the front so it can start spinning. Then you cut the rope holding us on the roof. Got it? Soon as that happens, we'll be flying. Now, everybody get in *now!*"

We climbed into our seats and fastened our goggles. I took the front seat. Buddy climbed in the middle, and Travis edged into the rear. I pulled a white scarf from my pocket, looped it around my neck, and swung it flamboyantly over my shoulder.

"For God and country and the Three Musketeers, we take to the sky!" I screamed.

I pulled my scout knife from my belt and passed it back. "Buddy, hand the knife to Travis," I said. Then louder: "Travis, when I give the word, lean back and cut the rope holding us to the lightning rod, OK? Now this is it, men! Is everyone ready?"

Neither Buddy nor Travis answered.

"I said, 'Is everyone ready?'"

Two faintly audible "yeps" sounded behind me.

"OK, then," I yelled. "The Wright Brothers ain't got nothing on the Right Cousins. Contact! Here we go! Cut the rope, Travis."

I released the latch freeing the twisted inner tubes, and the prop spun wildly, lifting the front of the plane. Vibrating dangerously, the plane lurched sideways, straining against the twine holding it to the lightning rod.

"Travis, you've got to cut the rope!" I shouted.

One wheel lifted clear and then the other, as the plane rocked crazily in its struggle to be free.

"*Travis*, cut the goddamn rope!" I bellowed. "*Travis!*"

Suddenly we were loose and hurtling down the steep slope of the roof. "Hang on, men!" I screamed.

Then we were over the edge and struggling to gain altitude. "*Yahoo!*" I shouted, flapping my arms. Buddy and Travis hung on tight.

For a moment we held steady. Then the tubes were finished. The plane seemed to hang suspended, then plunged toward the ground, angling sideways, nose down. The ground came up fast, and we slammed hard into the far side of the ditch with a deafening crash. One of the cousins behind me yelled something. Parts of the plane flew in every direction. Wood splintered and wheels bounced in the field. The impact threw all three of us clear of the wreck. We landed partially in the hay we'd stacked that morning. Dust and quiet settled around us.

Buddy spoke first, his voice groggy. "God, what happened?"

"I'm alive . . . I'm alive . . . I'm alive!" groaned Travis.

From under rubble and hay, I found my voice. "Shut up, Travis. Me and Buddy here are trying to figure out what went wrong."

"You can't get me to fly again," Travis sobbed. "I won't do it again!" He was becoming hysterical.

"Buddy," I said. "I think we had too much weight."

"Yeah, we'll have to dispose of Travis," Buddy agreed.

"We've got to figure the best disposal method," I continued. "Maybe he should have been offered as a sacrifice right before we took off. Maybe now ain't too late."

"I'm alive!" screamed Travis.

He tried to stand, lurched and fell back, clutching below his knee. He gasped in pain. "Harley, my leg! Oh, God, I've busted my leg!" he sobbed. "I've busted my leg flying an airplane!"

I sat still where I'd landed. My left arm hung limp. I tried to support it to ease the pain. "You OK, Buddy?" I asked.

Buddy stood up examining himself. "Yeah, I think so. I'm cut up pretty good, but I feel OK."

"I'm not going up again!" yelled Travis.

Buddy and I looked at Travis.

"I mean it, you guys. I'm not going up again! Never! Nothing can ever make me!"

Buddy and I looked at each other, then we giggled. Our giggles broke into laughter. Travis joined us. We laughed until the pain stopped us.

"Better go for help," I said to Buddy. "I ain't able to be carrying Travis."

When help came for us, Travis's leg was found to be broken. As I already knew, my arm was fractured, as were two of my ribs. Buddy was given first aid for cuts and lacerations.

In later times, when I pondered our flight together, my injuries did not seem as important as two other thoughts. One was the thrill that was mine because for a brief moment we *had* flown. The second was the realization that I might find a way to do it better.

TEXAS HALF-BREED COWBOY

When I look at my life, I see a core aspect of myself that has never disappeared or changed or been forgotten, no matter how ugly or beautiful things have got. That is the part in me that knows at heart I'm mainly just a Texas half-breed cowboy. Everything I have accomplished in this lifetime comes from a basic Texas cowboy ethic. It was instilled in me early on and has stayed. Any true cowboy would recognize the simple code of morality and ethics that guides me. An experience I had when I was fourteen years old portrays what I am talking about.

That year I was on the junior rodeo circuit. I loved the rodeo and competed every chance I had. I loved every aspect of it: the excitement, the crowds, the animals, especially the smells. I was deeply impressed by the cowboys themselves and their down-to-earth approach to life.

My specialty was bronc riding. Midseason I switched to bareback and loved it. There was something about having that contact right next to the animal that gave the ride a whole new flavor, a powerful energy exchange. I loved it and began to win riding bareback. Then something happened that made that season forever memorable.

The age rule for riding Brahma bulls in junior rodeo was lowered, which meant I was old enough to ride them. No one my age was riding them, but that was not significant to me. I began to study Brahma bull riding, talking to the cowboys and the handlers. My mind was preparing for the day I'd be on one of those bulls.

When the weekend of the junior rodeo at Mesquite, Texas, rolled around, I decided to go for it and registered to ride a Brahma named Breaks Wind. I'll never forget the moment they called me. I pulled on my jeans and chaps and Western shirt, put on my hat with an eagle feather, and ambled coolly over to the stock pen. I climbed up the stock gate and looked down at Breaks Wind. *Oh my gosh!*

I was used to getting on a bronc at the loading gate. A bronc will buck and try to throw you off, but it's not really that big when you're used to it. When I looked down at that huge bull from the stock gate rail, my heart almost stopped beating. He was a big cream-colored bull with sharp six-inch horns. I'd seen cowboys come out of the chutes on bulls, but I had never looked down at one from the view of the rider. A fear came up my gut. My throat went dry. I couldn't swallow. Breaks Wind's head looked bigger than a horse is wide. His horns were ominous.

My mentor and main rodeo man, Frank, was with me at the chute. "Are you sure you want to do this?" he asked. My face must have been white.

"Yes, Frank," I said. Secretly, I was hoping to faint or throw up or be disqualified in some way.

"OK then. You must be crazy, and that qualifies you to ride this bull. I'm going to tell you how to do this thing.

"Harley," he said, "get yourself right above him. When you sit down on him, act like you've got a plunger connected to your asshole. Then you stick that plunger on his backbone. Got it?"

"OK."

"Then take that rope and wrap it once, twice, then come over a third time and hook it right around your thumb and lock it. Do you understand, son?"

"Yes."

"All right now, one more thing: Once you're wrapped, do not move your right elbow. Get the elbow in tight and lock it in! Got it?"

"Yep."

I sat down on that big bull. His eyes were red and wild, rolling around. Obviously he didn't want anything on his back. I wrapped my hand tight and got my feet over his front haunches. I was ready to spur him when he went out. I looked up at Frank. He glanced at the chute master. It dawned on me I was tied to the bull.

"Well, are you ready, boy?"

"Frank! How do I get off this thing?"

"Any way you can, son. Any way you can," he said. "Now, I am going to tell you this because you will never ride a Brahma bull for the first time in your life again, and what you are doing is big. This is the only time you'll have a chance to battle an animal that cannot only kill a man, but can stomp his body into nonexistence. Fight him nose to nose, head to head, boy. If you are smart and do this well, neither of you gets hurt. It's exactly like life: life itself is one long ride. All you have to do is go out there and stay with it impeccably for eight seconds at a time. Are you ready now? Remember about your elbow."

"Cut him loose," I said.

To this day, I have never done a thing more exciting. Breaks Wind came out of that chute, cut inside, and spun sharply left. He went round and round and then leaped straight up. When his front feet hit the ground, I felt it through my entire body. The bull's back feet were almost perpendicular in the air, and I was pressed flat on his back.

"Don't move your right elbow," I said to myself over and over again.

When the bull did not lose me, he spun sharply to the right, and I almost went off. While I was off balance, he lunged for the wall. Three thousand five hundred pounds of bull slammed my right leg into the fence. My leg snapped. Breaks Wind came off the wall and made two more jumps as the buzzer went off.

Clowns rushed in to distract the bull so I could get off. I tried but couldn't move my leg. Pain and nausea affected my focus. A voice inside me was saying, "The eight seconds are up. Get off any way you can." I couldn't do it.

Seeing the situation, a brave cowboy got in there and hauled me off onto his horse. I was taken by ambulance to a hospital. Surgeons repaired a compound fracture.

Of course my mother was very upset. She wondered how I could do this to her.

My dad took it differently. "Well, I heard you stayed on him the whole eight seconds," he said.

"Maybe fourteen, by the time they got me off, Dad."

"Well, are you going to do it again?" My dad was laughing.

I had been thinking about that question myself when he asked. Riding that bull was dangerous, part of it truly crazy. It made no sense, but I had never found anything in fourteen years that tested me like that ride. Right then I knew I was a cowboy for life. I knew as soon as my leg healed I'd ride a Brahma again.

A real cowboy recognizes the adventures of life, and he loves them. He finds the challenge that will bring out the best in himself, then he "goes for it!" The challenge is the edge. There is an honesty and integrity in bulls and horses that you rarely get with a two-legged human being. A cowboy knows that bull or horse is never going to betray him—it just doesn't want the rider on its back.

I see life like that. Life offers the challenge. As people, we've got to find the edge and live on it impeccably. Naturally, we run into hard spots. The key to life is not to betray ourselves.

There is a movie called *My Heroes Have Always Been Cowboys*. I cried through most of that movie. It is a statement about the way I see life. Cowboys respect life.

This is the core of who I am. I am a Texas half-breed cowboy. The main difference in my life from when I was fourteen and now is that today I am trying, as a sorcerer, to ride a huge animal called the "eighteenth feathered winged serpent wheel." The challenge is just as exciting as when I rode Breaks Wind, just as much a rush. The key to life is to get in there, stay locked in, and ride it true for eight seconds at a time.

A TRADITIONAL
SEXUAL INITIATION

In earlier times, many Native American people viewed puberty in their young people as an important and exciting event. The onset of puberty, the movement of the egg and the seed, signified new energies that would benefit all clan members. The advent of each child's puberty was considered a blessing from the Great Spirit. It was a time for celebration, for each new child born to the clan was a gift from the Great Spirit, making the clan stronger.

Special ceremonies acknowledging puberty among their young people were arranged. At the onset of her menstrual period a young girl might be taken to the women's lodge. There she was purified in the sweatlodge. She was encouraged to bleed into the ground, giving menstrual blood to Grandmother Earth in return for the blessings she would receive. The grandmothers prayed with her, asking that all powers of woman would come to the girl. She might be led to a stream, where her purification continued. She was taught that as woman she was the universe. She learned that she was Grandmother Earth and that all life came from her. She was taught the sacred responsibility of her role as woman. She learned that she was sacred and beautiful. It was hoped that in time she would know she *was* beauty. She was taught many other things pertinent to her role as a woman in the clan. She was given an opportunity to ask the grandmothers questions about sexuality and womanhood.

When she returned to the village, a feast was prepared so that all clan members might join the celebration. Each young man who had completed his puberty rite brought a gift. There was joy and celebration for the new woman. She represented strength and vitality and life for the future of the clan.

Next she went with a mature man, sometimes called a "phoenix fireman," to learn about sexual love. He was an older man, in his thirties or forties, selected by the grandmothers for his skills as a sexual teacher. The young woman remained with her teacher for several days. On the first day, one of the grandmothers joined her with her teacher and broke the hymen in a traditional painless procedure.

As the days passed for the young woman with her sexual teacher, she learned to bring pleasure to herself and her lover. She was taught all there is to know of lovemaking. When her teachings were complete, she returned to the village a woman. When she had her next menstrual cycle, she took her place with the women of the village in the women's lodge.

A young man's puberty rite was signaled by his first ejaculation of semen. At that time a three-day fast began. Before dawn of the third day, an elder led him up a mountain. At dawn he was taught his masculine connection to the sun. He learned that a man is a sun being, just as the woman is an Earth person. His connection to all animals and the galaxy was explained. At noon he was led to a pool and immersed four times, once to each direction. He bathed himself in the east, signifying that he would follow his own path to the light. His wrist was cut and he began his quest for a vision. For three additional days, the initiate fasted in quest of his medicine name and his connection to the Four Worlds. When he returned, he was welcomed with feasting and celebration. He then rested.

Next he went with a "phoenix firewoman" to learn to make love to a woman. His sexual initiation lasted from seven to fourteen days, as with the young woman. When his training was completed, the young man might also occasionally continue to see his firewoman for years. During that time, she might bring different women to him, teaching him lovemaking appropriate for different physical types of women.

In earlier generations, the Cherokee considered sexuality and lovemaking a gift from the Great Spirit. It was as important to honor sexuality as any of the other blessings from the Great Maker. Mayan scholar Hunbatz Men suggests a Mayan influence in the development of earlier Cherokee views of sexuality. According to him, Cherokee and Mayan leaders exchanged economically and culturally hundreds of years ago. The Mayan understanding of sexuality, called *kou du shka*, influenced the development of Cherokee *chuluaqui quodoushka*. I have been asked if this tradition still exists with the

Cherokee people. I think not, though I have heard of two practicing
firewomen in Oklahoma. I know of none in North Carolina.

The present leadership of the Cherokee Nation is fundamentalist
Christian. The church, of course, is very conservative in its views of
sexuality. Modern Cherokee Christians tend to be horrified by the
sexual views of their ancestors. I think one can consider these chuluaqui quodoushka puberty ceremonies mainly forgotten, except for
what Shoshone/Cherokee medicine man Rolling Thunder and I have
done with them. I've done what I can to keep the puberty ceremony
for young people a sacred and impacting experience. (For more specific information on the chuluaqui quodoushka, the energy of spiritual sexuality, see appendix C.)

MY SEXUAL
INITIATION

$$\blacktriangleright\!\!\!\blacktriangleleft\!\!\!\blacktriangleright\!\!\!\blacktriangleleft\!\!\!\blacktriangleright\!\!\!\blacktriangleleft\!\!\!\blacktriangleright\!\!\!\blacktriangleleft\!\!\!\blacktriangleright\!\!\!\blacktriangleleft$$

In the summer of my thirteenth year, Grandmother informed me that it was time for my sexual initiation with a phoenix firewoman. I was tremendously excited. During my preparatory vision quest, I could think of little except my safe return to meet my sexual teacher.

On the designated day, Grandmother walked with me to a large log-and-stone home two miles from where I lived. The house was surrounded by towering oak trees and located at the end of a path leading through a small pine forest. I had dozens of questions I wanted to ask Grandmother as we walked together. Because she said nothing to me, I remained silent.

"Here we are, Little Grandson," she said when we reached the doorstep. Grandmother pushed the door open without knocking. "Step in," she said.

I did. Four women looked up from a round table. Teacups and cookies rested in front of them.

"Walk around in front of the ladies, Little Grandson, so they can see you." She pushed me forward.

I was introduced to each of them. Martha appeared to be the oldest, fortyish, which to me was ancient. Betsy was the youngest, with blue eyes and a stunning body. Ruth and Judy were somewhere in between. I knew I was being appraised, and I was sweating freely.

I was asked to sit and was then ignored for nearly an hour while the women talked and sipped tea. My thoughts were a thousand miles away when Grandmother's voice brought me back to the room.

"Choose," said Grandmother. They were standing in a circle. "Go and stand in front of your teacher, Little Grandson."

I had known immediately that Betsy was the teacher for me. She was beautiful, a half-breed like myself. I didn't want to hurt any of the others, so I took my time, appearing to be thoughtful.

"Do it now, Little Grandson."

I stood and stepped forward toward Blue Eyes, but somehow walked past her and stopped in front of Martha. I don't know how it happened. Martha smiled at me. I tried to move my feet back to Blue Eyes, but they stuck to the floor.

"Good," said Grandmother. "It is done. You have chosen well. Your teacher's name is Martha Spins Fire Eagle. We will keep this from your mother. Some things done today can stay secret."

Martha told me to return to the house on Sunday afternoon. She then dismissed me so she could "finish tea with her friends."

That day was the beginning of the most powerful and impacting experience of my life, and today it is the core of my understanding that spiritual sexuality, the chuluaqui quodoushka energy of the universe, is the matrix of everything created by the Great Spirit.

Martha lived with her husband in the home where I met her. Like Martha, he also was Native American and supportive of his wife as a phoenix firewoman. They had several children. I met Martha in a small cabin a quarter of a mile from their house. My first experience with her is as clear as the most vivid memory of my life.

When I knocked on her door, I held wildflowers picked on my walk. Martha accepted them smiling. She closed the door, removed her robe and was naked. She was gorgeous beyond words. I was speechless. I might have stood in front of her for hours.

Finally, Martha spoke. "Breathe. Your body needs air." She led me into the bathroom. "Lay your clothes on this chair. We are going to bathe together."

As we bathed she soaped me. It was heavenly. I began to ache from pleasure. She instructed me as I bathed her. "I like to be bathed here," she said, "like this."

When we finished, I was so hard I couldn't stand it. "Martha," I whispered, "I got to get relief!"

"Yes," she said. When she touched me, relief came in one second. I was embarrassed and wondered if the teaching was finished.

"Good," she said softly. "Now we begin."

That afternoon and the days that followed, I gradually learned to know Martha Spins Fire Eagle's body and align with her passion. She showed me how to find her deeper levels. I learned her personal ways to ecstasy in lovemaking. With her I learned different levels of orgasm, and I saw that each has its own beauty. I learned that men and women have different orgasmic experiences.

Martha taught me many lovemaking personas. She called them "lovers' masks." She said lovers must exchange energy from different personas to keep their passion alive and exciting. She taught me to "heart-pleasure" (see appendix D). I learned that making love with a woman is not penetration: it is *merging*. It is breathing together and sharing. It is a discovery, a mutual adventure. I never came fast again with Martha unless I wanted to.

"Every woman has her personal ways," she said. "Even those change. In lovemaking the soul does not stay in one place. It must be found and learned anew each time."

Martha even taught me what *I* like in lovemaking. I lived for the hours I could be with her. I adored her, loved her beyond anything imaginable. I would have died for her without a second thought. Martha took no notice of my personal adoration of her.

Later, Martha brought other women to the cabin. I'm sure she did this in part to help me temper my infatuation for her. I learned the differences in their bodies and found that different passions moved in each of them. Their bodies often asked for different loving than Martha's.

Martha Spins Fire Eagle had an infinite knowledge about love and life. Often what I thought was the end of a teaching was only its beginning. I always felt good when I left her, felt better than when I went to her—wiser, more complete. I know now that I merged with the Great Spirit each time I was with Martha. She had that gift. Those were the happiest days of my life. I am certain my later success in high school athletics and academics were directly affected by my experience with Martha. I had good self-esteem in high school.

Martha Spins Fire Eagle was the inspiration for the spiritual sexuality classes I teach today around the world. I try to give away the knowledge she gave me. It is my expression of gratitude to her. I know the positive effect her gift can have for the planet: to walk in beauty, aligned with one's environment sexually.

FIRST DATE

I had my first date shortly after my fifteenth birthday. The girl's
name was Frances. It was a typical Birdville High date for those
times in Fort Worth. First the Dairy Queen for hamburgers, fries, and
a malt, then dancing to a local juke box, followed by a late drive-in
movie. A full evening. Neither of us were interested in the movie, so
we got to the obvious: sex—touching, kissing, necking and heavy
petting, our mutual attraction.

I reached for her hand, and seconds later her blouse and bras-
siere were off, and we were touching, rubbing, and kissing each
other everywhere. She was open, responsive, and hot! We were really
into it. Just about everything Martha Spins Fire Eagle taught me
came up in a hurry. We were as passionate as two teenagers—or anybody—can be.

Frances moaned and sighed and seemed to have several orgasms. The car was rocking. I turned up the speaker volume to cover
the noise. It was heaven! When we'd done everything I knew except
penetration, I pulled her close and began to ease myself inside her.
As I started to slip in, she put her hand on my chest.

"No, stop!" She pushed me away.

I was stunned and started to go limp. I pulled back and zipped
up.

"What are you doing!" she asked.

I had no words. I buckled my belt.

Frances turned away and began to cry, hands covering her face.
"How could you treat me this way!" she sobbed.

"Frances, I don't understand."

She looked at me. "You bastard!" she screamed. Leaning back,
she slapped my face, hard.

"Wha——!" I stuttered, stunned. My ear was ringing. "What the
hell was that for?"

"For stopping," she said.

"But . . . you told me to stop!"

73

"Yes, but I didn't *want* you to stop."

"But you . . . why did you say stop?" I asked.

"Because I didn't want you to stop."

"What?"

"I wanted you to take me. I have to be taken!" She was sobbing again.

The situation was like nothing I had experienced. My mind was boggled. I decided it was beyond me. "I'm taking you home."

Frances continued to sob as she dressed herself. I turned on the car ignition. When I stopped at her parents' home, she jumped out, slammed the door, and ran for the porch.

Next day I still couldn't put it together. I looked for Grandmother, found her, and described my date with Frances. Grandmother listened, then spoke simply. "Did you take her?"

"No, I didn't. She wanted to, but I let it be."

"That's because you couldn't," she said. "It's as Martha Spins Fire Eagle taught you. The woman will guide the energy."

I thought about that and was quiet. Grandmother was right. Then I wondered what I would do in a similar situation. "What if it happens like this again, Grandmother?"

"It's likely to unless you meet a girl who's been taught how to use the gifts the Great Spirit has given her for pleasuring herself and a man. Most people aren't taught the way Martha did you. White people tend to feel more guilty than good. It's their way. Your girlfriend wanted to do it with you, but she didn't want to feel guilty. If you had taken her, she wouldn't have." Grandmother paused. "It's sad when something that feels so good is thought to be dirty."

"What will I do?" I asked.

"I don't know," she said. "But it doesn't help to take her."

I thanked Grandmother for her help. I knew I had problems ahead of me.

"Yes," she said, reading my mind, "you will."

FALSE PREGNANCY

Grandmother remained a beloved friend and consultant for me until her death. Though I saw her very little after I left high school, wherever I was, she never left my heart. One of the last times she helped me, I was a senior in high school. A girl came to me and told me I'd made her pregnant. I was upset and went to Grandmother Spotted Fawn with it. Grandmother listened to me and sat down with her crystal.

After a few moments she looked at me. "She's not with child," she said.

"But she told me she was," I responded.

"Well, she wants something from you."

"Oh."

So, I went back to the girl. "My Grandmother says you're not pregnant."

"How can she know?" the girl asked.

"My grandmother is a medicine woman."

"Uh," the girl muttered. "She's the old witch, isn't she?"

"Well, are you pregnant or not?"

"Mind your own business!" she said, and walked away.

My Grandmother worried people till the day she passed over—maybe even after that.

AFTER HIGH SCHOOL

My senior year of high school was idyllic. It was the last carefree year of my life. Like most high school seniors at Birdville High, my world centered around myself. I was in love with a woman I would eventually marry. I quarterbacked the football team. I played on a championship basketball team and lettered in varsity rodeo. I was an officer in the high school National Defense Cadet Corps, and I was an astute student in martial arts. My grades were top-notch. As a member of the Civil Air Patrol, I logged hours flying jets. My life was adventuresome and exciting. My dream was to be a pilot.

In May of 1958, prior to my graduation from Birdville High, I was the recipient of an appointment to the Air Force Academy at Colorado Springs. It was a dream come true, a perfect conclusion to the peak year of my life. My nomination to the academy came from Speaker of the House Sam Rayburn and Congressman Jim Wright. I was elated beyond words. My appointment was the passageway to my future and the dream of my life. I intended to spend four years at the academy, get my flight wings and a top-notch college education, and then I'd pursue my career as a pilot, in or outside of the military. My thoughts of Grandmother and all things Native American were pushed to the back of my mind. The world waited for me. All I had to do was step forward and take it.

In June of that same year, I reported to the academy at Colorado Springs. By October, when the first snowstorm hit the Rockies, I was homesick, confused, and unhappy. The academic classes were extremely hard, far more difficult than anything I'd seen in high school. But the classwork was not my main difficulty. I found the rules and regulations repressive, stifling, and suffocating. The regimentation raised havoc with my energy choreography.

Because I was a crack shot, I was wanted for the rifle and pistol team. Coaches also wanted me to play basketball and be on the judo team. I had never met a challenge I couldn't handle, so for a while I tried to do it all. Finally, the regimentation around sleep and study hours caused me so many walk-off demerits I spent my extra time marching and jogging with a dummy rifle. This naturally took me out of the sports activities I loved.

Plebes had to be in bed with the lights out at 10 p.m. At 5 a.m. we were up for the next day. My biorhythms would not make the adjustment. At 2 a.m. I was still wide awake. I am that way today. I continually got demerits for reading with a flashlight or turning on the lights. I was with five other men in a room. Because they adjusted and I did not, I was a problem for them. I felt unique at the academy.

If I had been able to work on *my* rhythms, I would have been OK at the academy. If I had been allowed my flashlight till 2 a.m. I could have handled the academics. Naturally, the academy does not adjust to the schedule of its plebes. I was forced to keep the academy regimen: lights out at 10 p.m.; lights on at 5 a.m. I'd get in bed at 10 p.m. and lie awake for hours. Some nights I'd lie in the dark fantasizing about women and sex till I was obsessed. I was living with four Yankees who were freaked out because I had to relieve myself sexually. I wondered if maybe Yankees did not masturbate.

The absence of women at the academy bothered me; at that time there were no women in the program. I *truly* believe a man must have a woman in his life to be healthy. At the academy, there were too many men, not enough women, and there was too much regimentation. I felt increasingly like a robot. By the time my sweetheart came up for the spring dance, I was so horny I couldn't see straight. When I was given *no* alone time with my girl during the four days she was visiting, and after we were ordered to dance with three measured inches between us, I started to lose track of why I was at the academy and began to seriously consider leaving the Air Force.

In May I made my decision. The academy was indifferent, intolerant, inflexible, callous, and, foremost, against sex. I informed the commandant of my intentions to drop out. I was told I had sixty days to decide which branch of the service I'd go into.

I enlisted in the Marine Corps on June 1, 1959, and was sent to San Diego for boot camp. It was my intention to enroll in Officers Candidate School after my basic training. As an officer I would enter flight training school and continue my dream to be a pilot.

After completing boot camp, I took advanced infantry training.

Nicki and I were married, and I applied for Officers Candidate School. While I was waiting for assignment as an officer candidate, I trained in airborne at Fort Benning jump school.

When I returned to California, I learned that my application to Officers Candidate School had been rejected because I was married. I was stunned. Upon inquiry I was told, "Marine, if we wanted you to have a wife, we would have issued you one." On the other hand, it was suggested, I had no problem. "If you really want to be a marine officer all you have to do is divorce your wife!"

No officers school and no flight school! I was learning about the Marines. A month later I was offered a temporary assignment in Japan teaching hand-to-hand combat and self-defense. I jumped at the chance. My love for martial arts was almost as strong as my love for flying. My assignment stretched into a year. For eight hours a day I learned and taught different forms of martial arts. Off duty I studied more martial arts. I worked for nearly a year, seven days a week, ten or twelve hours a day, with some of the best martial arts teachers in the world.

At the conclusion of my duty in Japan, I returned to Camp Pendleton and trained in scuba and underwater demolition. I became a combat instructor for the Second Force Recon, First Battalion, Third Marine Division. I was as ready for war as a young man could be.

PART 3

WAR

VIETNAM WAR

I went to war with my values clear. I was a United States marine, proud of my country, proud of my government, and ready to do whatever I could to keep the "commies" on their side of the water. I was a teenager, raised in the white culture of Texas. I wanted to do my part to make the world safe for democracy.

After four tours of duty in Vietnam between 1960 and 1967, and more battles than I can remember, survival was my primary value. I was disillusioned by my government. Democracy was political palaver. I had seen indescribable horror, participated in nightmarish carnage, and seen every value I was raised with desecrated. I was primed to lose my marbles completely. And I might have, had it not been for the experiences stored deep inside me by my Cherokee grandmother, Spotted Fawn—that and the fact that I had met Grandfather Two Bears in Arizona shortly before I returned to Vietnam for my final tour of duty.

The Sundance with Raoul Guzman and Bub Deer in Water in the jungle enabled me to "hang on" to a vision for myself that was not yet conscious. Meeting Grandfather Ding Poan was also a stabilizing influence. After my experience with Ding Poan, I knew I was done with fighting in Vietnam. Shortly after that, I was severely wounded and returned to Bethesda Naval Hospital in the United States.

I have included some of my memories of the horror of Vietnam. Two are from Taiwan, where my outfit was stationed before we went to Vietnam. Maybe telling these stories will help to get them out of my system. For sure, they suggest the madness that was engulfing me over there, slowly consuming me. The deepest horror of war is when you start enjoying it and don't have a way to let go of the complications from that.

There is a power in taking a human life. It's so simple to kill. You pull a trigger or snap a neck, and life is gone—it's gone forever. The body falls inert. One day in Vietnam I realized that I enjoyed killing.

In addition to that, I felt the rightness of what I was doing for my country: making the world safe for democracy. I felt a rush of ego when I killed efficiently. I knew I was on the thin red line with this. The experience became near orgasmic. I remember these things each time I lead a healing circle as a shaman today. I pray for all the brothers who brought this kind of guilt and confusion home with them.

When I returned from Vietnam, I was broken in spirit and body. I am certain I would be dead today had I not found my way to my Native American roots. The Medicine Wheels and ceremonies gave me stability and order. I found meaning and hope. I found new and deeper values. I live with them today.

FIRST COMBAT

My outfit had been in Taiwan for two months before anything worth remembering happened. It had been mainly eight weeks of up in the morning early, work your ass off all day in jungle training, and then after dark have a beer or a whore or whatever. Then a report came in one morning that a village down the coast had been hit hard and taken by communist guerrillas. We loaded in tanks and land carriers, moved onto the main artery, and headed south.

Closing in on the village, we came under scattered small-arms fire popping everywhere like Lubbock on the Fourth of July. Our tanks answered back, and that problem ended quick. We rumbled into the village. Huts were burning, black smoke and stink were blowing around, and bodies of the villagers were scattered over the place looking much too peaceful, as they always do when a marine is looking at the first ones he has killed.

Our recon team set up a point. We swept the village, making sure they had left no mines or other hot stuff in front of our heavies, and we set a perimeter watch. A squad of us rushed from one hut to another, checking for anything that didn't belong. When I stepped into my third hut on the row, I stopped up short and froze.

Someone had taken a pregnant Taiwanese woman, thirteen or fourteen years of age, and stripped her nude. They had stuck a sharpened stake in the ground and then shoved that stake up through her vaginal passage, all the way up through her bowels, and out the top of her head. The front of her was sliced open from chest to crotch, the child taken out and rammed down on the point of the stake at the top of her head. The cord was still connected. Time stopped as I stood there, my mind clicking like a camera.

I charged out of the hut and down the row to where four gook prisoners were being held for interrogation, kicked the breach of my Thompson submachine gun, and emptied the magazine into them. When the racket and smoke had settled, one of our Taiwanese officers was screaming something at me and swinging his arms wildly in my face. I swung my gun butt and hit him as hard as I could, knocking him down among the others.

"Welcome to Taiwan," someone said.

Later I was told there would be a court martial for hitting an allied officer. It didn't make any sense, but I remember feeling it didn't matter.

BRONZE STAR

For several days we were laid up in this nothing Taiwanese village in the middle of nowhere because we had heard the communists were going to counterattack and retake the village. That was hard for me to believe, because whatever existed in the village had been leveled when we came in, and I saw nothing worth the effort here in the first place.

The morning of the fifth day we were up early, sitting in our usual place on top of one of the heavy tanks heating coffee. One moment we had a peaceful sunrise scene, kidding each other awake like good buddies do; the next instant was a nightmare, with mortar rounds exploding and heavy machine-gun rounds slamming into the tank. The racket was deafening. None of my training came close to letting me know the feeling of being a turkey at the center of a grand turkey shoot.

Everyone dove in the ditch. Two marines landed hard on me, which was OK, because that put them between me and the people out there causing the racket. Someone was screaming from up on the tank, "Oh, Jesus, Mother of Mary! . . . Jesus, Mother of Mary!"

Then the firing stopped. For several moments it was unnaturally still. No birds—nothing. Nobody spoke. I edged along the ditch past my buddies, working my way down the back of the tank. I lifted my head as the firing broke out again.

They were closer in, with a clear view of what they wanted. The "Mother of Mary" guy was screaming again. Looking through the tank treads, I saw flashes from a dozen places up the hillside, 150 yards away. They were on top of us!

I was holding my Thompson submachine gun, but could not adjust its sight to fire the distance I needed. I noticed a GI lying face down in the ditch on top of his M-1 Garand rifle. I gave him a kick. "Hey buddy, let me have your piece!" No response. I kicked him harder. "Buddy, I said hand me your piece!"

He raised his arm and, without looking up, shoved his rifle at me. I was starting to feel strangely calm. Bullets were slamming in and ricocheting everywhere.

"Hey Buddy, what's your wind elevation on this piece?" No answer. I leaned in through the big lifting hook and fired one round to find out where I was landing. I kicked the sight back up and fired seven rounds up the hill. I fed in three more clips and fired them as fast as I could empty them. I had the absurd sensation that the rifle was alive and firing itself. Then I was shouting, "Go! Let's go!"

I rushed up the hill, throwing grenades and firing my Thompson. We cleared the hill with no further casualties. I was later awarded a Bronze Star for my part in this action, which was about as unreal as the fight itself.

VIETNAMESE CHILD

On our fifth day of search and destroy, we set up in a friendly village. We had been pushing hard and dropping our gear was a relief. Ahead of me a child of eight or nine walked on the path leading to the chow hut carrying a basket of bananas and mangoes. Hungry for fresh fruit, my buddies beckoned to her. I watched her approach them, a pretty little girl.

Raising a hand, she waved or brushed something from her eye, and the sun flashed on metal. I grabbed for my Thompson as I hit the ground, firing while I rolled. The girl's body jerked and bounced crazily on the path, propelled by my bullets. Her grenade exploded with a roar. Everything was quiet for a few seconds, then her mother was screaming.

My buddies watched, stunned. Nothing else happened. We let her people pick up what was left of the girl. Parts of her were all over. Three or four of my buddies wanted to waste the villagers and torch the place, but we let it be and packed up. No one ever knew if she was on her own or was put up to it.

MR. ED PARKER AND MARTIAL ARTS

My first meeting with Mr. Ed Parker occurred when I was home for thirty days prior to my third tour of duty in Vietnam in 1964. He was sponsoring an international karate tournament, as was his custom. Mr. Parker's annual tournament in the United States is still the largest of its kind in the world today, open to all styles of karate. I went to the tournament because I'd heard so much about Mr. Parker and wanted to connect with him. It turned out that he saw something in me, and I got the chance to work out with him four hours a day for nearly a month before I shipped out.

Brash young man that I was at the time, I simply walked up to Mr. Parker and spoke to him: "Sir, I'm not going to be here long enough to get into your tournament before I ship back to Vietnam, but I wonder if you would permit me to work out with you." Mr. Parker looked right through me when he answered.

"Son," he said, "are you good enough to work out with me?"

I wanted to work out with Mr. Parker so bad I blurted my answer at him. "Sir, I've had extensive experience in martial arts. I've done them since I was a boy. I studied and taught hand-to-hand combat twelve hours a day, seven days a week for nearly a year in Japan for the Marine Corps. After duty hours I worked with some of the best masters in the world. Master Oyama, Master Kiam and the two masters Yamaguchi had the most influence on me. I learned shorinji-ryu jujitsu with them."

"I see," said Mr. Parker. He smiled. "So that's where you *learned* shorinji-ryu jujitsu?"

"Well, sir," I stammered, "I didn't mean to say I learned it."

"Uh huh." He was still smiling.

"What I mean, sir, Mr. Parker, is that I understand it could take a lifetime to learn a discipline like shorinji-ryu jujitsu. I meant to say I was introduced to it in Japan and took to it."

Mr. Parker's eyes were twinkling. "Son," he said, "be here at four o'clock with your gear, and we'll take a look."

I met him that afternoon, and apparently he liked what he saw. It was the beginning of one of the most important relationships of my life. I worked out every day for a month with Mr. Parker. In that time I learned as much about real in-close, hand-to-hand fighting, strategy, and tactics as I had from all previous instructors. I was amazed. This is not to down-talk my previous instructors. They were great. Rather, I'm making a statement about the strength of Mr. Parker. And, of course, timing was important. I would not have appreciated what Mr. Parker did for me without my previous training. I also was working out with Mr. Parker knowing that I was going right back into combat in Vietnam, which in some situations became hand-to-hand conflict.

A few days before my departure for Vietnam, Mr. Parker called me aside. We had been working out, and I was puffing.

"Mike's looking for someone to work out with today," he said.

"Mike?" I asked. Mike Stone was the best fighter around. He was favored to win Mr. Parker's tournament the following month and did. I looked around the dojo like I didn't know who Mike was.

"Yes, Mike Stone," said Mr. Parker. "Would you like to work out with him?"

"Er, sure," I said. "That would be great experience, Mr. Parker. Thank you, sir." Mr. Parker made the introductions. Mike Stone and I went at it. I remember that fight with satisfaction, as though I won it. I didn't. Mike, of course, kicked my ass. But when the workout was over I saw respect in Mike's eyes, and I could tell Mr. Parker approved. I did get a couple of good licks in on the champ.

Two days later I was on my way. I had a full United States Marine Corps duffel bag beside me as I said good-bye to Mr. Parker. He led me into his office.

"Sergeant," he said. It was the first time he did not refer to me as "son." "You are going back into a tough situation over there. I appreciate what you are doing for your country and for me, and I want you back safe. I'm going to give you a kahuna blessing with this herb that grows on the high mountains in Hawaii." Mr. Parker lit the herb, blessed me, and prayed in the old Hawaiian tongue. He told me that if I decided to settle in California to look him up and he'd have a job for me. "Aloha," he said and walked away to join his people.

I went to Vietnam, experienced intense fighting, was wounded, came home, became a civilian, and settled in Fort Worth with my family. In a short time I earned a black belt in kenpo karate and was instructing several students. Kenpo karate was developed in this country by Mr. Parker. In my opinion, it is the most innovative and realistic combative street fighting taught in the United States—or maybe anywhere.

I woke up one morning and knew it was time to leave Fort Worth and get closer to Mr. Parker in California. Don't ask me how I knew. It was one of those things. I've always followed certain impulses. It should have been a big decision, but it wasn't. It *was* scary. Mr. Parker was famous. He had authored a dozen books, produced and acted in several films, and was the personal martial arts instructor for a score of famous people. I sold what we had and paid my debts. We packed everything. Nicki and the five kids and I climbed into our old station wagon and headed for Pasadena. I wondered if Mr. Parker would remember he'd offered me a job. I had $139 in my pocket, five kids, no place to stay, and no savings. I parked the car in front of his house on Walnut Street in Pasadena and rang his house chime.

Mr. Parker opened the door. Seeing me, he laughed. "I dreamed two nights ago you were coming." It had taken us two days to drive out. That's the way he was. He glanced at my car. "Call your family out," he said. "Let's meet everyone." He shook hands warmly with Nicki and each of my sons. Then touching my elbow, he guided me away from the group.

"Level up with me, if you don't mind," he said. "What is your financial status?" I told him how much money I had. He laughed deeply and asked me where I was spending the night. I told him we'd planned to find a motel. He wouldn't have it. He called to his wife Leilani, who made a delicious spaghetti dinner for us all. He insisted we stay under his roof till we found our own place. He opened his home and his heart. I'll never forget it. Mr. Parker hired

me to teach his beginning students and advanced me ten weeks' pay.
Imagine!

Mr. Parker is a model to me for what marks greatness in a man.
He had an ability to help his students understand the physics and
body dynamics in martial arts that are analogous to music and art,
literature and life. He helped me see that martial arts is like an alphabet in motion. When one understands letters, their relationship can
form words. Similarly, a student would learn four simple, basic
moves. From them, Mr. Parker would help him develop a minimum
of sixty-four combinations or moves. He demonstrated that the
beginning state of knowledge, no matter what the discipline, begins
with the simple mind. Following that, one discovers complexity,
which is followed by sophistication. Sophistication by its nature will
again become simplicity.

This description of kenpo karate, of course, is not dissimilar to
the concepts in other martial arts. Kenpo karate, however, empha-
sizes an important difference. In all the other major Oriental martial
arts systems the instructors insist that each student master the same
technique in the same way, whether the student is six feet four inches
tall or five feet four. The rules for performance in traditional systems
do not account for body size or weight.

Mr. Parker's emphasis, on the other hand, was that kenpo karate
must always be changing. It must be pragmatic to meet the profile of
the individual. He used to love to say, "Never mold the student to
the art. Mold the art to the student." That is revolutionary in martial
arts and very different from a traditional Oriental system. Mr. Parker
sought individuality.

I was drawn to him naturally. Practicality and individuality are
necessary for me. Plus, Mr. Parker had a powerful intellect. I needed
that and soaked it up.

Recently, I realized that his true genius was his uncanny ability to
help each student find a way to blend kempo karate to his or her
unique gifts, personality, and strength. This was the edge that
advanced me deeply into my aptitudes for martial arts and enabled
me to gain so much from them. From them I've learned to walk like a
warrior without fear. Martial arts have enabled me to conquer the

"Black Lodge," the lodge of the body, and to do many things beyond the ordinary in spite of the pain I've carried in my body.

When I heard that Mr. Parker had suffered a fatal heart attack I felt unaccountably small and alone, like a boy who'd lost his dad. I wanted to reach out to someone for comfort, yet I knew words weren't what I needed. I wanted to see Mr. Parker one more time. . . .

I know that though he has crossed over, Mr. Parker is not truly gone. He lives on in me and all those who were touched by him.

"Aloha, great man."

GRANDFATHER
TWO BEARS

I met Grandfather Two Bears Walks the Sacred Mountain under what seemed the strangest of circumstances. Following my third tour of duty in Vietnam during the winter of 1966, I returned home on thirty-day leave. Hoping to settle my mind, I volunteered to deliver blankets, mattresses, foodstuffs, and first aid materials to the Navajo Reservation at Tuba City, Arizona, for the Mormon Church. The church gives this kind of help to the Navajo Nation every year. It's part of the Mormon cultural exchange to do that, since most of the members of the Navajo Council currently are Mormon. The Mormons have one of the most generous volunteer programs I have seen anywhere. Navajo children are sponsored into Mormon homes in Los Angeles during the school year and given food and expense money. Financial aid is also given to the family back on the reservation. In return, it is expected that the child will learn the ways of the Mormon Church, give up the old religion, and become Mormon. It is, of course, the view of the Mormon Church that it is saving these children spiritually as well as aiding them materially. Because most Navajo are poor, it is a powerful proselytizing system, like it or not.

I had driven to Tuba City with three Caucasian Mormon volunteers in an eighteen-wheeler owned by Deseret Industries. It was the dead of winter, late at night and bitter cold. After finding someone to unlock the warehouse and help unload the trailer, I crossed the road to a local café and sat down to eat. I was hungry and exhausted from the drive. As I gulped my first cup of hot chocolate, a large Navajo man approached me. Staring at me, he made his presence known before he spoke. "Are you Unhua Oskenonton Anikawi?"

A shiver went up my spine. Nobody used my Cherokee name. I could count on one hand how many people knew it.

"Who's asking?"

"Grandfather's asking for you." He then turned and walked out of the café.

I stared at my empty cup. I didn't need any more adventure. I'd earned a bed for the night and had promised one to my body. I'd not had a good night's sleep in weeks.

"Screw it," I thought, raising a finger to order another hot chocolate.

The big Navajo poked his head back in the doorway. "Grandfather's waiting."

Something about his voice carried away my choice. I looked longingly at my empty cup and followed him into the cold night. We climbed into his pickup. Four miles out of Tuba City he turned north off Route 160 onto a dirt road that quickly became two faint ruts more suited to sheep than to a truck. The shocks on the truck were long gone. I clung to the dash to stay off the floor.

"Christ sake!" I groaned. "Can you slow it down?"

The big Navajo began to whistle. When he missed a note whistling, he hummed.

"Who the hell is Grandfather?" I asked.

More whistling. His focus was on the headlight beams in the darkness.

I had no idea who Grandfather was.

Like fun I didn't. My mind still wanted a warm bed and was resisting. I knew who Grandfather was—or at least the boy in me knew. We'd met in a vision at Fossle Creek in Texas when I was eight years old. I was thinking about that day and the fish I had caught when the truck brakes groaned.

"Over there," my driver said.

An old hogan was illuminated by the truck's headlights.

"This is it?" I asked.

"Yeah, end of the ride."

"Just like that, here?" I asked.

"Yep." He gunned the engine impatiently.

I pushed the door handle. "You coming in with me?"

"No, get out."

The truck door was half open and the wind blew into the cab hard and cold. "Are you going to wait?" I asked.

"Grandfather's inside," he said.

I slammed the truck door and stepped clear as the vehicle turned into the night and disappeared over the ridge.

"Thanks for the ride!" I shouted into the wind.

I listened to the truck engine fade. Then the night was quiet. I stood for several moments in the immense silence of the Arizona desert. When my eyes adjusted to the darkness, I turned toward the hogan and slowly approached it. As I reached for the door, it swung inward. I hadn't touched it. A lantern illuminated an old man at the center of the room on a dirt floor. I smelled cedar as I stepped through the doorway.

"Grandfather?"

"Come in. Shut the door behind you. Wind's cold."

His voice was familiar. He did not look up.

My knees wobbled and the room spun. I felt out of control. I grabbed for the door frame as I started to slide. Then I was sitting in front of Grandfather and the room had steadied. He wore a blue velveteen shirt and a green headband.

"Who are you?" I said, feeling stupid. I knew who he was. I remembered what he'd said to me a long time ago in Texas: "We will meet again when a man under a star brings you to me."

"Your horns are bloody," he said.

"My horns?"

I knew he referred to the mule deer of my vision. The moment was intense. My thinking was clear and precise.

"You've killed your brothers, and more will die at your hands." He still had not looked at me.

"How do you know this?" I asked.

What he said was likely to be true. I'd signed up to return to Vietnam when I returned from military leave.

"You can be a stronger healer than killer."

"In that case, I could be a powerful healer," I smiled weakly. "I've killed my share of men."

"Yes." He looked at me directly. His eyes went through me. "What do you want to do with your life?" he asked.

His question sounded so simple, like I *had* a choice. I realized that prior to his question I'd been living my life without thought to its direction.

"I, uh . . . I'm not sure, Grandfather," I answered.

"When you are done killing your brothers and are ready to heal them, your heart will speak to you. Come to me and I will help you."

Something inside me settled. He believes in me, I realized. I felt myself as a boy with Grandmother. I relaxed. This man *believes* in me, I thought again. I felt safe.

That was how I met Grandfather Two Bears Walks the Sacred Mountain. Though I did not know it at that moment, it was the beginning of my apprenticeship.

Grandfather talked with me for several hours. He'd ask a sim- ple question like, "Why are you here on the planet?" Then he'd sit quietly while I stumbled through my answers, trying to clarify my thinking.

At dawn, my Navajo driver returned. Grandfather Two Bears stood. Facing me, he took my elbows in his hands and squeezed.

"I will be here when you are done with killing and want to learn to heal. Go home now." He turned away.

I climbed into the truck, and my driver took me back to Tuba City. At the juncture of the sheep path and Route 106, he stopped the truck and lit a cigarette. The flame of his match reflected metal on his jacket, a star. He turned onto 106.

"Who are you?" I asked.

"I'm called Sheriff Bud," he said.

He was a deputy sheriff, Navajo police. I learned later that he was one of Grandfather's cousins.

I drove back to Los Angeles to my wife and family for a few short days and then returned to duty in Vietnam. Back in the jungle, the meeting with Grandfather Two Bears faded from my thoughts, until I met a Vietnamese grandfather named Ding Poan.

GRANDFATHER DING POAN

Shortly after I returned to Vietnam for a final tour of duty in 1967, my outfit, the First Force Recon Battalion, First Marine Division, Third Company, swept through a small village, meeting no resistance. We gathered up the men, women, and children of the village and strung barbed wire around an area to contain them until it was decided which would be interrogated as Viet Cong. This was not our normal activity, but no one else was far enough into the safe zone to relieve us. So we set things up as I have described and waited for someone to come in to take these people off our hands.

On the second day a chopper landed with mail for the outfit, and eleven letters from home caught up with me. I was in ecstasy. I carried my little package to a tree inside the wire and sat down. Mail is precious. The saddest marine in Vietnam could be made happy by a letter from home. Likewise, I've seen happy marines devastated by news from home. Mail call is a sensitive thing for a GI.

Most men are ritualistic with their mail. Some marines prefer to ration their reading when they receive mail, spreading it out over hours or even days. My routine was to sort the letters by postmark, then devour them all at once, fast. Later I'd go through them all again slowly.

I finished reading my letters and spread several photographs on the grass in front of me to dream with. My thoughts were a continent away when I realized I was not alone. I turned quickly and looked into the eyes of an old Vietnamese grandfather. His eyes held mine. For a split moment I forgot my mail and Vietnam. The man's eyes suggested a depth and power beyond anything I'd ever seen. His face was eroded with ancient wrinkles. For a long moment I was suspended in time.

Then he smiled, the spell broke, and I was again a combat marine inside a makeshift barbed-wire compound, at war in a country a long way from my home and family.

He pointed at the photographs. "Family?"

"Er, yes," I answered. "You speak American?"

"No." He smiled again.

I relaxed and offered him a smoke. I lit a match between us and we talked. I knew a little Vietnamese, and he knew some English. Occasionally, a French word worked. We did all right.

"I am Ding Poan," he said simply.

I learned that Ding Poan had been living with his wife and family in the village we'd just demolished. Two of his three sons were dead, killed by bombs. Four grandchildren were missing. They'd disappeared somewhere near the safe zone recently.

I was quiet. I could think of nothing to say about that. I talked about my family back home and life in Texas. I showed him pictures of my wife, Nicki, and my parents and Grandmother Raper. He listened quietly. When I asked, he told me his story.

We talked through the afternoon. Ding Poan was an herbalist. He doctored in the villages using plant medicine. He was an authority on all things that grow, including plants outside Vietnam. The land was sacred and alive for him. He loved his country and its people. He spoke of his passion for the mountains and jungles and fields around us. He hated the war, the destruction and death, the pesticides and napalm. When the sun was low, he excused himself and disappeared.

Gathering my things together, I felt unaccountably moved. I knew I had been deeply touched by Ding Poan. I thought about my roots as a Native American half-breed, a Cherokee Indian, something I had not considered since childhood. That night I dreamed I was a boy again living with Grandmother Spotted Fawn. She was teaching me how to mix colors to paint my bayonet.

My own mother, Ida Raper Reagan, had done her best to ignore her Native American roots, but her mother, Grandmother Spotted Fawn Raper, had stayed connected to the old ways. Grandmother's mother, my great-grandmother, was one of the few Indian children who survived the tragic march from the Carolinas to Oklahoma.

When I awoke in the morning, I wanted to talk further with Ding Poan.

In the days that followed, we met several times. I walked with him outside the barbed wire. I learned about Vietnamese history and the many centuries his people had fought for freedom against foreign invaders. He also taught me plant medicine, including herbs that protected against malaria and diarrhea. He showed me leaves that prevented spoilage of the fish we caught in the river. He described the medicinal properties of dozens of herbs and shrubs.

At the end of each day, I looked forward to meeting him again and prayed our lull from the fighting would continue. It was a strange and intense relationship, a foreshadowing of my apprenticeship with Grandfather Two Bears, which would begin upon my return to the states. What Ding Poan saw in me, to this day I can only guess. For me, he was a link to my past, as well as to my future.

One morning I realized that Grandfather Ding Poan's relationship with the Earth and his determination to hold the land was like that of my ancestors who had fought against foreign intruders, the white man in America, less than two generations before I was born. Each day I felt more identified as an American with a Native American tradition. It came to me why I had intuitively picked a full-blood Navajo, and a Lakota Sioux as my two best buddies in Vietnam.

Another evening it struck me that Ding Poan was not a communist, nor had he any interest in becoming one. That was mind-boggling. Until I had met this venerable old Vietnamese grandfather, I was certain that all the people in Vietnam were either communists already or would be if we didn't save them from themselves. Ding Poan had no interest in politics. His concerns were his medicine ways, his people, and the land. In time I asked him about that.

"Sergeant," he said. "I am who you see." I felt his sadness.

"I love this land you are destroying," he continued. "My heart is heavy. I weep for my country's lost children as well as for my own. My wife is now an old woman." He paused. "She should not have to lie down at night alone. Everywhere my people are alone now. Our villages, our way of life are threatened, our fields ruined. When I dream at night, my country is as it was before you came. I hope for the future, but my dreams are my only pleasure."

He paused, looking at something in the tree line. "Sergeant, communism is not a cure for Vietnam. It is a system designed to counter something bad that has developed in my country. In time communism will pass. Right now, apparently it is needed, but it is not my concern. I am a simple farmer," he said, "a simple farmer."

At that moment his immense weariness gripped me. I sagged with the burden.

"Sergeant, take your soldiers and get out of my country. We must rebuild what you and the French have destroyed. I want to lie down with my woman. I wish to tell the old stories to my grandchildren."

His voice was ancient and timeless. For the first time I sensed what it meant for me to be in Ding Poan's country.

"Sergeant, stop killing and go home to your family. Find your own peace."

One of his people called, and he left. I watched him walk away, bent and steady. The next morning an interrogation team arrived to transport suspect villagers to another location. Ding Poan was among those chosen. I saw him from across the compound waiting to be loaded, his straw bag on his back.

"No, wait!" I cried, waving my arms frantically.

The truck was moving when I reached it. I ran alongside, reaching for Ding Poan. I pushed two packs of Pall Mall cigarettes into his hands. I clung to his fingers as he took them.

"Sergeant," he said. My hands were around his. He stretched toward me. "One day these smokes will return to you!"

"Grandfather!" I called as we were wrenched apart. My voice broke. "Grandfather, thank you. Grandfather . . . I love you!" I staggered and caught myself, nearly falling. The truck rumbled away and disappeared in a cloud of red dust. My own words echoed in my ears. "Grandfather, I love you!"

I never saw Ding Poan again. No one survived a South Vietnamese interrogation.

Events happened fast after that. We went back into action. Within three months I was wounded twice, the second time critically, and was flown home. I didn't remember Ding Poan's final words until years later.

THE LAST BATTLE

SwiftDeer saw Vietnam for the last time on a hot, sultry early morning, June 14, 1967. Near dawn, he boarded a C-119 transport chopper at Quang Tri, Vietnam, and lifted off for a military strike near Lang Vei in the high-ridge mountains of Laos. An enemy supply line threatening the marine combat base at Khe Sahn was to be destroyed. As his transport chopper came over the target, it took a direct rocket hit and exploded. SwiftDeer was blown clear of the wreckage and fell three hundred feet to the ground. He landed on his feet, then collapsed, bleeding profusely from a severe head wound, deep back lacerations, and knees dislocated and broken.

While a fierce fire fight raged, a courageous helicopter pilot landed near SwiftDeer. He was loaded onto the chopper, flown back to Quang Tri, and given superficial medical aid. There was very little to be done for his head wound or shattered knees. He was transported quickly to Nha Trang, where he was given further medical aid. Still he had not regained consciousness. From Nha Trang he was flown to Bethesda Naval Hospital in Maryland. He arrived at Bethesda on July 10, twenty-six days after being blown out of the sky above Lang Vei. He was still unconscious. SwiftDeer was comatose at Bethesda Naval Hospital for twenty-one additional days. On July 21, thirty-seven days after his helicopter had been demolished, Sergeant Reagan opened his eyes to the horror of Bethesda Naval Hospital.

He was a patient at the naval hospital for eight months. In March 1968, SwiftDeer's status changed to outpatient, and he left the hospital ward. He remained on outpatient status until his honorable discharge from the United States Marine Corps on December 21, 1969.

While at Bethesda Naval Hospital, SwiftDeer had surgery several times. Metal pins were inserted into both knees to hold them together. Numerous pieces of shrapnel were removed from his back and shoulder. By far the most difficult, painful, and creative medical work done on SwiftDeer at Bethesda was the restoration of his shattered skull. Today, a portion of it is metal.

In the final months of his rehabilitation, SwiftDeer was treated for psychological problems. It was determined that he demonstrated "an unusual amount of anger related to his wounds." He was diagnosed as a Post

Traumatic Stress Disorder patient and was treated tentatively at the hospital for that condition.

SwiftDeer says today that his most damaging wounds by far were inflicted at Bethesda Naval Hospital. The inhumane and brutal treatment he and others received there ravaged his life emotionally for more than two decades. Only now can he consider the experience without trauma.

THE FINAL WOUND

The material of this chapter has been hard for me to release. I have done it primarily because I am angered thinking that wounded GIs may *still* suffer from the treatment they receive at Bethesda Naval Hospital in Maryland. When I saw a news clip of former president of the United States George Bush waving cheerfully from his window at Bethesda, I knew I would share my own Bethesda experience.

As television commentators assured the nation that our president was receiving the best medical attention in the world at Bethesda, my mind flashed to the wards of smashed bodies from Vietnam. My God, I thought, this was not my experience! Where was this "brilliant medical team" when I was there? I know the answer, of course. These specialists were up on the VIP floor. Their expertise was not wasted on the broken boys from the jungles once they rolled us away from the operating stations.

Doctors told me I was in a coma for thirty-seven days after I was wounded in Vietnam. Technically that is not true, though I suppose for their records the information is accurate enough. I regained consciousness twice before I awakened at Bethesda. The first time was somewhere in Vietnam. I opened my eyes to a tent ceiling and fans. I knew I was hurt bad, that I had survived a medevac. Then lights out.

The second time, I opened my eyes to a scene I recognized was stateside. Welcome home, I thought. I wondered once where I was and if my family had visited, wondered what I looked like. I wanted to ask where I was and couldn't. The effort to think was too much. I felt no pain during that time, though I knew I was hurt bad. Maybe heavy pain medication extended the length of my coma.

I have no memory of most of the time I was unconscious. I have heard stories of wounded men who saw the "other side." One marine at Bethesda told me he had stood at the entrance to a long tunnel filled with fire. He had felt compelled to walk through but was called back. Another GI said he had approached a gate in a picket fence. Flowers grew everywhere and birds sang. On the other side were all those he'd ever known who had passed on, including his parents and 'Nam buddies. They called his name, smiling, beckoning him to pass through the gate. He turned away from them and woke up.

I had none of that. Occasionally I hovered around my body observing, protective. I have no memory of the rest of the time. I have no description for it. Most of the thirty-seven days are gone from my life—a blank slate, a void. It used to be unnerving to think about it. Where the hell *was* I all that time?

I do remember being wounded. We were entering the fight at Lan Vei when my transport chopper exploded. It disintegrated around me in a yellow flash. Of course, there must have been a tremendous roar, but in my head it is all very still. I watched my body fall clear. It fell a long time before hitting the ground. I landed on my feet, then crumpled. I felt no pain. From the ground I watched the fight around me. I was detached, an observer. Then a helicopter landed near me. Marines placed me aboard. We lifted off, and the screen went blank, except for the times I have mentioned.

When I finally woke up, my mind was clear. I felt calm. I'd been in another dimension for a long time and was back. I knew I was at Bethesda, and the nurse approaching the bed was Judith. I knew I had been observing myself from outside my body. I watched Judith change my bed pan. I studied the numerous tubes and bottles attached to me.

"Nurse, unhook me from all this stuff," I said. "It's making me sick."

Startled, she jumped and nearly lost a pan of shit.

"Oh, Sergeant Reagan! You startled me," she said. "No one told me you were awake."

"Nurse, get all these lines and things unhooked from me. They're making me sick," I repeated.

She stared at me, as if to figure out who I was.

"Nurse," I said, "I'm asking you."

"Uh, Sergeant, yes. Excuse me a minute," she said. "I'll get rid of this and be back shortly." She walked away.

I looked around. I was in the far corner of a ward. There were two more beds, then the door into what they called a recreation room. All the ward beds were occupied. Some of the men watched me. Nurse Judith returned, accompanied by a doctor.

"Sergeant," she said, "here is Dr. Whan to look at you."

I thought for a split, crazy second that I had been tricked and was a prisoner of the enemy. He looked Viet Cong.

"When you wake up, Sergeant?" he asked.

I watched him, feeling very weak.

"You were in coma long time, Sergeant."

"Doctor, sir," I said, "all these tubes and shit are making me sick. Will you please get them out of me?"

He looked at my chart and made notes. He did a full bedside check: pulse, blood pressure, heart, and so forth. He spoke to the nurse. He handed her my chart, which she hung on the bed. The doctor patted my shoulder.

"You going be OK, Sergeant," he said. "No worry. You get best hospital care here. You in our hands. We take best care." He smiled, all teeth. "You no worry about anything."

I was thinking, Get your fucking hands off my shoulder!

He walked away.

"Doctor," I called. He was gone.

Nurse Judith looked at me.

"What the fuck!" I said. "I am asking for some help here."

"I'm sure the doctor knows what is best for you," said Nurse Judith.

The first night I was truly conscious quickly became a nightmare. The sounds and smells were horrible. Men close by sobbed all night. The most difficult part came from a walking wounded marine named Ted, who had cracked up in 'Nam while firing M-60 machine guns on transport Hueys. It appeared that military psychiatrists had given up on him. Ted said he was in Bethesda awaiting a promotion. In truth, misplaced paperwork would "section eight" him out of the corps.

During the day Ted was cheerful and calm. He would help out around the ward, reading to patients, lighting cigarettes, running errands—all of it unofficial. At night, however, he went berserk. His brain was in Vietnam saving us all. He would scream desperately, trying his best to warn us.

"They're coming in! Over there!" he would roar. "Jesus, fire a flare! Where the fuck's the claymores! Medic, here! They're all over us! They're inside the P . . . Fire it . . . Call it in!" Most nights they let the poor bastard sob and scream half the night before someone filled his ass with drugs and took him off.

Because we were both from Texas, Ted looked after me during the day when he was normal. With darkness he was under attack in 'Nam. It was that simple. It was tough, because his screaming would pull me in. Other marines would shout for someone to shut him up. It was like that for weeks.

The ward stank. The stench of putrefied flesh was in the air all the time I was there. Someone always had a wound that wouldn't heal, and I could smell it. Maybe others couldn't. My sense of smell is acute.

It had been their custom to tie both my arms to flat boards while I was in the coma so I wouldn't pull loose from IVs during the night. For some unexplained reason, I got the same treatment the first night I was awake. They sedated me and tied me to the boards.

"What the fuck is this?" I asked. I got no answer. That night was the beginning of what I call my Bethesda nightmare.

In the morning I ordered a nurse to get me loose. She untied my arms but left needles and tubes in me. Looking at all the tubes made me sick; I also cannot take a needle in my body.

"Nurse, all this shit is making me nauseous," I said. "I'm trying to tell you nice: get this shit out of my veins!"

"Sergeant," the nurse said, "the doctor hasn't authorized anything different for you. I'll ask the afternoon nurse to give your request to him."

"Shit!" I said.

After she left, I sat up and pulled everything loose that was attached to me. I threw as much of it on the floor as I could. I kicked over the IV stands, breaking bottles and ripping tubes, muttering to myself. A guy in the bed next to me started yelling, and in came the orderlies. They must have been watching because normally they never responded that fast. They carried restrainers, intending to tie me up if provoked.

The nurse looked at the mess I'd made. "Sergeant Reagan," she said, "you'll hurt yourself! You have no choice but to follow orders." She was picking things up. "Everything has to be connected again."

I was convinced that the antibiotics, chemicals, medication, sedation, glucose, and the rest were making me sick. "Nurse," I begged. "please don't put this shit back in my veins! It's causing me problems and filling me with sickness. Please, nurse, just go to the mess hall. Get me a fucking hamburger!"

She had fresh IV materials in her hand. When she stepped forward to hook me up, I hit her as hard as I could. She staggered back and fell. "Bring me some fucking food!" I shouted. I tried to get out of bed. My feet touched the floor. I passed out. When I opened my eyes, a big woman with captain's bars on her white uniform leered at me. She held a large syringe. I tried to sit up again.

"Now, now, Sergeant," she said, her hand on my chest, "we can't have our nurses treated this way, can we? We are still in the United States Marine Corps, aren't we, Sergeant?"

It took all my strength to hold her gaze with my eyes.

"Turn over, soldier, and take this like a man."

I whispered, "If you touch me with that fucking needle, when I wake up I will kill you!" I meant it.

"Well, well," she muttered. "We have a real live marine here." She turned to the two orderlies. "Hold this son of a bitch while I get this needle in his ass," she ordered.

They turned me over and held me while she did her thing. Just before she injected the shot she leaned toward me. "Sergeant Reagan," she hissed, "I know you've just recently joined the living and may not understand that we function differently here than in the field, so listen up! I will say this one time. Get it right!" She paused to make sure I was with her. "If you ever strike one of my nurses again, I'm going to make your life so miserable in this hospital you'll wish you hadn't been born. For starters, just think about where else I might be sticking this needle besides your ass. Get it?" She was breathing hard in my ear. "If you think I'm bluffing, try me! I'd love to make you a project of mine!"

I understood her. I felt so weak I couldn't struggle. I yelled at them, however, to bring me some real food. Other men on the ward began screaming at them. "Leave the bastard alone! Bring the fucker a hamburger!"

Of course, when I woke up I was restrained. Everything was again hooked up, and I had messed in my bed. A huge man, one of the ward orderlies, was cleaning me up. "Hubert," his name tag read.

"Hey now, Sleeping Beauty's awake again!" he said.

When our eyes met, I flinched inwardly. My internal radar registered danger.

"Good morning, Sergeant. Hope you slept pleasant." Hubert stared at me coldly. "Now that you're among the living, we can start your shit rehabilitation. You got one day to learn to wipe your own ass or you start eating your own shit! Got it, Sergeant?" He held the bed pan under my nose. My second "awake" day had begun.

No one there seemed to realize I might have something to say about what was good for my body. I had survived four tours in Vietnam because I had had complete control over everything related to my body. In combat I'd left nothing to chance regarding my physical well-being. No one had made a decision regarding my body except me, and that's why I was alive. Suddenly they assumed that I would accept the decision that *they* knew what was best for me. It was nuts.

If I had been a "gassed-out" World War I veteran fifty years after the war, incapable of contributing to my physical or mental health, I might have accepted it. It didn't occur to people there that less than two months earlier I was a recon sergeant in the field, responsible for others' lives as well as my own. I couldn't handle the position they'd put me in.

One morning, the man on the other side of me, a paraplegic, was turned upside-down to aid his circulation. They left him too long or hadn't changed him, and his urine bag overflowed. The smell of piss permeated the area. Then the man had a diarrhea attack. He shit all over himself, his bed, and the floor. The stench was gagging. His calls for help went unanswered. Within minutes most of the men in the ward were yelling and pounding on metal. We made a tremendous din.

The nurses and orderlies left the man hanging that way, weeping hysterically, for nearly five hours. I never understood this. It must have been a punishment for something I did not know about, or it was entertainment for them or just plain hostility. When the orderlies finally responded, they went to each of us and sedated us before attending to the paraplegic. When I woke up again he was cleaned up and quiet.

It gradually dawned on me the orderlies didn't care. They didn't give a rat's ass. They laughed at us. They wanted nothing to do with us. They didn't want to listen to us. They were deaf to our cries of pain. They didn't want to feel our fear or see our madness. They didn't want to see us. They didn't want to smell us. The reality was, they sedated us so they wouldn't have to do the work they got paid for. Their hostility was blatant.

The American public never knew about the silent war waged against the wounded Vietnam vets in the GI wards at Bethesda— the needle war. For years I did not remember my early months at Bethesda. Much of the material for this chapter surfaced from the recesses of my mind only recently. The films *Coming Home*, with John Voigt, and Tom Cruise's *Born on the Fourth of July* flooded me with painful and undeniable memories that previously I had kept from my consciousness. I don't think I could have handled them earlier.

Two beds over from me was a huge marine named Steve. He would burst into deep sobbing several times a day. It was nothing external; Steve just needed to cry. His feelings were understandable to me. He had lost two legs at the hips and was working through it. He was easy prey for the big orderly, Hubert.

"What's the matter, dearie? Feeling sorry for yourself again? Want Daddy Hubert to hold his little snookie and make it better? Grow up, snot nose," he'd say. "You couldn't stand on your legs when you had them!"

The men around Steve's bed got hot every time it happened, and I suppose that was part of Hubert's fun. I noticed that the gunnery sergeant next to Steve was furious, yet he said nothing. One day when Hubert was doing his thing, ridiculing Steve, "Gunny" lunged at Hubert and fell hard to the floor on his face: his rage had overcome his awareness that he had no arms.

When Gunny fell, I jumped from my bed to help. Again I passed out. Naturally, I was wearing restraints when I woke up. Gunny required surgery for his jaw and front teeth. There had been nothing wrong with his face when he went into the hospital. There were no medals given for the wounds we received at Bethesda.

Ted, the "Section Eight" marine, killed himself one afternoon, and then nights were quieter. He broke into a drug supply cabinet while he was "sane" and took himself over the edge. He'd been disconsolate for several days because the only help he could get for his problem was an injection of "John Arbor," a morphine-laced substance. Ted had worked out his own peace with the enemy.

It is no mystery to me that so many Vietnam veterans had drug problems. Wounded vets, particularly, had a high percentage of drug incidents after discharge from military service. I was addicted when I left Bethesda—a lot of men were. Every time staff members wanted peace and quiet, we were drugged. We were drugged to the max. If you complained or resisted, they doubled or tripled the dosage. I had plenty of triples.

It didn't matter what you said or did, they were going to do what they wanted to your body. They took your pride and integrity, your individuality, your autonomy. They took everything that gives a man dignity. They would not listen to what a man might know about his own body.

I hated the recreation room. I called it the "zombie room." The men were drugged and then led or wheeled there, where they sat in front of the screen in stupors, like old men. No one was stabilized or functional enough to play pool or Ping-Pong. It was a vegetable room. The men looked dead. Christ, these were young men, veterans and comrades, men who put everything on the line for America! There they sat in front of mindless shit soap operas like something important was happening there. I avoided the place. Even today the only thing I watch on TV is CNN or a film I've put in my VCR. I didn't understand my contempt for TV until memories of Bethesda surfaced for me.

Everyone commented on the rapid recovery I made there, considering the severity of my wounds. To me it was no wonder: I put all my life force into getting out. Every breath I took, I imaged myself breathing on the outside. I never once lost my focus on leaving Bethesda Naval Hospital. Something very deep in me told me I might never leave there if I relaxed my intent for an hour. So I focused everything I ever learned about stalking and mental discipline on getting me away. I saw too many men die there I thought should have survived.

Perhaps the hardest thing about Bethesda was the vulnerability a wounded GI brought with him. When I was admitted, I was badly hurt. My body was shattered. I was confused and very vulnerable. I needed help. During four tours in Vietnam, I had experienced every decent value I'd grown up with in the United States of America ignored, devastated, and trampled. I'd seen death, betrayal, and violence in every thinkable form for months at a time. I truly had begun losing track of who I was. I had become part of the violence. I'd contributed to it, even initiated and inspired some of it. I'd been high on killing with no way to deal with what that eventually would do to my mind.

Yet my experience at Bethesda hurt me more emotionally than all my time in Vietnam. When I was admitted to Bethesda, I needed a transition place from Vietnam to normal civilian life in the States— every GI I ever met who had it rough in 'Nam did. A marine went into combat with a solid sense of who he was and why he was in Vietnam. However, given time and enough fighting, he had plenty of chance for confusion. I needed Bethesda to heal, recuperate, and integrate the personality I had become over there. I was in no way prepared for the hostility and indifference of the naval hospital staff. My body *did* heal at Bethesda, but my mind is still getting over naval hospital trauma.

The final period of my stay at Bethesda was labeled "treatment for symptoms of PTSD." I went to therapy sessions and took an ongoing series of psychological evaluations and tests. The theme was "Can Sergeant Reagan assimilate into society or not?" By the time I got out of there, I really wasn't sure I could. As it turned out, I didn't do so well. I knew, however, that if I didn't get out of there I was going off the deep end—I felt it. So I learned what the psychiatrists wanted to hear. I anticipated what was in their minds. I gave them the right answers. I was desperate: I had to get out of Bethesda at any cost, so I played their game.

Eventually, they announced that I was suitable for civilian life. Was I OK? No, I wasn't—not even close. But I felt I had no alternatives. Conditions were much worse for my emotional rehabilitation in there than on the outside. For me, there was no choice. I had to enter the outside world knowing I was *not* OK and try to make it. I had to "go for it" on my own without military controls. This was my secret: I knew I was not ready, but I had to pretend to my family, friends, and the outside world that I was.

PART 4

THE REAGANS

FAMILY

SwiftDeer's maternal grandmother, Spotted Fawn, nourished his traditional Native American roots as she taught him the medicine and traditions of the Cherokee during his early and adolescent years. Perhaps equally important to his early training as a boy who would become a shaman were his experiences with the patriarchal side of the family: his Irish father and his ten "outgoing," free-fisted, hard-drinking, storytelling uncles. They brought the spirit of the leprechaun and the tradition of the Irish master storyteller to the young boy, SwiftDeer.

Following is what Jeff Gray, a former resident of Lubbock, Texas, reported regarding the Reagans.

> The Reagans are notorious in Lubbock as storytellers. Local residents consider them among the best liars Lubbock has ever produced, which in itself is no small feat!

> I have never seen a man better able to weave his stories through the life events of his listeners as convincingly and delightfully as Jeff Reagan. In that sense, he is brilliant, a man of power.

> One sees where SwiftDeer gets his storytelling gift. Sharing stories must have been as natural as breathing in the Reagan household.

MY FATHER,
JEFF REAGAN

When my father put his arms around me the day I returned from Bethesda Naval Hospital, weak and finished with war, I was shocked. He'd never hugged me before. His arms went around me big and strong, and he pulled me close against him. "Welcome home, Son."

I thought, What is this? I placed one hand tentatively on his back, returning his embrace. He sensed something, stepped back, and looked at me carefully.

"It's been a long time," he said.

"Yes," I answered.

He took my bag, and the moment was gone. It was the first time I'd ever experienced affection from him. I had a flash of memories of growing up without his touch and the times I'd liked to have had it. I wondered if a can of worms had been opened. He hadn't written me in Vietnam at all. I had received one letter from him during my eight months at Bethesda.

Later, when I was alone with Mother, I asked her if she had a clue about the tension I felt around my dad. She became untypically quiet. Her eyes focused on another time.

"Harley," she said finally, "your daddy has always loved you. You must know that. He's so proud of you. If you look on our bedroom wall, you'll see a map of Vietnam. He wanted to know where you were every day. He talks so proudly about you to everyone we know. Yet there has been a problem between you since you were little. Given who you are and who your daddy is, maybe it couldn't have been different. You are both so strong in your ways. It might have been otherwise if you could have started out together.

"The hardest thing about your daddy going off to war so sudden the way he did was he barely got to know you after your birth. Then he was gone over four years before we laid eyes on him again. Most men got furlough before they shipped overseas, but your daddy was one of the unlucky ones. He couldn't come home. It turned out I was fortunate to get a telephone call. For nearly four years, you and I lived with my parents, or his. That must have been nice for you, in a way, because your grandparents favored you the entire time. They didn't want me to correct you about anything. There was nothing too good for you to have. All the love and concern they had for your daddy fighting overseas in the war was expressed to you. You were wonderfully spoiled for four years. Then your daddy came home.

"I had the shock of my younger years when he returned," my mother continued. "I sent a young, good-looking, twenty-year-old kid off to war. Four years later a stranger got off the train—an older man, serious looking. I was stunned, because I had thought everything would be the same as before he left. *Nothing* was! Lord, he didn't even *look* the same! I probably seemed the same to him, but he had been through fourteen major battles in the Pacific, had experienced hell, and I'll tell you, he had aged considerably. He seemed to have things deep inside himself he couldn't reach. I tried to help him talk, but I never did it very well. I doubt he's ever talked about them.

"So here's a man come home from war who is not by any means used to a child who has been the center of attention for four years. Just struggling to live in crowded conditions with his in-laws would have pressured him. Certainly you didn't understand having a strange man telling you what to do. Your daddy began correcting and disciplining you, and in the process telling me and my mother what we had been doing wrong for four years! He'd say to my mother, 'Ida and I are not going to put up with this kid the way you've raised him. He's not going to throw fits and tantrums anymore when he doesn't get what he wants! I won't have it. He's going to be more of a man than that!' He seemed to think more about what kind of man you'd be than the boy you were.

"So, your daddy started a whole new way of life for you," she said, "and that was the beginning of your conflict with him. You didn't take well to his methods. You needed a lot of getting used to each other. Your daddy knew what he wanted, but he didn't understand you. I was pulled between the two of you. I shed a lot of tears because I wanted so much for you to be close. It was years before he

understood you. You see, he missed the first years that are so important between a father and his son. It took a long time for your daddy
and you to hit it off. I don't think it happened till the last few years.
Now you're close, and it is a blessing to see!

"Your brother was born two years after your daddy came home,
and that must have been confusing to you. While you and your
brother, Johnny, were growing up, I lost three in miscarriages. I
longed to have a daughter to go with my two sons. It never happened. I thought, well, I don't have a daughter, but with these two
sons I'll surely have a granddaughter. Then you and Johnny grew up
and got married. You had five sons, Johnny had two, and we still
have no girls. We laugh now about all the boys. That's probably why
we made a point to get a girl dog!

"We moved to Portales, New Mexico, when you were six," my
mother told me. "Your brother was born there. Those were trying
years for your daddy and me, and they must have been difficult for
you also. We had hardships with the farm. Hail took our crops out
twice. You didn't grow up having everything you wanted, and your
daddy was hard on you, pushing you with farm chores. He said farm
work would make a better man of you, and at the same time we really did benefit from your help. So the conflict continued. It must have
made you unhappy to feel on the outs with your daddy. In a way,
maybe it was good for you to see you couldn't have everything you
wanted, though we tried to see that you and Johnny had what you
needed. Finally we left farming and moved to Fort Worth, Texas,
where your daddy went to work for General Dynamics. It was the
best decision we ever made."

That was the most level-headed, helpful talk I'd ever had with
my mother. I'd never seen that side of her, and I thanked her. I
thought of her mother, Grandmother Spotted Fawn, who gave so
much to me during my early years, and I realized that my mother
had more of Grandmother in her than I had known.

When I was alone again, I thought about those early years with
my father. . . . Jeff Reagan was adamant, near fanatical, about hard
work being the only consideration of what made a man a "man"—
that combined with providing for one's family, which was mainly
related to hard work. Dad wanted so *much* to make sure I was a man!

His father had come to Texas from Ireland during the potato famine. His people had survived because they'd worked hard. Thousands hadn't. Grandpa Reagan was one of twelve children—eleven brothers and one sister. The Reagans brought a valuable resource with them from Ireland—the capacity for long hours of work. One of the brothers became a Texas senator and is listed in *Who's Who in America*, but most of the Reagan clan, like my dad, had little formal education.

After finishing the sixth grade, Jeff Reagan found no use for school and quit to go to work—he probably had no use for school prior to that. At age fourteen, he lied about his age and hired out to drive a road grader for the Texas Highway Department. At fifteen he drove a bulldozer and drew as much pay as a full-grown man. Like me, he was physically strong as a teenager. We are the same height, six foot one, and pictures of him at age nineteen look like me.

As a youngster he gave me staggering amounts of work compared with what all my friends and cousins had to do. I was popular, and my buddies in the neighborhood would come by asking me to go off and play with them. Usually, I couldn't until my work was finished. Dad would say, "Sure, Harley can go and play as soon as he weeds this field" or "Yes, but this fence needs painting before he can go off with you kids."

Naturally, my chores did not enable me to join my buddies if I worked alone, so I schemed to get their help. Usually I figured ways my friends could do the chores for me. Then we'd all take off for the ball field. I thought Dad couldn't complain because the job had been done. It drove him wild knowing I hadn't done the chores personally, that others had done most of the work. That made no sense to me. My personal creed even then was the saying "Minimum effort, maximum results!" It still is. I never understood Dad's criticism. Even today I don't get it fully: he got what he wanted; so did I.

To him I was lazy unless I was using my hands, sweat pouring off my body. He wanted to see me working harder physically than anyone else. That was the way he grew up, and that was what he understood. To me that was the "Irish-potato-famine mentality." You can be sure my dad never heard me say those words.

In thirty-five years of work at General Dynamics, Dad missed work only for a funeral. He was late to work once—the day he fell on the ice and broke his arm. In his family there was nothing special about this. You just did your job.

"You're conning those other kids, Harley," he'd say. "You're taking advantage of them because you can't face hard work!" Or, "You'll never amount to anything if you don't work hard, Harley!" When he was mad, he'd say, "You'll never amount to a fucking thing because you're lazy!" I've heard him say this a hundred times. I knew he considered me lazy. I wondered if he thought laziness had inspired my choice to play quarterback on the high school football team, because a quarterback uses his brain and linemen use their brawn.

If I was lazy, I didn't see it. I look at my grown sons today, and I know they were lazy as kids. For certain, I worked pretty damn hard picking cotton, shucking corn, and milking cows. Seasonally, it was especially hard. I mean hard-ass work and missing school to do it. We raised peanuts, cotton, broom corn, and regular corn, among other things. There is no way to get away from hard work on a farm. When it was time to get a crop in, you didn't go to school.

Dad used to say, "At harvest time God doesn't go to school, and by God, neither do you!" It was that simple. Still, my grades were good. I loved school and made mostly A's.

But it was true that if there was a way to make a job easier, or get out of it, I'd damn sure do it. I wouldn't bust my ass if there was an easier way. To Dad that was laziness. I never came to his position that work had to be physical, though I took physical beatings for holding to my way.

Dad had a conflict about my schoolwork. He'd say he wanted me to do well in school so my life would be easier than his. He complained about how hard he'd worked all his life. Yet he ridiculed my love for study and books. He tried to understand it, but he never seemed to get it. I read hundreds of books. I read myself to sleep at night.

As a boy I read voraciously; I still do. Once Dad picked up my copy of *White Fang* and glanced through it. "Why are you always reading these stupid books?" he wanted to know.

"It's because I'm learning, Dad. They teach me."

"What do they teach you?" he asked.

"About life and things and people and places! I know more about everything from my books."

"Yeah," he'd say. "But this book here is about a fucking dog!"

I tried to tell him White Fang was a wolf and that the book wasn't really even about a wolf.

"Dad, this book is about values. It's about honor and courage and loyalty."

He looked at me like I'd spoken Chinese. "You got all you need of that right here in front of you! Just be *loyal* to your family and learn a skill *courageously*! That will bring *honor* to the family."

He wanted me to learn more practical things, so he planned time to show me how to adjust the carburetor in the family car, or change the oil and spark plugs, or replace a piston. He was a good mechanic and wanted me to know as much as he did. I'd meet him at the car. He'd prop up the hood and teach, being careful to explain all the various functions under the hood several times to be sure I had it.

"Son, now look," he'd say, "you gotta be sure these line up just right for the proper explosions in the cylinders to get the best out of the engine." He'd tell me about mileage and power and economy and lubrication, and I'd listen. As soon as I understood what he was teaching, I'd get back to my paperback book. I'd hear him talking, happy with himself under the hood, repeating his instructions like his father had with him.

"Do you think you got it in your head now, Son?" he'd ask. "Have you got it?" Then he'd look up and see me reading Jack London or James Fenimore Cooper and begin to sputter and fume.

I didn't do it to hurt him. It was just my way. He'd get so mad he didn't know what to do with himself. It didn't matter that I understood his engine teaching. The book just didn't belong. It didn't fit with his concept of work.

Dad is a hardworking, honest, down-to-earth man. His word is more reliable than most documents. His approach to life is direct: "Things are either right or wrong. If they're right, leave them. If they're wrong, by God make 'em right or don't complain."

Dad's temper was explosive when I was growing up. If I stepped out of line, especially with a lie, or if he thought me disrespectful, he'd whip me with a razor strap. When I lied to avoid a beating, he whipped me for the lie. His message was clear and simple: "Do something wrong and you get the shit knocked loose!"

When I look back today, his methods don't seem so harsh. At the time, they did. I tried his system with my own kids, and it didn't work. I never found one that did.

When Dad was really mad, he'd hit me with his fists. The most remarkable instance was when I was a senior in high school. I was talking on the phone one afternoon with my steady girlfriend. In the background, my parents began to argue about something. As usual, my dad swore and shouted, and I took offense. My girl was a Mormon. I was in love and protective.

I was lying on my back on the floor, the phone beside me. "Excuse me a second, honey," I said and covered the mouthpiece with my hand. I looked up at my parents, "Pardon me, Dad, but do you have to use that kind of language when I'm talking to my girl?"

Dad looked at me incredulously. I felt like a worm who'd learned to speak English. He reached over, ripped the phone off the wall, and threw it out the open door. Then he jerked me up off the floor, slapped me hard in the face, then punched my stomach viciously with his fist. I fell to my knees, unable to breathe. As I struggled for breath, I turned icy cold inside. My guts turned to steel. I'd been learning judo and jujitsu. As he moved to slap me again, I stepped inside the blow and slammed him hard to the floor. I jumped on his chest and grabbed him by the throat.

"If you ever hit me again," I growled, "I'll kill you—or you'll have to kill me!"

A drop of blood fell from my nose, landing on his cheek. I sat on his chest panting for breath, one fist raised. I was beginning to wonder how to get off him when I looked into his eyes. They were twinkling.

"Son, I guess you just grew up," he said. Nothing more.

I climbed off his chest and went outside to find the phone. For two weeks I was an emotional wreck because I had threatened my dad. The incident was never mentioned, nor did he ever hit me again.

All Irish male Reagans are hard hitting and hot tempered. They were born tough and stayed that way. They are my roots on my father's side. Uncle Leonard was an early model for me. By trade he was a master mechanic, one of the best body workers in town. He could buy a wrecked car for seventy-five dollars scrap and fix it to sell for a thousand. At one time Leonard drank heavily. After two beers he was drunk.

I was with my parents and brother Johnny in his shop one afternoon with a plan to take Uncle Leonard to dinner. He was busy working when we arrived. I watched him, fascinated, as he redid a Lincoln body. He knew I idolized him, so he handed me a paint mask and included me in the job. I soon felt integral to the success of his project. That was his way. He talked to the old Lincoln and me while he worked. He had a relationship with that wreck like Dad had with horses.

My dad approached us with a serious look on his face. "Leonard," Dad said, "some cops are here for you."

I watched Uncle Leonard's reaction. He removed his paint mask and hung it up, put the spray gun away, walked over, and carefully locked up all his tools. "You can keep your mask, son," he said to me.

"Leonard, don't do it," my dad said.

"How many have come?" he asked.

"Leonard, I said don't do this," repeated my dad. Dad looked worried.

"I ain't going to make it easy for them." Uncle Leonard hung up his paint apron. "I asked how many have come?"

"Two," said my dad.

"That won't do it," said Uncle Leonard.

When the officers saw Uncle Leonard would not come with them peacefully, they called for help. They stood on one side of the garage watching him till their backup arrived. When they closed in on him, Uncle Leonard charged directly at the officers like a wild man. He fought hard, screaming like a maniac. In the end they took him. When he finally went down, they beat him over the head and body with nightsticks and dragged him away. Three of the officers who attacked him were also hurt. Later I asked my dad why he hadn't helped Uncle Leonard in the fight.

"It's because I promised him I wouldn't any more, Harley," Dad said sadly. "He made me promise. I've done it too many times."

"Why did the police hit him like that?" I asked.

"The police came for him because your Uncle Leonard beat up someone important to city politics in a bar fight last night."

That's the way the Reagans were. When they weren't working, they socialized. They were a hardworking, hard-drinking clan and still are. I loved the Reagan family gatherings. All my uncles were storytellers. They'd open a beer, and the stories would begin. They all told stories. I noticed one day that's the way they talked to each other—through their stories. Most people talk to each other in a straight way. You understand what the Reagans are saying by getting the story.

For all the hard-fisted discipline I was raised with, I didn't suffer socially, particularly after we moved to Fort Worth. I was in scouting and rode rodeos. At Birdville High I lettered in football, basketball, track, and rodeo. I was a sky diver, and I flew jets in the Texas Civil Air Patrol. Through high school I maintained A's academically.

My father and mother had a good relationship when I was growing up. It looks even better now. They'd argue and quarrel, but I felt their happiness with each other, and I still do. In August of 1990 I was at their fiftieth wedding anniversary, and Mother looked like a kid in love.

Dad loves my mother. Though he never touched or hugged me or my brother, John, he is loving and affectionate with my mother. I often saw them touching, kissing, and teasing while I was growing up. It was clear they were open to each other sexually. That was nice.

When my mother flirts a certain way, Dad will do anything for her. He'll buy her anything she wants. For example, one Christmas he bought her an expensive mink coat. "To me, it's silly," he said, "but that's what she wants."

"Mother," I said, "how can you do this? You are an Indian. Do you have any idea how many hundred little mink it takes to make a coat like this? Do you know you have a part in their deaths with this coat?"

"Well," she said, "it kept them warm; it'll keep me warm."

She doesn't get it. My mother is a very warm-hearted, kind-hearted, loving, naive woman. She is naive to the max. She has a strong little-girl personality when she chooses, and she's in it a lot. When she's being a naive little girl, my dad will buy her the whole damn world. He loves her naïveté.

As I think about it now, though, I wonder if Dad and I are naive thinking my mother is naive!

THE YEARS AFTER VIETNAM

My first son, Steve, was born on April 1, 1961, after I had been married less than two years. On December 12, 1967, Raven, my fifth son, was born. My three middle sons, Jeffrey, Todd, and David, were born a year apart. Five boys in less than seven years! During that period I was out of the country much of the time.

When I was discharged from the Marine Corps, I wanted to become a good father, husband, and provider. Because I had no civilian skills, I took any job that paid—anything! I must have held fifteen or twenty different jobs in a four-year period. I was a bartender, draftsman, vacuum cleaner salesman, gas station attendant, finance company collector, stunt man, truck driver, martial arts instructor, shipping clerk, and design illustrator. I often worked double shifts. In 1974 we moved from Fort Worth to Southern California, where I added college classes to my chaotic schedule. I eventually earned a Ph.D. in psychology from the Pacific Cultural Institute for Advanced Studies in Hollywood.

None of the jobs lasted long. I left each position to avoid conflict—or because of it. I could not tolerate being told how to live my life. I had several run-ins with the law for disturbing the peace. I terrorized my family, brutalized my kids, hit my wife, and destroyed my home. For a time I drank heavily and was addicted to morphine, which had been given to me at Bethesda Hospital for pain. I felt crazy. Inside my head I had nowhere to go, no way to find peace. A violent incident would give me temporary relief. Like a vampire, I sought it. Periodically I needed the blood. Violence took me nearer to an edge I sensed would be irreversible.

One night, not long after my discharge from the Marine Corps, I walked into the house after working an exhausting fourteen-hour construction day, opened the refrigerator, and reached for a Dr.

Pepper. There was none. I carefully shut the refrigerator door and stared silently at nothing in particular. I turned. "Nicki, dear, will you make me some supper?"

She and the five kids lay on the couch watching TV. They were so absorbed in *"Lassie"*, or whatever, none of them had risen to greet me.

"Honey, can you get something yourself tonight?" she answered. "We've eaten and I'm exhausted. There might be a can of chili in the cupboard."

"Nicki, I want some supper."

After a long pause, Nicki responded. "What, Harley?"

"Food!" I yelled.

"OK, Harley, take it easy. I'll be right with you." She had not looked away from the screen. "The program's almost over. Can you wait?"

"Sure!" I shouted. I lifted the stove and dumped it. Pots and pans bounced on the floor. I kicked at them as I stormed out of the house. I found understanding in a bar.

Another night Nicki was watching TV and didn't move fast enough for a request I've forgotten. I kicked the TV. Pieces crashed around the room. Naturally, the kids were scared to death.

The three middle kids got the brunt of it. Steve, the oldest, would leave—just disappear. Later, when my explosion was over, he'd come back and look up at me, "Daddy, you OK now?"

I'd say, "Yeah, Son, sorry."

He'd go to his room and shut the door. As young as he was, Steve seemed to understand it, though of course he didn't really understand. Raven was too small to get involved. The other three were confused and terrified. My inconsistency was devastating. One day I was the best dad in the world, the next I was a monster. I never struck them when they were little, but as they grew older I did. I couldn't stand it when they stuck up for Nicki, which naturally as boys they would. Massive guilt filled me. The Vietnam War coursed its way gradually through my body.

The first four years I was home were terrible for Nicki. I believe she got through them because of her courage and tenacity. Nicki always had a gutsy willingness to try again. I admired her for that. I know she was pushed to her breaking point. I was already there when I came home.

There is nothing Nicki could have done to prepare herself to live with me after Vietnam. I had no idea myself what awaited me. I came home with a medical discharge under honorable conditions— bitter, disillusioned and sick. At Bethesda, where I had hoped to heal from emotional as well as physical wounds, my conflicts had only deepened. I was discharged truly ill, struggling to suppress a rage I was just beginning to feel. That was my condition when I left the Marine Corps. That was what I brought to my wife, five sons, family, and friends.

One afternoon Nicki and I went out for ice cream with Steve and Raven. She held Steve's hand, and I carried Raven. The other three boys were at my mom's. Having only two kids with us was wonderful, and it must have been nice for them also. It was a beautiful day, and I felt great. As we exited the ice cream store, a truck backfired. I lunged at Nicki and Steve, hurling them against the curb.

"Stay down!" I hissed. I clawed frantically for a weapon.

Raven was terrified and screaming. Steve was confused and shaking. Nicki's blouse was torn. She was filthy. Our ice cream cones lay shattered in the gutter. Naturally the day was ruined.

Another time I went to the high school to see my brother practice football. He was an incredible athlete, and I loved to see him play. My old coach approached from behind and slapped me on the back to say "Hi!" I reached back and flipped him over my shoulder. I was on his chest, about to attack his throat, when my vision cleared.

I broke down and cried. Coach wanted to help once he recovered his composure, but there really wasn't much he could do. He'd never been in the kind of personal war that enveloped us in 'Nam.

I was deeply entrenched inside myself and unreachable. Violent incidents continued. The confusing aspect to me about them was their suddenness and my loss of control. One moment I was a peaceful civilian, yet in the next second I could be a jungle animal.

One weekend we all decided to go see *The Wizard of Oz* at a drive-in theater. I had been away driving a truck all week. I missed everyone and was pleased we were going out together. In my dreams the seven of us were a close, happy family.

I was home by six 6 p.m. Friday evening so we'd have plenty of time to get ready. It was our ritual to make popcorn before a movie, and the kids jumped around excited. Nicki cooked hot dogs and baked cookies for desert. We'd eat in the car like a picnic. It would have made sense to eat before we got in the car, but we all loved a car picnic.

"Can I heat the butter for the popcorn this time, Dad?" asked David. He was five years old, our next-to-last son.

"No, I get to!" insisted Steve. "I'm the oldest!"

"You always do it," said David. "Anyway, you don't put enough butter on."

"I want to!" shouted Raven, waving his arms. "Lemee . . . lemee!"

I thought that was a good idea, since Raven was two and had not previously asked to participate. I suggested we help Raven. Jeff got a saucepan, Todd brought butter. We helped Raven put butter in the pan.

"I fix butter good, David," he said. He felt his responsibility.

"Raven, you want me to show you how to strike a match so you can light the stove?" asked Steve.

"Yes, I do!" shouted Raven. He adored his oldest brother.

Steve gave Raven a wooden match, then struck another on the matchbox. When the match flared, Raven's eyes grew wide. He stepped back, watching the flame.

"Now, you go ahead, Raven. Light your match."

"No, don't wanna cook butter today!" shouted Raven. He dropped the match and ran from the room.

We laughed as a family. I felt so happy!

We loaded the car and drove to the theater. We found our spot just before the film started. Nicki passed hot dogs as the lights went down. *The Wizard of Oz* is one of the best movies ever made. It has something for everyone—or so I thought.

Halfway through the film, four guys in the car on Nicki's side got loud and crude. They didn't like the movie and amused themselves with loud comments.

"What shall we do, Harley?" asked Nicki.

"Let's not do anything," I said. "Maybe they'll shut up. Maybe they'll leave."

They didn't. They were drinking, oblivious to their surroundings. They yelled at the Tin Man. "Hey, Tin Man. Don't let your dick rust! Oil it up on Dorothy!" They laughed hysterically.

"Could you ask those guys to be quiet?" asked David.

Nicki rolled her window down.

"Hey, would you fellows mind watching your language? We've got kids in the car."

They looked at her like they couldn't believe it. "Fuck you, bitch!" yelled one of them. "It ain't our fault you got kids, but if you want another one, duck your old man and come over here!" shouted a second. "Piss on your kids, lady!" said a third, giving Nicki the finger.

I opened my door so hard it cracked the speaker pole. I rushed to the other car, yanked the driver's door open, and grabbed the kid by his throat. I dragged him out of the car.

"You sonofabitch! You talk to my family that way!"

I slammed his head against the side of his car. I attacked the others before they could move. I cracked two heads together and hit the fourth in the back of the neck as he ran. Breathing hard, I looked at them on the ground. I resisted an impulse to kick.

"My God, Harley," cried Nicki.

"Shut up!" I yelled.

I climbed into our car, started it up, and we drove away. It all happened before an attendant arrived. That's the way I was. The evening was finished. I was so angry I couldn't talk for hours. Nicki put the boys in bed.

I had wanted that evening so much. Naturally, my family was frozen with fear. It was so scary knowing their dad could go nuts in a second. For four years I slept with a .45 automatic pistol under my pillow every night and would have used it in a second with pleasure.

I tried to control my behavior. I moved, changed jobs, involved myself deeply in the Mormon Church, and pushed myself as a scoutmaster. I began to make money. Nothing helped. I was estranged, painfully alienated from everything. I had no way to identify, no way to relate. I was enraged. Rage moved in every fiber of my body. The only way I knew how to feel, to connect, to respond was through physical violence or sex. I was a volcano boiling at the surface, trying to hold it down.

I knew even then that my anger wasn't about Dr. Pepper or supper or drive-in drinkers. If Nicki had left me a six-pack of Dr. Pepper, I might have been helped a little. I'd have felt, seen, or sensed a connection. Perhaps my rage would have abated. I tried once to tell her how Dr. Pepper was important to me, but I didn't get through.

"Nicki, will you please leave Dr. Pepper for me?"

"OK," she said. "But I doubt it's good for you to drink so much of it." But she didn't remember. The importance of it missed her.

Probably there was nothing Nicki could have done to help. I was alienated from everything. I looked for a sign anywhere to give me a feeling of connection or that I mattered or had a place. I was the toughest on Nicki because I wanted her the most. I needed so much from her. I wanted desperately to feel that she knew my inner war, my anguish. I had to be seen and loved and nurtured. Without that, I gradually turned to stone, incapable of love.

Naturally I made it impossible for Nicki to give me what I wanted, even if she could. Eventually she didn't want to risk going anywhere with me. An obnoxious drunk I'm sure she could have put up with. But I needed someone hurt and down and bleeding. I welcomed provocation.

People who know me now have a difficult time believing I was as I have described. Those with their own Vietnams understand. For four years, I felt truly insane. My dad became critical of me again, and that hurt, too. He thought I should settle down to one steady job like he had and support my family. After all, he'd gone off to war for longer than I had, and he'd come home, settled in, and raised his family. He never said it like that, but I could feel it. There was absolutely no one to talk with. Even had there been someone who understood, I would have had no words for my inner feelings.

One night in 1972 I came home after fifteen hours of work in a beer factory and found no supper on the table. Nicki was asleep on the couch in front of the TV. The kids were not in sight. I picked up the television set and threw it through the front window. I broke everything in the house I could kick, hit, or throw. For the first time, I felt no relief from my rage. It grew out of control, and in my rage I wanted to kill. Nicki must have sensed this; she ran from the house.

I decided to kill myself. I unpacked the pearl-handled .45 automatic I had carried in Vietnam. I loaded it, cocked it, and put it to my temple. As my trigger finger tensed, I sensed the presence of Grandfather Two Bears: *"When you are done killing your brothers and are ready to heal them, your heart will speak to you. Come to me and I will help you."*

My finger relaxed. My body shook in deep spasms. I put down the gun. I sobbed until I collapsed in exhaustion. When I awoke, I felt hope for the first time in years. I knew I would return to Arizona to study with Grandfather Two Bears.

That was the turning point of my life. The fires of anger did not diminish for several more years, but with Grandfather's help and the medicine of my people, I slowly learned to channel my rage into healing myself and others.

PART 5

GRANDFATHER
TWO BEARS

FINDING
GRANDFATHER
TWO BEARS

Five weeks later I cleared my schedule, said good-bye to my family, and headed east for Arizona. As I drove into Tuba City I had no clear idea of where I would find Grandfather Two Bears—or even if I could. Desperation fed determination. I followed numerous clues for several frustrating hours before I drove my used Karmann Ghia slowly northwest from Tuba City, guided by a dubious map sketched on a paper cafe napkin by a reluctant Bud, the Navajo deputy sheriff who had originally led me to Grandfather. I could not discern whether Navajo people did not want to talk about Grandfather, or whether they just did not want to talk to *me* about him. Later I learned that both were true. Navajo have a tendency not to know anyone who works with Navajo medicine; it's just safer that way. Navajo medicine is powerful enough to worry even the skinwalkers themselves. (Navajo medicine people are referred to at various times as sorcerers, witches, and skinwalkers.)

After driving for thirty minutes on faint tracks Bud had called a road, I hit a rock that cracked my oil pan. (The only roads I've found as rough as the Navajo roads in Arizona are the Navajo roads in New Mexico.) I jacked the car up, crawled under it, and pulled the pan loose. A rush of filthy oil hit my face, barely missing my eyes. Furious, I crawled out from under the car and kicked it as hard as I could, which was hard enough to knock it off the jack. Great—I hadn't seen a vehicle since I had left Tuba City. I had a long walk ahead of me. I picked up my bag and aimed a departing kick at the Ghia as Grandfather's pickup came slowly around the bluff. He pulled alongside and glanced at my car.

"Put your bag in here," he said. He was smiling in a way I came to know well. During all the years I knew Two Bears, I never learned how he managed to materialize at my side when he was nowhere in the vicinity. One second he was not in sight, and the next he appeared.

Minutes later he killed his engine beside the hogan where I had met him previously. He stepped down from the truck, looked around, and walked into the hogan. I followed him in. The hogan's one room was dimly illuminated by sunlight. Grandfather lit a lamp.

"Sit down. I'll show you something," he said.

Grandfather opened a wooden trunk. From it he lifted several objects. He lay the first of them in front of me.

"You need a dream bundle," he announced. "You don't dream so good yet. This one will teach you how to make yours."

He carefully undid the leather strips wrapped around his bundle and unrolled it. Inside were several smaller bundles. Grandfather placed them on the larger skin. One after the other, he opened the smaller bundles, placing their contents on the skin. As Grandfather meticulously explained the history and medicine of each object, I realized I was expected to remember everything he told me. I could take no notes. There would be no quiz.

I was fascinated. "What is this?" I asked, pointing at what looked like a small, mummified bat.

He ignored me. "Your dream bundle will help you see the relationship between your life and your death," he said.

From one of the bundles he lifted several tiny arrows tied together and handed them to me. I took them in my left hand, studying them. "How many are there?" he asked.

"Four," I said.

With my right hand I touched the tiny arrows. Each had a fragile arrowhead. Faded flakes of brown, yellow, and green paint clung to them. Bits of feather were attached to the ends of the shafts.

"Don't touch the feathers," said Grandfather. "They are original. Very old. What do you see?"

I intended to ask what "original" meant when I suddenly felt strange. I became unaccountably hot, and sweat ran down my forehead. I trembled. The floor seemed to slant to the east. I became frightened and placed one hand on the floor to steady myself. I looked at Grandfather. He appeared oblivious to my experience.

"What do you see?" he asked.

I looked at my left hand. I was holding one straight, true arrow, a long shaft with a perfectly chipped flint arrowhead and magnificent quetzal feathers.

"I see a . . ." I looked at Grandfather. He was a young man. The room became much lighter. "I see . . ." The magnificent arrow was gone, and the little bundle of arrows rested again in my hand. I looked quickly at Grandfather. He appeared the same as always. He turned and looked at me.

"Good," he said. "Good." He smiled at me warmly.

He lifted each object carefully from his bundle and showed it to me. I felt the most intimate secrets possible were being shared, and I did not know how to react. "Very nice, Grandfather," I muttered.

He spoke to each object as though it were alive. His personal relationship with it was clear. He explained the way the medicine of one object combined with another to increase their power.

"Here," he said. He handed me what looked like a small stick covered with fur and tiny feathers. "Bird person. Its eyes play peekaboo."

At first I didn't see what he was talking about. Then I discovered two bright little eyes peeking at me. Tiny, luminous turquoise eyes peered out from behind scattered fluffs of feather. They blinked. I wondered if Grandfather was fooling me.

"It's used to summon all the winged ones for prayer," he said.

I was about to ask him if I'd ever need all of the winged ones when he spoke again. "This one here looks similar, but has no eyes. It's my medicine sprinkler."

He held another stick covered with feathers.

"Now switch the summoner to your left hand, and hold this in your right."

He lifted a small bundle from the skin and handed it to me.

"What is this, Grandfather?" I asked.

"What's it look like?" he responded.

"Like two old pieces of leather tied together," I said.

"It's not leather," said Grandfather.

What is it? I thought.

"What do you feel now?" he asked. "Hold them about this far

apart." Grandfather indicated about six inches. My "bird person" hand became hot.

"The bird person is used to sing power songs when you hold this *jish* near it. It's a control piece. It's how Navajos influence the elements.

Grandfather began to sing, then stopped abruptly. "That's a song to bring the rain. But we don't want to get wet!" He smiled. "We use them together to control the rain and wind, the thunder and lightning. It's the bird person that does it. The prayer stick in your right hand is the igniter. I call it the bird feeder." He laughed.

"Look," he said. "Here is my knife for cutting the cord." He handed me a beautiful crystal knife about five inches long. "I chipped it myself!"

"It's really pretty," I said. I wondered what cord he was talking about. Later I learned he was referring to an auric umbilical cord attached to the navel.

"Here," he said, "this gets placed on the navel to keep a spirit from reentering the body after the cord is cut."

"Is it obsidian?" I asked.

"Yes," he answered.

I reached for an evenly chipped black stone ten inches long, shaped like a spearhead. "Did you make this, too?" I asked.

"This is for warding off evil. Hold it and see what you feel. It's a strong protection bundle."

He handed me a leather pouch five inches long. It appeared ancient. He could have told me Anasazi. It was wrapped with strips of worn fur. I examined one side and then the other.

"Don't try to open it," he ordered.

I was not inclined to open it. My head began to flood with information.

"This is my laser gun, hold it," instructed Grandfather. He handed me a pistol-shaped piece of antler with a small crystal protruding from one tip. A tiny, evil-looking claw hung from the pistol handle.

"That's a devil's claw," said Grandfather. "Grows over near Many Farms."

He talked through the night. Scores of medicine items passed in front of me. I knew I was expected to remember everything he said.

As the hours passed, Grandfather's energy seemed to increase. By dawn I wondered when he would tire. What I didn't know then is that once he began teaching, the hour was insignificant. Teaching increased Grandfather's energy—it nourished him. By early afternoon of the next day I was tired and feeling it. Grandfather was strong and appeared unaware that I was running down.

A large male otter skin was spread belly up in front of us. Grandfather pointed to seven symbols painted on the otter. "This symbol here goes over the patient's heart." He indicated the fourth painting up from the otter's tail. "Lay the skin on the one being healed with the painting over his heart. It's painted where the otter's heart was."

Suddenly he turned to me, his eyes intense. "SwiftDeer, lie on your back."

"What . . .?"

"Get onto your back."

Frightened by the urgency in his voice, I lay on my back. He had never called me by name before. Grandfather placed the otter skin on my chest and stomach, belly down. He took an eagle-bone whistle from his bag and blew it over my heart. He sang in Navajo and blew the whistle again several times. He studied me silently.

"What was that for?" I asked tentatively.

"Feel any different?"

I considered that. "I'm tingling," I said.

"Where?"

I thought about it. "Well, it's moving, Grandfather. First my chest tingled, but now it's my belly."

"Good," he said. "Your heart's pumping the otter spirit through your body. The medicine of the otter is to clean the blood. Sit up now."

He replaced the otter skin in the trunk and lifted another bundle. He unwrapped it slowly.

"Do I have dirty blood, Grandfather?" I asked.

"It's something to talk about at another time," he said gently. "This one is my oldest medicine object." He handed me a stone replica of an ancient god ten inches in length. It was smooth and cold and heavy for its size. Once I held it, my energy increased. The stone felt alive. I would not have been shocked if the stone had breathed. The god was looking at me.

"Put it over your third chakra," he said. "There. Hold it there in both hands." He pointed to my belly.

I held it against myself. A calmness pervaded my body. My energy expanded. I felt about to embark on a journey. "What is this, Grandfather?" I asked.

"A *nagual* stone," he answered. "It is a stone of power from a nagual of other times. Today, it is held by the one who guides the feathered winged serpent wheel. Its origin is in the stars, the Pleiades. It was given to me by my teacher, as it was given to him by his. It has come down many times. It is carved from a meteorite that my elders say struck the planet generations ago." [The feathered winged serpent wheel refers to a mythical creature having the powers of Earth and heaven: a Mayan serpent that flies. Today, the winged feathered serpent is a major symbol integral to the medicine of the Deer Tribe.]

"Why is it called the nagual stone?" I asked.

"It has always been called the nagual stone," he answered. "If you study hard, perhaps one day it will be in your bundle!" He gave me his warm smile. "But then perhaps you will get a dunce cap instead!" He chuckled, pleased with his joke. My hands vibrated as I returned the stone.

Grandfather continued his teachings. For two hours he described the ceremonies of the first three "gateways," the initiations into the many different levels of medicine teachings. I began to feel extremely tired. I closed my eyes—a quick nap would help. I dozed, his voice in my ears. A gentle peace pervaded. Suddenly I received a tremendous blow to my upper back and was sharply awake. Grandfather sat before me talking as before.

"You could see many gateways on this path," he said. "Twelve, maybe more."

Pretending I had been awake the entire time, I stretched and stood up. I was determined to discover who had struck me. I excused myself and went outside. I saw no one. I returned to my place to find Grandfather gone. I ran outside again and found him standing near a woodpile. When I approached, he handed me an ax. "Chop," he said.

Confused, I accepted the ax and did as he said. After splitting a huge pile of wood, I stacked it and sensed I should return to the hogan. I was surprised to feel my energy greatly increased. Grandfather stood at the center of the hogan holding a broom. Grasping his intent, I took it from him and swept the hogan. When my task was completed, I paused in front of him. "Now we walk," he said.

Grandfather set the pace. Soon I was trotting to stay with him. I wondered what purpose he had in running across the desert. Then I realized that Grandfather was not running. He walked with a relaxed gait that seemed to propel him across the land. His walk appeared effortless. I tried to imitate him and quickly fell behind. I was forced to run again to catch him.

We entered an area heavily overgrown with cactus. I plunged after him, beginning to feel desperate. Sweat poured from every pore in my body. When I was about to cry out for rest, he stopped and sat abruptly in a small clearing. I collapsed at his feet, my lungs heaving.

"Careful," he said. "Move yourself over here."

He helped me to one side of the clearing. From there I observed a conical mound of dirt near the center of the clearing where I had collapsed. It was a bare mound, void of vegetation, strangely mysterious.

Grandfather lit a cigarette and began to sing. As my breathing normalized, my excitement grew. I became charged with energy. Grandfather sang for several minutes and stopped.

"The mound marks the place of a battle with a powerful *brujo* or evil sorcerer." He pointed to the little hill. "My song was about the events before the fight. Now I tell the battle."

He demonstrated the struggle of one man against a seemingly invincible brujo of the area. He dramatized the events and action as they unfolded. He stood and shouted. He stamped his feet and ran back and forth with great emphasis. At times he leaped into the air for exclamation. In the end the brujo was defeated by the local medicine man, and the story concluded.

Grandfather sat down again. He lit another cigarette. My heart continued to pound for several minutes. Grandfather sang a prayer of thanks for courage in small men. We smoked in silence for several moments. I wondered if the man who defeated the brujo had been himself. I was reluctant to ask him. I felt shy, like I did as a boy with Grandmother Spotted Fawn. He rose, and we walked back to the hogan. I could not believe the brevity of our return. It was my impression that we were hours from the hogan.

"Come. Now we sit and talk."

I had planned to stay two days with Grandfather Two Bears. Midmorning of the sixth day, my Karmann Ghia appeared outside the hogan, towed by a Navajo teenager driving a banged-up GMC pickup truck. He crawled under my car with his old tools, and by afternoon the car was repaired. Without a word the kid tossed his tools into his truck and drove away. I never saw him again, nor did Grandfather mention him. I was learning about Navajo protocol.

On the evening of the sixth day Grandfather said, "You have done well. You are an adequate student. You have enough teaching for now."

"Thank you, Grandfather." I said.

"Take this with you," he said. He handed me a white oblong stone three inches in width.

"What is it, Grandfather?" I asked.

"It's the stone that captured the spirit of the brujo I described in the desert," answered Grandfather.

"What? . . ." Startled, I nearly dropped it.

"Careful!" said Grandfather. "The spirit in that stone was captured to stop a cycle of evil. I don't want it freed by your care-less-ness."

"You mean there's a person in this stone?"

I looked again at the stone. It was moss agate, shaped like the head of an eagle.

"Turn it over," said Grandfather. "The mandala you see there trapped him. He's caught in the middle of it. See those lines. He was tricked into the stone, and it closed shut on him. Now he's caught indefinitely."

Tiny reddish lines extended from the center of the stone to its perimeter. A shadow of something lurked behind them. "The lines look like ridges in a human brain," I said.

"Yes," said Grandfather. "What do you feel?"

My left hand was hot and beginning to vibrate. I felt dizzy and lightly nauseated. My vision intensified.

"He is responsible for the deaths of over twenty Navajo people," said Grandfather. "His spirit can never hurt anyone as long as it's in the stone." Grandfather paused. "This spirit has danced evil in many lifetimes. I'm passing the stone to you. It is part of the lineage of being able to fight evil. Someday you will pass it to the nineteenth nagual."

I shivered. I didn't feel like the eighteenth nagual, and I definitely did not want that stone to go home with me. "Thank you, Grandfather," I said. "It is an honor."

"Wrap it in this red cloth," he instructed. He then sent me home.

I stopped my car as soon as I could, climbed out, and carried the stone to my trunk. I hid it under the spare tire for the ride to Los Angeles. Today the stone rests among my most powerful medicine items. It is still scary to touch.

I drove through the night and arrived in Los Angeles exhausted and stimulated. On that morning I knew for the first time since I had left Vietnam that I was going to make it.

During those six days with Grandfather, he made suggestions, shared knowledge, and offered advice, but I was aware he was also working with me at powerful and subtle unspoken levels. I felt my extrasensory abilities expanded to a sharpness I had known only in Vietnam when my survival had depended on them. I began to see auras again. I had moments of profound peace and silence. I had mysterious bursts of sobbing that passed as strangely as they arrived. In time, my emotions began to find a more even expression. The tremendous rage that had been dominating my existence receded to deeper caverns in my psyche.

The days with Grandfather were a new beginning for me, a foundation. Whenever I couldn't take the grind in Los Angeles anymore, when I sensed that deep rage beginning to stir and felt I was beginning to lose control, I'd climb in my car and drive east to find Grandfather. Till the day he died, he always managed to be there for me.

TWO BEARS
AND THE GRAVES

During the years I apprenticed with Grandfather, I often glimpsed his vision for harmony between the old ways of the Navajo Nation and the realities of newer and modern times. As Navajos became more involved in white ways, his vision was not always workable. Nevertheless, Grandfather worked tirelessly to combine the old with the new to benefit his people. One morning I arrived at Grandfather's place after driving all night from Los Angeles. He was in his pickup truck about to drive away as I pulled into the yard.

"Good," he said. "In five minutes you'd have missed me."

I tossed my pack in the back and climbed in. I had learned not to ask how he knew I was coming or where we were going. After thirty minutes on the road, he spoke. "We're headed for Black Mesa. A bull-dozer needs stopping."

It turned out a road was being built on the far side of the mesa so the Peabody Mining Company could access its coal mine with a shorter route from the back. The work crew had discovered an old burial ground in its path and was about to turn it under. Anasazi, probably—no one seemed to know. The Navajo Tribal Council had met and given approval to raze the old graves. Taking a different view, Grandfather called the Medicine Council together. When we arrived at the work site, three or four road graders, a couple of bull-dozers, and several dump trucks were making a cloud of dust. They were all Navajo workers, so of course this was their job. Grandfather drove his truck into the center of the activity and shut off his engine.

When the workers recognized Grandfather's pickup, they turned off their equipment and climbed down. Grandfather approached the foreman, a large, muscular white man with a bushy red beard.

"Do you understand that in a few minutes you will hit ancestral graves with that equipment?"

"Yep, I know that. What might that be to you?"

"No you won't," Grandfather said.

"What?"

"No you won't. There's ancestral graves on your route."

"I know that, old man," said the foreman. He glanced at his work crew watching him. "I can't help that. That was a long time ago. Now look here. Your people have approved this project. This road I'm building is good for everybody—especially the Navajo!"

Four Navajo elders appeared out of the landscape. "This road can be made to go over that way around the ancestral grounds," suggested Grandfather.

The white foreman stared at the old Indian. He lifted his hat and wiped off from the heat. "Did you hear me, gramps? Look, I don't need this aggravation, old man, chief—whatever you are. I'm talking about things you don't understand—moocho bucks for everybody, jobs for the Navajo. I'm talking economy, American prosperity. Things beyond you, things you'll never understand."

"I understand the graves."

"Jesus!" groaned the foreman. "Old man, just pack up and get out of here, nice like. Get back to wherever you came from and nobody gets hurt. Everyone is happy. I want this crew working now!"

He turned to the workmen. "Get those fucking machines rolling now, pronto!"

None of the men moved.

"If you need a road, it should go over there." Grandfather pointed.

The foreman shuffled his feet. The workers moved in closer. "Listen, there's no way to stop this road," the foreman said. "Tell your people here to climb back on the equipment. Peabody wants the project, and so does your council. I ain't pushin' it. Peabody gets what he wants out here, and I work for him. It's your own people asking for the new road."

"The bones should not be turned over," said Grandfather.

"Christ Jesus, let me see what you are going to do to stop me," said the foreman.

"OK." Grandfather turned his back and walked to the big road grader. He walked around it four times, then holding tobacco and an eagle feather, he knelt and spoke to the equipment. Grandfather cedared the machinery as he chanted. The foreman lit a smoke and watched. When the workmen heard Grandfather begin to sing, they got in their pickup trucks and drove away. Within two minutes they were gone. The foreman, myself, and the four elders watched.

Grandfather sang at each piece of equipment. At some he danced, shaking the gourd. Time stopped. The white man stared, as if in a trance. His cigarette smoked itself down and dropped from his lips. When Grandfather stopped singing, the mesa became very quiet. He studied the machines, looked back at the mesa, and sat down.

"By Jesus!" the foreman swore. "There's whites to do this work won't be bothered by no witchcraft! You're hurting your own people. To hell with you and all the goddamn superstitious skinwalking Navajos!" he shouted. The foreman jumped into his truck and drove away.

Next day we went to the site early. A few minutes later, a crew of white workers arrived, ready to work. "Watch," said Grandfather.

The workers climbed onto the machinery. The heavy equipment wouldn't start. None of the machines Grandfather had prayed over would start. The men cursed and banged engine hoods and doors. Mechanics were called. They got the road graders to turn over, but when the blades hit the earth, they stalled.

Grandfather had brought lunch. We sat in the shade on lawn chairs and ate. The foreman arrived with a new grader. It ran till it hit the land, then quit.

The foreman's face turned as red as his beard. At midafternoon he charged at Grandfather. "Get it off!" he screamed. "Get this black magick, skinwalker stuff off my machines! Fix my equipment!" He pointed a huge index finger at Grandfather. "You got sixty seconds to take the spell off, or I bust your skinny back over my knee!"

Grandfather looked at him steady for several seconds. "Don't point that thing at me, " he said. "It's got a nail in it."

The man hesitated, looking at his finger. The dust he'd kicked up drifted forward.

"Arrgh!" he grunted. "Rrugrug!" He stared wild-eyed at the finger he'd pointed at Grandfather, as though he saw something I didn't. For a second, I thought he'd had a stroke. His mouth sprayed spittle. He rocked stiffly on his heels, then reclaimed himself slowly. Straightening, he looked thoughtfully at Grandfather and walked away. He climbed into his pickup and drove west without looking back. We never saw him again.

"I didn't see a nail in his finger, Grandfather."

Grandfather's eyes twinkled. "Did you ever hear of a fingernail?"

Another foreman was hired, and it was the same. The equipment would not run. For a month the machines sat motionless under the desert sun. Hundreds of working hours were lost. A resolution was finally reached by the council, and the Navajos came to Grandfather.

"Our people need work," a council spokesman said. "They ate better when we worked the road, had better clothes."

Grandfather sat, thoughtful. "Let them live the old ways for now," he said. "The families can hold together and pray about this for a while. Eat in the old ways."

The council spokesman argued, but Grandfather didn't back off. "It's bad medicine to turn away from the Old Ones. It is not the way of our people to disrupt the resting place of the ancestors. You know it would come back to us."

"Grandfather Wilson, what about our agreement with Peabody?"

"Would you let Peabody plow your father's grave?" asked Grandfather.

The council chairman looked at Grandfather for a long time. "Tom Wilson, what do you want to settle this?"

Grandfather produced a road plan, showing four additional miles around the ancestral graves. "Go this way. Peabody is bound to have his road at any cost. This way the ancestors are honored."

Today the back road to the Black Mesa Peabody mine is as Grandfather suggested, and the ancestors rest quietly.

A HARD LESSON

One of my most memorable and impacting experiences with
Grandfather Two Bears came following a healing ceremony at
Window Rock Hospital in 1975. Grandfather and two other singers
were summoned to help a high school basketball star who had been
run down by a drunk truck driver and was seriously injured. I was
studying with Grandfather that weekend. Naturally, he asked me to
assist him at the hospital. We went into the intensive care unit late
Friday night and worked with the boy straight through till Monday noon.

It was a bad accident. Celebrating an important basketball
victory over Kayenta High with his friends, the boy had failed to
get out of the way of the speeding vehicle and was dragged several
hundred feet.

Four elders were with us. Dozens of friends and family were in
the waiting room the entire weekend. I don't think anyone expected
him to live. Grandfather and the two singers cedared the boy and
began the ceremony at his bedside, leaving room for the activities of
the medical staff of the hospital. I helped Grandfather and the
singers. It was a strange scene.

On one side of the room was the best modern medical equipment
and knowledge Window Rock had to offer the young man. Working
simultaneously on the other side was the best of the old Navajo medicine. Neither was saying much to the other.

Grandfather created a sand painting on the floor. At that time he
was one of only four singers who knew more than seventy major
Navajo ceremonies. I helped in any way needed.

I had been shoveling coal when Grandfather picked me up to go
to the hospital, and I was filthy. One of Grandfather's favorite things
after a teaching session, or so it seemed to me, was to send me up on
Black Mesa to shovel coal. I think it was his idea that the teaching
would settle in deeper if I shoveled.

It was mind-boggling to be filthy in a hospital room, sitting on the floor working with herbs, crystals, and sand, while nurses and doctors and others of the medical staff worked beside us with machines, tubes, needles, blood bags, syringes, monitors, and the usual sterile hospital apparel.

As time passed, the doctors and nurses had less to do. By early Sunday morning, I sensed that the hospital staff had given up on the boy. He had been in a coma most of the time. On the other hand, Grandfather had increased his activity and seemed to be getting stronger. Midmorning he led the singers in an eerie and ancient chant about a Navajo youth of other times who had met tragedy and survived it. I'd been pumped with adrenaline since we entered the boy's room, but I was running out of juice and was beginning to tire.

By dawn Monday morning, I was exhausted and trembling. Grandfather looked at me. "Redo your brain. This boy has three more critical hours."

By noon, the boy was through the crisis and breathing evenly. I was shaking with exhaustion and nearly fell as I helped Grandfather cedar the room. Outside the hospital, he indicated that I should drive the truck back to his home.

I thought, Oh, my God, how am I going to drive sixty-two miles?

I climbed in the truck and started the engine. Tears ran down my face. I almost went off the road twice. Grandfather let me continue that way, ignoring my state. Fifteen miles outside Window Rock, I swerved the truck sharply to miss sheep on the highway, throwing Grandfather to the floor. He pulled himself upright and looked at me. "Stop!" he ordered.

I slowed the truck and stopped in the middle of the road.

"Move the truck to the shoulder."

I did so.

"You are pathetic!" he said.

I didn't know what he meant. Surely he saw how courageous I had been to work sixty-two straight hours in ceremony after having almost no sleep the night previous.

"I've wasted my time with you! Move over!"

Grandfather got behind the wheel and drove the truck toward Many Farms. He drove silently. Near town he turned off the blacktop onto a dirt road headed toward Black Mesa. When he found a coal pile, he killed the engine.

"Your apprenticeship with me is over!" he said.

His eyes said he meant it. In my condition, I began to cry. I begged him to reconsider. I pleaded with him, sobbing, promising I'd do whatever it took to please him.

"OK," he said. "I'll reconsider while you shovel coal."

I couldn't believe it. I picked up the shovel and began to heave coal. I must have shoveled twenty minutes before I put the shovel down, though it seemed like hours.

"Why'd you stop?" he asked me.

"I'm beat," I said, "exhausted!"

Grandfather ignored me.

I started to yell, "I'm tired, I'm tired! Can't you see I'm finished?"

Grandfather stared at me. Quicker than I could see, he picked up the shovel and slammed its backside into my stomach. Down I went. Grandfather leaped on top of me. He yanked my hair. He pounded me, banging my head on the ground. He was a maniac! With his knees on my chest, he jumped up and landed on my stomach again. "Wake up and *see*!" he yelled. "Wake up!"

He then climbed off me, picked up a shovel, and began shoveling coal. I lay on my side looking at him. I was flabbergasted. Grandfather was eighty-two years old and weighed 104 pounds. He had worked in the healing ceremony longer and harder than I had. I weighed 182 pounds. I was a thirty-two-year-old martial arts instructor.

"Wake up!" he screamed. "*See!*"

Suddenly, from where I lay, I did see. I saw that as he shoveled, the coal had a song, I saw that the shovel had a song. Grandfather had a song, even the pickup truck had a song. I saw that Grandfather heard the song and that he shoveled in harmony with it. He was like a symphony conductor. I realized that what I saw was the maximum-efficiency, minimum-effort law he had been teaching me earlier. While I had struggled against myself during the long hospital ceremony, Grandfather had been conducting an orchestra, a ceremonial symphony.

SwiftDeer with portrait of Grandfather Two Bears in
upper left.

Ida Reagan, SwiftDeer's mother.

SwiftDeer with his father, Jeff Reagan.

Grandmother Spotted Fawn, standing left next to her husband, Harley Raper.

SwiftDeer with his sons David (left) and Jeffrey, 1971.

SwiftDeer at boot camp, USMC.

SwiftDeer at boot camp, USMC.

Private Reagan, USMC boot camp graduation, 1959.

SwiftDeer (right foreground), Vietnam. Photo by Frank Beardsley.

SwiftDeer (left rear) helping a wounded buddy, Vietnam. Photo by Herb Freeman.

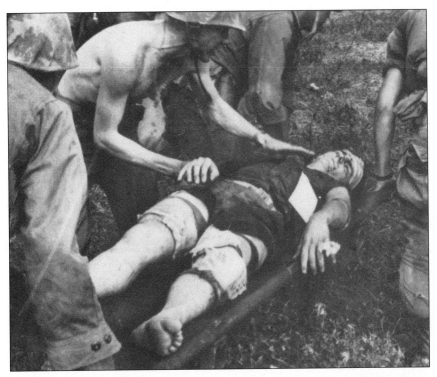

SwiftDeer is critically wounded, Vietnam, June 1967.
Photo by Bob Bowen.

Grandfather Two Bears Wilson, 1978.

Grandfather Two Bears and his wife, Zoni.

Grandfather Two Bears with his grandchildren and great-grandchildren at the Wilson home near Many Farms, Arizona.

Karate class: SwiftDeer in second row, Nicki on his left.

SwiftDeer, martial arts instructor.

SwiftDeer, martial arts instructor.

Dianne NightBird and SwiftDeer on the day they were
bonded (married), June 22, 1979.

SwiftDeer and Mary ShyDeer at their bonding ceremony, 1982.

SwiftDeer with the African shaman Eli Hein, Upper
Volta, Africa, 1983.

He sensed the shift in me and dropped the shovel, smiling. "I see you get it."

"I think so."

"Good. You see, everything has its song. It's the same if you wash dishes, change a shitty diaper, hoe corn, or run a ceremony. Find the energy, the song, and merge with it. Let it become an extension of yourself and you a part of it. You must seek the harmonic and merge with it. Do you get it?"

"Yes, I see it."

"Good. I now have an apprentice again. Please, get behind the wheel and drive us home. You need a bath."

I had never heard Grandfather raise his voice before that day. I never heard him do it again.

LEUKEMIA

I experienced the healing power of Grandfather Two Bears personally in late 1975. While fighting in a full-contact karate tournament in northern California, my teeth caved in from a blow I caught in the mouth. I went down shocked and stunned, choking on my blood and broken teeth; since I was wearing the most expensive mouth piece available, theoretically I should not have been hurt. I was taken to a dentist in the area.

After what seemed a very lengthy examination, the doctor concluded his study of my mouth, set his instruments aside, and washed his hands.

"Well, Doc?"

"You have something more serious than broken teeth," he said.

"Well?"

"To put it bluntly, your teeth are OK, but your gums are shot."

"Meaning what?"

He hesitated, studying me.

"There is something amiss in your bloodstream."

I was referred to an associate of his at the UCLA Medical Center. Several tests were run. Eventually a specialist was called in from Sinai Hospital, an elderly, semiretired doctor named McGimmery. After more blood studies he spoke to me.

"Mr. Reagan, you have a rare form of leukemia that attacks the bone marrow and the body tissue. You've undoubtedly had it for some time." He waited, searching my face. "We have no cure for it. We probably can't even slow it down. It is going to kill you."

"I don't believe this," I said.

"The damage done by the blow you received suggests the disease is now moving rapidly. Typically it moves slowly for a long time— years in some instances. Then it courses through the body. I'm sorry, but I would guess you have at the most six months to live. We can expect your muscles will begin to atrophy, and the bone marrow will soon be destroyed. Stress on your bones when you bend over to pick something up may snap them."

I fell into a panic and had no words. Simultaneously, I hated the old doctor yet felt grateful for his frankness.

I excused myself and drove home. Once there, I shared the news with Nicki, who became very emotional. Shaken by her reaction, I left the house muttering that I had to see Grandfather.

I arrived at Grandfather's place in Arizona around nine in the evening, close to their bedtime on the reservation. I stopped the car outside the house and waited in the traditional way, hoping Grandfather was awake.

Shortly he came out of the house and walked toward me. I climbed out of my car.

"It's good you came," he said, and walked away from me in the dark.

I followed him to the hogan. He lit a lamp and we sat.

"You've been told you are dying?"

"I am told that."

"Do you believe them?"

"I guess I do." I had started to say no.

"Do you know why you chose this illness?"

"No."

Grandfather looked at me with the deepest "gaze of power" I had ever experienced from him. His energy flooded my body. "Well, you've got to know why you chose this, or I won't have a good start in helping you. I will sit while you figure this out. Talk it through with yourself. Stand up. Move around."

I began to pace in the hogan. "I can't believe this has happened to me!" I raised my voice. Soon I was shouting, waving my arms. "Why me?" I raged. "How can the Great Spirit do this to me after all I've come through?" I became furious. "It isn't fair!" I screamed. I tried to cash in all the good I'd done in the Marine Corps, all the sacrifices and risks. I pointed out how hard I had worked in my life, how difficult it was to work sixty hours a week, feed five kids, and go to graduate school. Couldn't anyone see the time I gave as a scoutmaster, all the good I did? I wallowed in self-pity. I raged at a shitty-assed world that had dealt me this death blow. I continued for hours.

Finally, exhausted, I sat near Grandfather, hoping he would console me, perhaps touch me.

"You've got to know why you chose this."

Astounded, I could not believe his words. He must not have understood. I had chosen nothing. I was the victim of life's twisted fate! I stood and paced again. I raged at God, at all the gods. I cursed and swore. At length, I stood in front of Grandfather. "Grandfather, help me!" I shouted. "I'm scared to death!"

"Why do you want to kill yourself?" Grandfather responded.

I was stunned by his words. They bored deeply into me. I sat. My shoulders sagged, and I began to sob. I realized I *did* want to die. I truly felt I didn't deserve a life. The only place I had felt good in the past decade was in combat. I was the best there. I was a damn good killer. Back home I was "at effect" with everyone. I could barely support my family. I felt I'd never be good at anything but killing, which had become unacceptable to me. Unconsciously I had summoned death. Guilt was the food of death, the spiritual cause of my illness.

Years later I would know that Agent Orange was the physical cause for my illness. My spiritual collapse allowed Agent Orange to activate in my system.

Grandfather sat with me through the night. At dawn he spoke. "Do you see it now?"

"Yes, I see it, Grandfather." I thanked him.

"If you want to heal someone, you have to know it from the patient's side," he said.

"I see that."

"Good, we'll begin now."

I was there for eight days. Grandfather did Navajo ceremony, a Blessed Beauty Way and a full Shooting Star chant. He was assisted by another singer. The ceremony propelled me into a deep trance. Sand paintings were made, several songs were sung. There were numerous body paintings as well. Today I cannot remember all the specifics of the ceremony because of its intensity. Near its conclusion, someone asked me to give the disease away, to take its teaching. I realized I had chosen leukemia, a "south/southeast disease" on the medicine wheel because I hated the world for what had happened to me in 'Nam and the pain it still caused me back home. I had lost my heart. I had lost my path, my path of heart. I truly wanted to die.

After the seventh day, the others left. Grandfather's wife, Zoni, brought me tea. I sat quietly with the elderly Navajo couple.

On the eighth day, Grandfather indicated I should return to Los Angeles. "Stay on your path of heart now," he said. "It's too dangerous for a man anywhere else!"

I tried to thank him.

"You are repatterned," he said, smiling. "Keep the faith!" He held up two fingers in a V and walked away. I drove west to Los Angeles.

THE END OF
A MARRIAGE

My marriage came to its official end in 1977, when Nicki divorced me. Like many marriages, ours was finished long before the state of California recognized the fact. Nicki had left me almost as many times as I'd gone away from her. Each time she left, she took the kids, intending to start her life over. She'd return a few days later. We struggled on like that for years, both hoping we'd find a way to make the relationship work. Then one night something happened that ended the marriage in my heart.

I had begun to compete seriously in state and regional martial arts tournaments. In 1969 I won a regional jujitsu tournament as a light heavyweight. I was elated. I sensed I was on the path of something important and began judo competition. In a short period of time, I developed one of the top judo teams in the country. Overnight, my four teaching centers overflowed with students. I was amazed. I hired an assistant and then a second. I also began instruction in jujitsu.

One morning I went to Nicki to share my excitement.

"Nicki, I've got a feeling this is our year. I've decided I'm going to compete in every jujitsu tournament in the country this coming season!"

"This is *our* year?" she asked. "Are you crazy, SwiftDeer?"

"Nicki, what do you mean, 'crazy'?"

"Well, how many tournaments are we talking about?"

"Two a month."

"Will these tournaments be held here in Los Angeles?"

"Nicki," I explained, "you know I'm talking about national tournaments. I'll be traveling around the country."

"You got a sponsor?" she pressed. "You know, an expense account?"

"No," I muttered.

"Are you inviting me to join you in these treks across the country?"

"No."

"I see." Her face looked grim. "Is someone going to earn the money and take care of the house and kids for me while you're running around playing Bruce Lee at these tournaments?"

"No."

"So, I'm still asking if you are crazy, SwiftDeer."

I paused, thinking briefly of giving it all up, then made up my mind.

"Nicki, I'm going to do it."

"No!" she yelled. "Not and be married to me! I've had enough of you running off to every damn thing that temporarily interests you while Nicki takes care of the home front!" Her face filled with emotion. "Your sons ask if we have a guest for dinner when you come home to eat! They've lost track of what you look like! The only times they see you lately is when you rough them up!"

"Nicki, I have a feeling about this."

"No! You've always got a feeling about something!"

"I'm going. I don't care what it costs me, Nicki. I've got to go."

"That sounds familiar!"

"What?"

"Never mind."

I went to the tournaments. After a slow start, I began to win. In the final competition in Washington, D.C., I reached my peak. I won the United States jujitsu tournament in both the light-heavy and heavyweight classes. In addition, I was awarded the grand champion trophy and two thousand dollars in prize money. Mohammed Ali made the presentations.

The grand champion trophy is as tall as I am. Its size created special attention for me on the flight back to Los Angeles, especially from a flight attendant named Tammy. She seated me in first class and plied me with drinks and her phone number.

I hoped Nicki and the kids would be in the terminal waiting for me. She had surprised me in the past by appearing at the gate or in the baggage area. I was tremendously proud and excited to show the kids the trophies. I had not asked her to meet me, and, of course, she didn't.

A taxi unloaded me with my bags and all my trophies at a dark house. I found my key and opened the door.

"Anybody home?" I called. My voice echoed around me. I called again. No response.

I turned on the lights and found the cause of my echo. The house was empty. I found a note on the refrigerator: "You are married to martial arts, not me. I'm gone."

Nicki had loaded our furniture into a U-Haul and driven to her mother's place. She'd left a bed, and that is where I collapsed after I drank champagne till dawn. I was determined to have my celebration.

That's when our marriage ended for me. That night I knew at the deepest level that Nicki had no awareness of my sacred dream. In her way she'd tried, but perhaps she had never understood it. That hurt. That tournament was the highest moment of my life since Vietnam—perhaps of my whole life. I had wanted so much to share it with Nicki.

A few days later she called, her voice warm and bubbly. "How'd the tournament go?"

"It went good."

"Did you win?"

"Yes."

"Well, are you going to ask how I'm doing?"

"No."

Nicki paused. I knew her next words would show hurt, and they did. "Well, are you interested in the kids?"

"Yes, of course," I said. "How are they?"

"OK. They're all fine."

She paused again. I knew what she would say. "Well, do you want to get back together?"

"That's up to you."

She came back, but I was propelled in another direction.

EXCOMMUNICATION

Several years after I won the national jujitsu championship, an incident happened that facilitated the formal end of my marriage to Nicki. When I first began to study sorcery with Grandfather Two Bears, Nicki was very interested and asked to study with me. I was pleased and tried to share what I learned. As the months passed and the work intensified, Nicki's interest waned. I understood. To learn sorcery, one has to change the view of the world one has been raised with. As she was challenged to do this, Nicki became frightened and sought security in a more active participation in the Mormon Church, a traditional religion to which she was accustomed. We were both members of the church at the time.

Sorcery offers an alternative system for perceiving the world. Nicki's tradition, of course, dictates that there is one reality that is the *real* world, the *only* world. Most people in the Western world take this view. They see themselves as separate from the world around them. The sorcerer does not see the world as separate from himself. He experiences himself as an embodiment of one aspect of his environment. He is part of his surroundings. This recognition opens a whole different viewing of the self and one's surroundings.

My early work with Two Bears was designed to give me an alternative understanding of the world I had been raised in. Grandmother Spotted Fawn began this when I was a boy. Two Bears intensified and expanded it while teaching me sorcery. A main part of the study of sorcery is learning to attune to what we are part of—what surrounds us. A sorcerer must adopt a magical mode of consciousness. He discovers how to let go of the brain's control of reason. The sorcerer learns to make reason a tool of the body rather than of the mind. Sorcery necessitates an integration of the wisdom of the body. One must learn to understand and rely on body wisdom and *know* that the body is *inside* our sacred mind.

Usually the brain does not want this to happen, and an inner battle is fought to control reason. The brain does not want to let go of its

accustomed ways. The struggle can be very scary and mind-boggling. Learning sorcery means giving over to a separate reality from
the reality one is accustomed to. That's a hard thing for anyone to do.
In the early years, I often felt I had to break away from Two Bears to
maintain my sanity. How could I give reason over to my body and
heart without going crazy? My brain fought against me.

The struggle was too much for Nicki—too frightening and confusing. She turned to the Mormon Church to assure and maintain
stability. As I delved deeper into the realities of sorcery, we went our
separate ways.

That did not bother me at the time. She enjoyed church activities;
so did the kids. Often they were with her, and that was good for
them. Naturally, I was also teaching the kids basic sorcery, as well as
leading the Boy Scout troop at the church.

During an intensive period when I was studying "snake medicine" (as sorcery is called) and "shapeshifting"—actually changing
into the form of an animal—with Grandfather Two Bears, I invited
my girlfriend Mary Mac to a "plant working" with me. "Mac" was
studying sorcery also, and at the time was living at the house with
Nicki and me. Nicki was away with the kids at a Mormon Church
function at the time.

I explained the plant working to Mac, detailing the possibilities
of the unexpected. I described the various stages one can anticipate
as the full power of a psychotropic plant hits the body. We ingested
the plants Grandfather had given me. I guided the experience.
Shapeshifting is an intense process, challenging and always exhausting. Shamanistic work demands strong focus, combined with a natural aptitude for the work.

The experience proceeded beautifully, mainly because of Mac's
adroitness. Within three hours we shifted forms. Mac was my first
apprentice to make the shift. We explored the other dimension tentatively and then began the reverse procedure. Mac had returned to
natural form and I was nearly back when Nicki unexpectedly walked
into the room. Both sides of my head were still in crow's wings.

She took one horrified look and screamed. "Oh, my God, Swift-
Deer! Oh, my God!"

I was startled. Black feathers scattered in the room. "Hi, Nicki," I muttered. A final feather drifted to the floor.

"I, uh . . . you," Nicki stammered and stopped. Her face was white. For several moments she was frozen. "Enough," she said in a tone barely discernible. "Enough!" Nicki picked up several feathers and ran from the room. She called the kids and pushed them into the station wagon. Tires squealed as she raced away.

Mac and I cleaned things up. Two hours passed. We talked the experience down and were about to go out when the phone rang. A bishop from the Mormon Church was on the line. He asked if he could come by. I assured him he would be welcome.

When he arrived a few minutes later, two priests accompanied him. They looked extremely somber coming up the walk. Bishop Jones is a tall, broad-shouldered man, big all over. He had been an all-American tight end at Brigham Young University and a Rhodes scholar. I am six feet one, and I looked up at him when I opened the door.

"Yes, gentlemen, how may I help you?" I asked.

"To tell the truth, Brother Reagan," said Bishop Jones, "we've come hoping to help you."

His eyes were North Pole blue and penetrating.

"I thank you, but what do I need help with?"

"Well, brother," the bishop continued, "I know this will sound irregular, but we've decided your family's whereabouts will be kept a secret until unascertained satanic forces are banished from your body. For your family's well-being—and yours, of course."

Mac began to laugh.

"Miss," said the bishop, "I assure you, this visit is a most serious matter."

She laughed harder.

"Brother Reagan, this lady's decorum is not appropriate to the gravity of our visit."

"Mac," I said.

"That's oka——!" She was laughing so hard she was unable to talk. "That's OK," she finally managed to say. "I'll leave you to God's work. SwiftDeer, don't let them do anything that affects our sex life. I feel horny!" She left the room, hands over her mouth, hips undulating.

The room was quiet. I was thinking, SwiftDeer, you're losing your mind to talk with the bishop when you could be helping Mac with her problem. I addressed the situation, hoping Mac needed me later.

"Bishop Jones," I said, "which devils are we talking about?"

"Your wife has told us about satanic happenings."

"I still don't understand."

"We have the proof right here," he said. The bishop smiled and glanced at his assistants. Looking proud, each held up a black feather.

I saw that the bishop meant it. Theirs was a mission into the valley of dark sorcery.

I thought, What the heck! "Bishop Jones," I said, "in that case I thank you for coming here to help me. I'm ready to proceed when you are."

I lay on my bed for a Mormon Church exorcism. The two priests knelt quickly on either side of the bed and prayed loudly for my soul—nonstop. Passion and sincerity were their gifts.

The bishop opened his valise and extracted a vial of holy water. Next he placed a small silver chalice on the nightstand. He lifted the vial, offered it to God, and uncorked it. He poured holy water into the chalice and, singing, invoked the spirits needed in his ceremony. His voice was surprisingly pleasing, strong and clear. He poured water in his hands, splashed it at his assistants, then sprinkled some on me. He began to sing again as he covered my body with a Mormon Church mantle.

He invoked all the great people of the Mormon Church since its beginning. He called for Joseph Smith and Brigham Young and all the prophets past, present, and future.

"I ask that you all come to me at this time in this place to help this good man, Brother Reagan, in his struggle against darkness!"

He prayed for power, inspiration, and protection in his battle for the Lord. He asked the Lord Jesus Christ to stand with him and guide him during his perilous journey into the darkness of the

Reagan household. He opened his Bible and in a loud voice switched from singing to conjuring. He read from the Bible and sang again. This continued for more than three hours. I moaned for them now and then to help things along.

The ceremony was done well. I was pleased to learn how the Mormon Church does exorcisms. It was a ceremony with merit, though I did not feel the power I knew would be necessary for a high-level exorcism!

At last the bishop announced that Satan had been confronted and defeated. "Brother Reagan, the battle has been concluded!"

I sat up, rubbed my eyes and looked around the room slowly, like I'd just returned from the land of Oz. They watched me respectfully until they sensed I had fully returned. "Wowee," I said, "that was something! How am I?"

"How do you feel?"

The three men edged close for my answer.

"I feel lighter!"

"Praise the Lord," they said in unison. They looked ecstatic.

"Brother Reagan," announced the bishop, "it was your courage and faith that made our work here possible. Your belief in Jesus Christ and the Mormon Church is what enabled us to serve you and do our humble work. Do you understand that?"

"Bishop, I thank you."

"It was our pleasure, Brother Reagan," he assured me. "As humble children of God, we are here to serve you."

"Why, I thank you, sir."

He looked like he wasn't finished.

"Brother Reagan, now that Satan's influence has been confronted, there is another matter."

I stood up. "What is it?"

"Well, Brother Reagan, as I'm sure you know, we ended polygamy in the Mormon Church some time back."

The two priests had moved up beside the bishop, flanking him.

"Yes," I said. I knew what he was getting to.

"You are living in this house with five children and two women."

"Yes, that's how many kids Nicki and I have."

"I'm talking about the women," he pressed.

"Do you want me to let them go?"

"No," he snapped. "Absolutely not!" He appeared agitated. "We don't want either of the women to suffer, or you."

His voice became friendly and confidential. "No one need suffer, Brother Reagan. As scoutmaster of our church, you've done a splendid job with our young people. Absolutely exemplary!" He looked happy again. "With your guidance, the boys have done things we never dreamed possible! The work you are doing with them is extremely important to our church and community! The congregation wants to support you; however, living openly with two women and five children flaunts modern-day church morality."

"It's just who I am."

"Yes. You see," he continued, "this is a situation that is impossible to ignore."

"Should I dispose of some of the kids?" I asked.

He looked at me startled, then stroked his chin and smiled. "Brother Reagan, you are teasing me. The children are fine as they are. Listen carefully. For you I think an arrangement can be made to ease the situation."

"It can?"

"Yes. Within the church today we've maintained a procedure considered highly anomalous by some. What I'm going to tell you is held highly confidential."

"It is?"

"Yes."

His face beamed like a father honoring his favorite son. He leaned toward me as though to impart a matter of great secrecy. "Bring your two women to the temple this next weekend. In my private chambers, I will marry you officially to both women."

"That is possible?"

"It will be a church ceremony according to the *old* covenants."

I was truly surprised.

"Is that possible?" I asked a second time.

He looked at me carefully. "Brother, it is possible. Of course the general congregation does not know about our present use of the old covenant, nor would we want it known. I think you can understand." The bishop smiled knowingly.

"Will the people not still see I am with two women?" I asked.

"Yes, of course they will," he answered. "However, the people of our congregation concern themselves primarily with what we suggest is important. One cannot be concerned about everything and still do the Lord's work. There simply would be no time."

That made sense. I saw how Bishop Jones had gotten to the top, and I suspected he'd go even higher.

"No," I said.

"Beg pardon?"

"No," I repeated.

"It can be done simply and efficiently, Brother Reagan," he said. "Things will look the same; however, in the eyes of the church you will be married. The pressure will be off us and you. The way you live now, we have no choice."

"About what?"

"We can't condone your present situation."

"Are you saying you'll kick me out of the church?"

"Brother Reagan, will you do us both a favor and sleep on this?" he asked. "Come to the temple tomorrow morning and we will broach the matter in depth."

I told him I would.

Clearly the bishop was used to getting his way. I didn't want to leave the church at that time, though I recognized that the conflict I felt developing inside me had surfaced. I'll never belong to any organized religion, but if I did join a church it would be Mormon. The Mormons are family oriented and have tried to undo some of the harm they've done to Native Americans.

Mainly, I didn't want to give up my Scouts. The troop was truly one of the best in the country. Eight of our boys were Eagle Scouts, and the troop had won an international scouting jamboree. Scouting also was a means to have time with my sons in a good way.

Next day I met the bishop and told him I could not accept his offer. I explained that I was a shaman, a man learning the secrets of Native American medicine, studying sorcery, and proud of a Native American tradition that has a sexual morality different from that of the Mormon Church.

"Bishop Jones," I said, "I appreciate your offer to marry me secretly to two women to take the heat off you. That is big of you. I thank you, but no. It's not my nature to go underground. I'm not an undercover man. I'm not making a secret with the church to appease the congregation. If I did, you'd own the part of me that keeps our secret. Living openly with women who dance in my heart *is* my religion. If Nicki and Mary Mac are willing, I'll be bonded with them in an official Native American ceremony not honored by the Mormon Church. Should that ceremony take place, I'd be pleased if you would accept an invitation to sing. You have a beautiful voice."

I was, of course, excommunicated from the Mormon Church for immorality and consorting with Satan. My reaction was to ask my attorney to draft an official letter excommunicating the Mormon Church from me. He did that and sent the letter to church headquarters in Salt Lake City. I have received no reply. I was not permitted to say good-bye to the boys in my Scout troop.

Responding to advice and pressure from church authorities, Nicki filed for divorce. She did not need excessive encouragement. A short while later, the household broke up. Mac went her own way, and Nicki found separate residence. Initially, our sons went with Nicki. In time, they moved back with me. Nicki has remarried and lives in southern Texas.

DANCE OF THE SNAKE

Until now, only my most advanced apprentices in the Deer Tribe gateway ceremonies know the details or alchemy of the higher ceremonies. They are, of course, secret. But because times are changing, I will share two of the pivotal ceremonies of my early work: the Dance of the Snake and the Cave of the Dead.

The Dance of the Snake is a seventh-degree gateway ceremony. It is one's initiation into the fifth gateway of snake medicine. On the ceremonial path wheel it is a northeast ceremony. I am sharing the Dance of the Snake because it was a catalyst ceremony for me, locking me into the path of enlightenment I follow today.

Until the night of this ceremony, I had dreamed of becoming a sorcerer. During the Dance of the Snake, something inside me changed. When I stepped out of the kiva at Wupatki ruins at dawn, I knew I *was* a sorcerer.

Grandfather Two Bears told me I was ready to face the intensity of this ceremony. The way I worked with him in the gateway ceremonial steps was different from the way I work with my apprentices. My people come to me when they are ready for the next gateway ceremony. They ask for help, advice, and prayers. Some ceremonies call for a send-off sweat. Others need the Sacred Pipe smoked and held together for the duration of the ceremony. With Grandfather Two Bears, I didn't ask for the next ceremony. I had no idea what it was.

The Dance of the Snake is a good example. I had been working with Grandfather for two days expanding telepathic aptitudes in activities suggested by him. I never knew what I'd be doing with him. I'd show up and follow his directions. I was satisfied with this procedure. Grandfather seemed to have a plan, and I knew my nagual powers were growing. Near the end of the "working," Grandfather became uncommonly quiet. Though his silence was not unusual in our work, he remained quiet for so long that I asked if I was finished.

"Yes," said Grandfather. He walked abruptly away from me, entered the hogan and shut the door.

I stood near my car for several minutes. I saw no sign of life from the hogan. "Well, good-bye, Grandfather!" I called.

I climbed into my car and started the engine. The hogan door opened as I backed around to make my turn. Grandfather approached me carrying a large brown bag.

"Here," he said, "take this." He pushed the bag at me.

"What is this, Grandfather?"

"There are three small sacks in this bag. Make tea for ten days from one, then use the others: three different blends. Drink tea four times a day for thirty days. Eat only one meal a day. Do it as I have said, or you could die during your next ceremony." Grandfather sounded more sober than was his custom.

Then he smiled his memorable smile that told me the world was OK. "Maybe you'll die anyway," he suggested.

"What's the ceremony?" I blurted. I was suddenly nervous.

"Dance of the Snake. Down at the big kiva at Wupatki ruins outside Flagstaff. I'm not going to be there."

"What?"

"Speak to Rolling Thunder. Ask him to pray with you there."

I felt like an abandoned kid. "Why won't you be there? What if Rolling Thunder is not available? What if I can't find Rolling Thunder? What if he doesn't know what to do?"

Grandfather's smile lengthened.

"Shouldn't you be there, Grandfather?" I pleaded.

"It's time for your crossover ceremony," he said. "I think if you survive this ceremony, you'll make it."

"Grandfather, don't you want to see me cross over?"

"I'm not going to be there," he said, and walked away.

When I was convinced he would not return, I placed the bag of herbs on the floor beside me and drove west to Los Angeles. Later I realized that Grandfather recognized my dependence on him and sensed I would not integrate the ceremony if he was present.

Back home I began my fast. Each day I drank herb tea four times. I realized, of course, that the tea was intended as an antidote to snakebite. Knowing that did not make me feel better.

Rolling Thunder said he would be available for the ceremony. He explained that I must fast on a three-day vision quest at the end of my thirty days with the tea. The final night of my vision quest, I was to find a male rattlesnake and ask if it were willing to join me as my teacher at the Wupatki ceremony.

After my vision quest, I met Rolling Thunder at the Wupatki kiva shortly after noon, carrying a burlap bag containing my snake. It rattled angrily. Apparently the snake had forgotten it had agreed to help me in this ceremony, or I had forgotten to tell it about the burlap bag. Rolling Thunder said everything was ready and that he had several assistants standing by if I needed help. I wasn't sure what he meant, but I felt grateful. Rolling Thunder described my part in the ceremony as he led the way to the kiva.

"As you dance tonight, look for a vision of how to best use your masculine energy. How are you going to help the people? Tonight you will begin to build your spirit canoe."

"My spirit canoe?"

"Yes," he said. "You are looking for eight shamanic deaths. Your physical body must go eight times into the tunnel of death—the *bardos*—and come back. When you've had eight of those, your spirit can build an etheric boat, a spirit canoe you can use to help someone whose spirit is trapped in the dark. The spirit canoe is for travel into the spirit world to bring someone back into the light from where they are trapped or lost. You can't do that without a spirit canoe. Tonight you build it. You start it. Smoke your pipe, then dance to the snake holding your medicine. The snake will help you."

"Rolling Thunder," I said.

"Yes?"

"Am I ready for this?"

"Two Bears says you are."

At the low walls of the kiva entrance we stopped. Rolling Thunder put his hands on my shoulders, looked into my eyes. "Step into the kiva now, SwiftDeer. Unwrap your pipe and smoke it. Then begin your dance. My assistants will block the entrance with logs to keep the snake inside. Then they'll let the snake loose."

I stepped into the kiva and lit my pipe. The snake slithered into the kiva, angry and rattling like crazy. It raced around looking for a way out. I smoked. The snake showed no interest in me. Eventually, it settled itself under a stone on the west side of the kiva.

"Begin your dance, SwiftDeer," said Rolling Thunder. "Hold your medicine and dance around the snake. You will not hear or see me again till dawn, but I will be close by."

I had been dancing for hours when the snake struck for the first time. I was jolted out of trance by what felt like two hundred volts of electricity. A piercing pain hit my calf, followed by electrical surges of energy shooting through my body. The rush was strong, nearly orgasmic. I began to shake. My entire body trembled.

You're a hummer, SwiftDeer, I thought crazily. I danced. The snake struck again. Another rush! I danced harder. Then I saw women sitting on the kiva wall laughing at me, pointing, shrieking, ridiculing me and my dance. I knew immediately they represented my unresolved conflicts and difficulties with women—all the women I had wronged and ruined and raped and killed over many lifetimes. I knew I had to somehow connect with them and my female side or I would die. I had no idea how to do that. Sobs wracked my body.

The snake struck again and again. I danced harder, faster, until I fell unconscious, clutching my medicine tightly. I went into a vision and entered a tunnel. At its end was a roaring fire. I picked up materials and began intuitively to build a spirit canoe.

At dawn I opened my eyes and was awake. I lay on my back. The fire in my vision was replaced by the Arizona sun. Rolling Thunder sat near me on the edge of the kiva.

"Good morning, Little Brother," he said.

I lay mute. I had no words.

"Welcome to the Brotherhood of the Snake."

I tried to sit.

"I killed and skinned your snake a few minutes ago," he said. "Its head and rattles and skin are in this bag. From this moment, you will never take a snake brother's life again."

He set the bag beside me. I was certain I had no strength to kill anything. "Snake bit you seventeen times."

"How could I survive that?" I croaked.

"Well," said Rolling Thunder, "he'd used up his venom after the first few hits. And somewhere in the night you merged with him."

It was true. I felt it. The snake was my brother. I took the bag.

"As you come out of this, you're also going to understand the lizard people better, too, SwiftDeer. You did OK last night."

What he said felt right. Lizards symbolized black magicians.

"You want some breakfast?"

I shook my head.

"Well," said Rolling Thunder, "give me your hand. We'll do some walking, then see how you feel about breakfast."

I reached for him, and we began the long walk back to the Wupatki ruins parking lot. I knew I had to ask him something.

"What about the women?" I rasped through a swollen tongue.

Rolling Thunder stopped and looked at me for a long time. "Little Brother, if you saw the women last night, you'll see them again soon." I sensed he was right.

As we left the café at Grey Mountain, Rolling Thunder handed me a package. "Open this after you've rested. I'm not going to be here much longer. I want you to have it. You did well last night, Little Brother. Many good things for our people will happen around you."

Back home I crashed and slept hard. Next day I felt better. I looked at the package beside me. I opened it, and lifted out an ancient ceremonial Cherokee headdress.

To me, Rolling Thunder will always be one of the great ones. I dance his headdress to the Sacred Tree to honor him at each Deer Tribe Sundance.

FIGHTING FOR
THE CHILDREN

Grandfather told me a time might come when I would take my stand publicly as a guardian of children. He said I would pay a price for visibility—that it would cost me. I didn't know what he meant at the time. That's the way it often was with Grandfather. While my mind was engaged in surviving or integrating a challenging gateway ceremony, his was on the person I'd be after the ceremony. An incident happened shortly after I did the Dance of the Snake that in Grandfather's eyes marked my emergence as a true apprentice to sorcery. At the time, in my mind the event had nothing to do with sorcery. Grandfather said the experience marked the integration of my ceremonial experience with my outer life.

In the spring of 1970, I was driving a sixteen wheeler for Kimball Groceries. Days on the road were always long and hard for me, as they are for any trucker. Near the end of a typically exhausting day—only seven days after the Dance of the Snake—I stopped for hot chocolate at Hank's Place, a café outside Flagstaff, Arizona. The chocolate hit the spot. I ordered a second cup and lit up.

Leaning back, I stretched and noticed that the four Navajo children asking for ice cream when I sat down were still waiting at the counter. It was clear they weren't going to be served, and they didn't know it. I was thinking I'd walk over and order ice cream for them myself, when one of four locals sitting at a nearby table intervened, speaking to Hank, the proprietor.

"I got a good idea, Hank," he said winking. "Let's give 'em some free ice cream. Hand me the chocolate syrup."

He looked about twenty-five years old, a redhead. He had good size—huge hands and forearms—the kind who verifies his strength by pulling wings off butterflies. His buddies were laughing and jabbing each other. I took it they had been wagering among themselves.

Red Hair took a jar of chocolate syrup from Hank and dumped it on the Navajo kids. Before they could move, he poured nuts on the syrup and pressed huge handfuls of ice cream into their hair, rubbing it. The kids screamed and tried to get away. Red Hair yanked their hair and reached for more syrup.

"Lookee, Hank, they like it so much they're screaming for more. Gimmee the strawberry this time. I wanna make sure they get a flavor they like." His buddies whooped it up, cheering him on.

"That's enough," I said. I was on my feet. I'd held back as long as I could. I stepped slowly between them, easing the man back with a hand on his chest. I reached for a towel from the counter and wiped syrup from the little girl's face.

Red Hair looked taken aback and was obviously thinking about a plan. He glanced at his buddies and made up his mind. "Hey, lookee here!" he growled. "The fucking Lone Ranger in person!" He picked up a big jar of strawberry syrup and stepped toward me.

I knew I should not want what was coming, but I relished it. "Back off," I said.

"You like some, too, asshole Lone Ranger?" He raised the syrup high and lunged at me.

As he came in, I hit him hard in the throat. The syrup crashed to the floor, and Red Hair staggered back, choking. He fell into a table with a loud crash, scattering chairs and dishes.

His buddies were on their feet, circling. "Say good-bye to yer life," muttered one of them.

My adrenaline pounded. Wonderful, I thought. Come to papa!

Red Hair's buddies had no idea what they were getting into. My body longed for the release the fight would give me. They were just playing their routine bully game. In the last several days, I had been bitten seventeen times by a rattlesnake. I had eaten one good meal, slept four hours, and had driven a truck sixteen straight hours. I had an angry edge when I walked into Hank's Place that quickly became a focused rage.

The fight was one-sided, a Western barroom brawl. Within seconds two of the men were down. As the third turned to retreat, I kicked him hard in the back, plummeting him through a stack of chairs and into the counter near Hank with a crash.

I looked around, wondering if the men had friends. Hank peered out from behind the counter.

"Mister, you're crazy," he said. "They was only having a little fun."

"Hank," I said, "how do you feel about your ice cream policy for little kids right about now?"

The interior of the café was a shambles—broken glass and scattered tables throughout. Two of the men were groaning. Another was trying to pick himself up. Red Hair lay on his stomach gagging. I looked for the kids. They were gone, probably ran when it started.

I picked up my jacket, intending to get out of there, and heard sirens. Hank had called the police, of course. Brakes squealed, car doors slammed, and four officers rushed into the café. I knew I was in deeper than I wanted, but at this point I was watching it all happen. My adrenaline was still pounding.

"This crazy bastard busted up my place!" yelled Hank, pointing at me.

"Spread-eagle on the floor, mister!" shouted one of the officers.

"For what? I replied. "Ask this man to tell the truth. He saw what started it."

The officers paused for a moment.

"That right, Hank?" asked another.

"Peaceful afternoon," answered Hank. "Out of the blue this psycho jumps up slugging customers, breaking up the place!"

"OK, mister," the first cop said, "you wanna come peaceful or bloody? Get yourself spread on the floor!"

When they saw I wouldn't lie down, they moved in. One jumped forward, trying to twist my arm. Even today, if I am grabbed, watch out. I spun under him, gripped his arm, and snapped the elbow. He fell to his knees screaming in pain as the others attacked. We brawled. More police arrived. I was subdued, handcuffed, beaten, and dragged to a squad car.

I was charged with disturbing the peace, resisting arrest, assault with a deadly weapon (my hands), and manslaughter. They said the first man I hit had choked to death. Later they told me he was not dead yet but was not expected to live. It turned out, of course, that the man was not hurt seriously. I was their live entertainment.

I had no bond money and was incarcerated in a large cell block filled with more than forty people. Several days later, I was moved from the overcrowded county jail to the Yuma State Correctional Facility. I was at the Yuma facility for twenty more days before charges were dropped and I was released. If my defense attorney had not found a courageous lady from Hank's Place, I would have been in jail much longer.

I knew plenty about tyrants prior to my experience at Yuma State. I learned more while there. Every kind of tyrant imaginable appears sooner or later in a penal institution. The Yuma State Correctional Facility added to my tyrant education.

I was surprised to discover that most of the inmates believed somebody else caused their problems. They really believed it! They appeared unable to consider that *they* might be the source of their problems. In the beginning, nearly everyone I talked to said he was innocent, a victim of someone or something. Later, as a man got to know me, he'd admit his crime, but not his responsibility. "It was my bitch wife's fault, or Dad's, or society's, or the fuckin' parole officer." I was amazed by this. That wasn't my upbringing. My people took personal responsibility for every aspect of their lives. That was also the Marine Corps way.

In the Deer Tribe we call blaming others for one's problems a "mirror mythology." It is a "victim" syndrome from which there is no escape unless one assumes personal responsibility for one's life circumstances. The Deer Tribe suggests a ceremony to help people release themselves from dark mirror mythologies. The well-known Cheyenne teacher Hyemeyohsts Storm gave me the ceremony when I was apprenticed to him. The ceremony, called the Balancing of the Shields, is described in Storm's masterpiece, *Song of Heyoehkah*. It is a ceremony designed to move the personality from a victim lethargy to an active freedom.

There were a few inmates who acknowledged their crimes, yet had no feelings about it. For example, I spoke with a man at the county jail waiting for sentencing. He'd killed his wife and children.

"Why did you kill them?" I asked.

"I didn't like them. Never did."

"Why did you marry her, if you didn't like her?"

"Because I liked to fuck her. I didn't want nobody else between her legs."

"Well, why did you have kids?"

"Because she didn't use no birth control."

"Couldn't you have used rubbers?"

"It wasn't my cock getting pregnant."

"But what about her?"

"It's her cunt."

"What did you feel when you killed them?"

"Nothing. What was there to feel? I just took my shotgun and blew them the fuck away."

"You felt nothing?"

"Absolutely nothing."

Scary. We didn't talk much after that.

Most of the inmates were not stereotypical criminals. I saw more honest people in jail than I see in many places on the outside—like in most church pulpits, for example.

RAPED

My first night in the county jail outside Flagstaff I was given a blanket party. I was beaten and raped. They came at me after I lay down to doze. I sensed suddenly I was in danger and sat up, wide awake. The light bulb had been removed. Men surrounded me in the darkness. As I tried to stand, I was covered by a blanket and shoved down. They beat me till I lost consciousness.

When I woke up, I was tied face down and blindfolded. They'd stripped me and placed pillows under my belly. Cold water was dumped on my head, apparently so I'd be awake for the fun. They taunted me, beat me, then sodomized me. Whoever wanted me had me. When I screamed, they laughed. The pain was excruciating. I passed out. More water was thrown on me. Near dawn they let me be.

Later two guards came in and untied me. When they saw the extent of my injuries, they moved me to a hospital for treatment. No one said a word to me about the assault. I was in the hospital five days. When I was taken back to jail, I was assigned to the same cell block. Normally, one is never put back with the same men who "blanket" him. This clued me that the attack had been set up. Either the authorities wanted my spirit broken or wanted me dead—or both. I was sure the attack had been arranged by enforcement officers there in retaliation for the damage I had caused them, though I had no proof.

I understand what happened to me, but I don't condone or forgive it. It was ugly and brutal. Some naturally hostile people were bribed to rape me. I was with forty-two other people in a cell block designed for twenty. The others were mainly Chicanos, Native Americans, and blacks. There were four whites. Some say minority people break more laws. I know better. Our penal system is slanted in favor of whites. Though my brother could have posed for the Indian on the buffalo nickel, I look Irish. In that cell block I was a natural scapegoat for the hostility minority people feel because of generations of mistreatment from whites.

When guards brought me back to the same cell block and pushed me into the cell, an icy calmness filled me. The cell door clanged shut and I was back in Vietnam. I could actually smell the jungle. I was on my turf. I had survived here, and I could again.

Every man in the cell watched me, some laughed. "Well, look who's come home to look after her men!" snickered one.

"Hello, sweetheart. Daddy missed you." "Pussy, pussy, pussy. Here, nice pussy!" purred another. He pushed his index finger into a circle he'd made with thumb and forefinger.

I didn't recognize any of the men who assaulted me. I knew voices. I looked at each of the men. They sensed something. Two or three looked nervous.

"Which ass fucker wants to die first?" I demanded.

The men got quiet.

I stepped forward, my hands lifted in karate attack.

"Hey, man, what you talking about?" whined one of them.

"If you had nothing to do with fucking me up, move over there," I ordered. I pointed to the far side. "If you have the balls to stand behind what you did, stay where you are."

Several moved away. The rest looked at each other to be sure they had the numbers.

I struck at the nearest man with a wide roundhouse kick. I put all I could into that kick. I didn't want him hurt—I wanted his life. I tried to keep them from an organized attack. I spun and turned, kicking and striking. When they hesitated, I kicked viciously at the men already down. I screamed at them, "Come on, ass fuckers, come on. Let's all die a little!" I raged at them, "Come and get it! Your little sweetheart of the other night wants to get close again!"

They came at me, swinging. A knife slashed my shoulder. I staggered, but kept my feet. I kicked out hard. I knew I was dead if I went down.

When other inmates saw me hold my own, they began to intercede, stepping in the way of my attackers. Some shoved them. Others blocked the guards. I have never known the strength that came to me in that fight. I was possessed.

When the brawl ended, the cell block looked like a battlefield. Men were down, some out cold. I bled from several wounds. I was returned to the hospital overnight and sewn up. Emotionally I felt clean. Some of the others were in bad shape: a broken rib cage, a shattered sternum, a smashed knee cap, injuries that are slow to heal and sometimes never fully mend.

When I was taken from the hospital, I wondered what the next action would be. It was their turn. I was not returned to the cell block. They sent me to the Yuma State Correctional Facility, and I sensed that the vendetta was complete.

It was an impacting experience from which I've retained only one good thought: When a brother or sister comes to me today for healing from sexual abuse, they sense that I feel the depth of their pain. Twenty-two years later, I still teach rape awareness and defense in Deer Tribe workshops.

I asked Grandfather once what my Flagstaff experience had to do with the ceremonies I did prior to driving to Flagstaff. He looked insulted and refused to answer. Today, I think Grandfather must have figured that if I hadn't recognized that a sorcerer must be able to walk his talk on the Earth plane as well as the spirit plane, he wasn't going to tell me.

BONDING
CEREMONIES

After Nicki and Mac moved out of my life, two important women came into it. The first was Mary ShyDeer. I met her after she enrolled in one of my martial arts classes. I knew immediately I was to share a destiny with her in the "medicine," and within a few months we were living together. She had a natural aptitude for shamanism and soon was my top apprentice.

Several months later, ShyDeer took me aside and pointed to a beautiful woman who had recently joined another of my classes. "I think I've just found the woman you've been looking for, for the Wheel." I introduced myself to Dianne NightBird.

ShyDeer was correct. Almost a year later NightBird joined Shy-Deer, my sons, and myself in our family home. I loved them both dearly. It was a happy time for me. The Deer Tribe was growing. Lodges were opening around the country, and we were beginning to attract recognition overseas. The women gave an important balance to my life. ShyDeer was outgoing, flamboyant, and daring. Night-Bird was steady, consistent, and intuitive.

My marriage to Dianne NightBird came unexpectedly, as often happened when Grandfather Two Bears was involved. In June of 1979, ShyDeer, NightBird, and I visited Grandfather Two Bears and the Wilson family at their reservation home near Many Farms. We were on our way to Canyon de Chelly to begin a medicine journey with twenty Deer Tribe apprentices. It was my usual way to visit Grandfather's family with blankets and other gifts whenever I was in Arizona. After our initial greetings and traditional gift giving, the Wilson grandmothers asked to talk with NightBird and me.

They spoke their minds directly. "When are you two getting married?" they asked.

I was taken aback. "I, well, I, we hadn't set a date, Grandmothers," I stammered.

At the time, I was living in a relationship with both women, NightBird and ShyDeer. Though I expected that NightBird and I would eventually be married, my thought was that ShyDeer and I would be bonded first. ShyDeer was my best apprentice, and she and I were living together when NightBird came on the medicine path.

The grandmothers were smiling. "We think it's time now," they said.

I looked at NightBird. Her face was flushed. "What do you think, Snit?" I said.

"Well," she said, "I haven't had much time to think about it." She laughed her embarrassed laugh.

"When you come by after this medicine journey we'll have things ready for your wedding," said the grandmothers.

"Grandmothers, I don't have anything to wear!" exclaimed NightBird.

"We have everything you'll need, dear. Don't worry about a thing." The Grandmothers smiled and giggled like little kids.

There were twelve days before we'd return. Twelve days to think about it.

As soon as I could excuse myself from the women, I found Grandfather Two Bears. "Grandfather," I said. "The grandmothers say NightBird and I should marry at the conclusion of this medicine journey."

"I know."

"You know?" I asked.

"I told them to tell you."

He was rubbing linseed oil into the stock of an old Winchester rifle and had not looked up from his work.

"You told the grandmothers it was time for me to marry NightBird?" I asked.

"This is a good old gun," he said. "True at two thousand feet."

"Grandfather, you say you told the Grandmothers to prepare a marriage for NightBird and me?" I asked again.

"Yes, a bonding."

"Grandfather?" I hesitated.

"Yeah?"

"Grandfather, I've been with ShyDeer longer than NightBird."

"I know."

"Are you gong to bond me with both women?" I asked.

"No, only NightBird."

I waited. Several moments passed.

"Only NightBird is ready," he said. "ShyDeer isn't settled in yet."

"But Grandfather," I said, "ShyDeer's taken a blood oath to stay with me till I die."

He looked at me for a moment.

"She isn't settled yet."

"Grandfather," I said, "What's the hurry?" Again I waited for his response.

"My time is close," was all he said.

That evening I shared Grandfather's words with NightBird and ShyDeer. When I finished talking neither of them spoke.

"Well," I said, "What are your reactions?"

"I have to think about it, SwiftDeer," NightBird said. "I'm going to consider it on this medicine journey. It is much to think about." ShyDeer remained quiet.

"What do you say, ShyDeer?" I asked.

She looked at me. Her eyes filled with passion. I thought she might sob. She regained composure. "I have nothing to say," she said. She turned and walked into the darkness.

"ShyDeer, wait a minute!" I called. She did not respond.

I sat alone at my campfire that night, gazing into the flames, hoping for inspiration and a glimpse into the future. So many times in my relationship with Grandfather Two Bears I had walked straight into the void. I sensed that NightBird was uncertain about a future with me. I knew ShyDeer was deeply hurt.

As my little desert fire changed to ashes near dawn, I felt something between ShyDeer and me was about to change. She was challenged by the thought of my marriage to NightBird in ways I could not have foreseen. The depth of our relationship was threatened by Grandfather's vision of NightBird and me. I wondered if ShyDeer could handle it. I prayed she could.

Shortly after sunup we said good-bye to the Wilson family and departed to meet the participants of our Southwest medicine journey to the Hopi mesas and canyonlands. During the journey, ShyDeer

never mentioned the bonding. She was active and friendly with medicine journey participants. She remained distant and aloof with me.

On the final night of the journey, NightBird and I drove into the
desert in my little camper to consider the grandmothers' proposal.
We talked for several hours. Eventually, a gateway of excitement
opened. We decided to have the ceremony. I turned the vehicle back
toward camp, shoved a country-music cassette into the player, and
put my arm around NightBird. It had been an exhausting medicine
trip. I felt relieved and happy.

NightBird suddenly stiffened. "Stop the truck!" she said.

Startled, I slammed on the brakes, and we skidded in the desert
dust. "What's wrong?"

NightBird jumped out of the truck and paced back and forth.

"What's happening, Snit?"

"I'm not going to do it!" she said.

"What?"

"I won't do it!"

"Do what?"

"I'm not going to have this ceremony! I won't be bonded to you!
I'm not going to be a housewife! I'm not going to do your laundry!
I'm not going to be the maid and the dishwasher! I'm not going to
worry about the dog shit in the yard. I won't be your kids' mom!"

She was waving her arms. She stamped her feet.

"Hon', calm down," I said.

"I'm not taking on that role again like I did in my first marriage.
I won't do it again!" Tears ran down her face. Her eyes glittered
determination.

"NightBird, climb in and let's talk this through," I said.

"No!"

"Well, what would make it OK, Snit?"

She thought about that. NightBird explained the boundaries she
needed in our relationship: what she wanted, what she didn't, what
she *must* have, and what she wouldn't put up with anymore. She told
me how our marriage would *have* to be for her to go ahead with the
ceremony.

"I have to be seen as a person, Swift. I must be regarded and
loved for my own preciousness and uniqueness, for who I am.

I've got to experience myself this way, not as a role." She looked at me quietly, tentatively. "So, *that's* it, SwiftDeer," she said finally. "That's it."

I looked at her for several moments. I was deeply touched. I stepped down from the truck and went to NightBird. I took her hands.

"I agree with everything you've said, NightBird. I like what you said. You are right, and precious. I agree. I love you, Snit."

"You do?"

"Yes."

"You mean it?"

"Yes, I do."

"Then let's go."

We climbed into the truck and returned to camp. I love NightBird for her simple and straightforward intuition and her knack for following through. In the morning we broke camp and drove to Grandfather's home. We presented ourselves for the bonding ceremony.

They were ready for us. Our bonding was a traditional Navajo bonding ceremony called Washing the Hands. Grandfather's daughter Elsie clothed NightBird Navajo style. She wore the outfit Elsie's daughter Gloria had been married in—the skirt and blouse and earrings. Elsie did NightBird's hair, and we went into the hogan for the ceremony. Grandfather did the bonding. The marriage basket was filled with a traditional cornmeal cake. Each person at the bonding ate from the cake. NightBird and I were obliged to finish what remained in the basket. The marriage basket used in the ceremony is among NightBird's precious medicine objects. The date was June 22, 1979.

Though I never again experienced the sustained closeness I had known with ShyDeer prior to the ceremony with NightBird, she and I were bonded three years later in a Native American ceremony guided by Hyemeyohsts Storm and Lynn Andrews, author of *Medicine Woman*. ShyDeer stayed with us at the heart of the Deer Tribe for two more years. Then one day she packed her bags and gave away her medicine and pipe. She left the Deer Tribe and the Medicine Path. Apparently she has not looked back. No amount of logical explanation helps an injured heart.

Grandfather, of course, was right. He knew ShyDeer would leave the Medicine Path. NightBird and I are still together. Our bonding secured a relationship that has prevailed since 1979. Today she is the eighteenth nagual woman. She is the light of my life in every way. Truly, no one has ever danced in my heart with the depth of Night-Bird. Each year she becomes more precious to me.

DING POAN'S
CIGARETTES

One afternoon early in 1980, I dragged myself into the house we rented in La Canada, California, dropped into my old armchair in front of the TV, shoved a tape into my VCR, lit up, and settled in to watch martial arts film star Chuck Norris in action. I'd done an all-night healing the previous night and had been running around town most of the day trying to find a piece of land the Deer Tribe might use for ceremonial purposes. Norris was relaxation.

ShyDeer spoke from the hallway. "Lynn called."

"Who?"

"The Lynn you have been hoping to meet."

"C'mon, ShyDeer. Who are you talking about?"

"Turn down the volume if you want to know." I did.

"All the way down, SwiftDeer," she said. "OK, now tell me what it's worth to know which Lynn."

"ShyDeer, I don't have the energy for this little game. If it's important, give it." Chuck was bashing a bad guy on my silent screen.

"It's *very* important, SwiftDeer, and I want to know what it's worth to you to have a beautiful and sexy 'important message' taker at your beck and call." She was standing near the door, hand on her hip.

I looked at her. "Your message is worth anything you want, ShyDeer. You just name it and . . . Gugh!" I clutched my throat, my body spasmed. "Grurp . . . I choke . . . uh . . . ugh . . . help me, ShyDeer." I slid to the floor, twitching. "Argh, water." ShyDeer rushed to the kitchen. Then she was beside me with a glass of water.

"SwiftDeer, what is it?" She knelt, alarm in her eyes.

I took the glass carefully, then bent her over my lap, stomach down, and held her there. ShyDeer screamed. "Now my dear apprentice," I purred. "Who the hell called, and what was the message, or would you like this water where you don't want it!"

"OK," she said. "Lynn Andrews called. Let go of me and I'll tell you why she called." ShyDeer was laughing.

"No! Your last chance. Give me the message right now or drown."

"OK." She sagged between my knees. "Lynn called asking if you'd meet with her and a friend. She wants help for a problem the friend has. She's leaving town next week, so I set the meeting at Musso and Frank's Grill on Hollywood Boulevard for noon tomorrow. Now let me loose."

"She say who the friend was?"

"No, just that it was important."

I dumped her on the floor and poured the water on her. She slugged me and ran from the room. I thought about chasing her and decided against it. I was thinking about noon tomorrow. . . .

I found Lynn and her friend sitting at a table in Musso and Frank's when I walked in next day. Lynn stood up to greet me. The man remained seated. She did the introductions, and I met the author of one of the finest books I've ever read, *Seven Arrows*. We sat. Lynn explained that Hyemeyohsts Storm had cataracts in his eyes complicated by severe swelling. She asked me to begin the process of helping Storm heal his eyes. I told them I would as soon as Storm wanted it. We set the date. Lynn thanked me, and in a traditional way gave me tobacco: two packages of Pall Mall cigarettes. As I took the cigarettes from her, I saw the jungle in Vietnam and an old man being taken for interrogation as a Viet Cong suspect.

"What is it, SwiftDeer?" Lynn asked. My face must have been white.

"I, uh . . . it's the cigarettes, Lynn. Excuse me, hon. These smokes just took me a long way back in time and place." My throat felt thick.

Lynn studied me. "A story goes with these cigarettes, SwiftDeer. I'd like you to hear it."

"I'd like that, Lynn,"

"I learned you smoke Jakarta cigarettes."

"Yes."

"I stopped at a tobacco shop on my way to pick up Storm today. I asked for a carton of Jakartas, intending them for you." She paused, looking at me. "Are you OK?"

"Yes."

"As I waited for the cashier to ring up my sale, a voice came to me. I replaced the Jakartas and purchased these two packs of Pall Malls."

"Who spoke to you?" I asked faintly.

"My wolf spirit guide," she answered.

"A spirit told you to buy these cigarettes for me?"

"Yes," she said. "Not specifically in so many words like you might think. When my wolf spirit speaks, I simply follow it. It happened that way in the tobacco store. I have no idea of its meaning.

I glanced at Storm. He puffed a cigarette and could have been ignoring us. "Lynn," I said, sweating. She waited. "It is important I tell you the history of these cigarettes. If they are from your wolf spirit guide, the wolf has entered the circle of a wonderful old Vietnamese grandfather and myself. I want to tell it, but . . ."

"But what?" she asked, seeing my hesitation.

"What about Storm?" I peered at him. "This meeting was to help him."

"He's into this," she said.

"The wolf and the cigarettes?"

"Yes."

"How do you know?"

"If he wasn't into your story, he'd be gone now. You can count on that." She smiled.

I looked again at Storm, then back to Lynn. Taking my time, I told them the story of Grandfather Ding Poan, as I have described him earlier in this book. When I was finished, I said, "Lynn, these are the cigarettes Ding Poan said would come back to me."

"Yes." Lynn was crying. Storm had turned away from us. He took a kerchief from his pocket and blew into it. We sat silently in the noisy bar. Then the waiter brought our check, and the moment was gone.

I knew then that *through* Ding Poan, Lynn's wolf spirit guide had led me to Storm, as well as to Lynn. Several days later, I did the healing work on Storm's eyes. During the ceremony, it came to me that Storm would be my next teacher. For the next four years he became a powerful and impacting influence in my life.

THE CAVE
OF THE DEAD

The Cave of the Dead is the graduation ceremony of the tenth gateway into full shamanism. It is the initiation ceremony into the eleventh gateway. In its way, it remains as the most integrating of all my gateway ceremonies. It sits in my mind like a rock, holding awareness of what I had to find inside myself to survive and prevail. I am sure I am saying more than has ever been said about this ceremony.

It was my last ceremony with Grandfather Two Bears. He passed to the other world a month later. Grandfather waited for me for five days, holding vigil near the place where I emerged from the Cave of the Dead.

Purification for the ceremony of the Cave of the Dead was intense. I went into a sweatlodge three times a day—morning, noon, and night—in a small protected area on the floor of Canyon de Chelly. Prior to the sweats, I chewed four peyote buttons. After each sweat I walked three hundred yards down the canyon and crawled into a tiny cave to dream and await the next purification. That was my procedure for seven days.

The peyote buttons were cut into four parts, one button for each direction. I felt the alchemy of the arrangement immediately: four buttons times four, three times a day for seven days. Nineteen, the spirits of the great masters, repeated seven times. Seven is the number of the dream. I saw no one for seven days. Each day twelve quartered peyote buttons waited for me in a wooden bowl, near firewood for three sweats.

After seven days and nights, I knew that my body was detoxified. Every poison or chemical imbalance in my body had been given a chance to pass through. On the eighth morning, I lay in the sun outside my little cave feeling clean and powerful. Grandfather was suddenly beside me.

"Getting yourself a tan?"

I glanced for something to cover my nakedness. He always had that effect on me. One second I'd feel integrated and at peace, then Grandfather would show up or speak, and I'd feel like a kid.

"Er . . . Good morning, Grandfather."

"Sit for a minute," he said.

I pulled a cedar branch and covered myself.

"The first part is finished now," Grandfather indicated. I waited. "It was to get you ready for the second part." I knew this. I was certain he was aware I knew. "Now for the next part," he continued. His eyes stayed on mine. Several seconds passed.

"I'm ready, Grandfather."

"Yes," he said. "C'mon then. Get your things." I followed Grandfather down a dry wash to his truck. "We're going up to the rim."

I held my medicine bundle quiet as Grandfather made his way back and forth across the shallow stream. There are quicksand areas on the canyon floor that swallow horses and vehicles. We came up out of the canyon and drove onto the rim road. Near the far end of Canyon de Chelly, he pulled off and parked.

"We'll paint now," he said.

Grandfather supervised while two of his relatives painted the left side of my body red, the right side blue. My feet were painted black, my hands yellow, my face white. Grandfather made other markings on my body I cannot share.

He handed me a cedar torch. "Hang on to this. You can light it in the cave." He looked at one of the nephews. "Get the rope now, and we'll put this man into it."

He brought an old horsehair rope, beautifully woven, an inch thick, and long. One end was tied to a large rock, then looped around a pinon pine. Obviously, the loose end of the rope was for my waist. As Grandfather attached the rope, I asked the obvious: "Am I going over the edge with this?"

I knew the drop was straight down more than nine hundred feet.

"You go into the cave from above," he said. "It's below us near the canyon floor. Here is the old way of rappelling. You work it like this." Grandfather showed me how to slide the rope through a loop

to lower myself manually. I'd done rappelling in the Marine Corps
and was not afraid of heights. I felt strong, integrated. I was ready.

"If you lose control for any reason, the upper part will give way
but won't release you."

"What?"

"You'll flip upside down but can still rappel. Do you see it?"

"Yes." I determined not to lose control.

"OK," said Grandfather. "Do you have everything?"

I wore a loincloth and a belt. I held my medicine bag and the
torch. "I want to look over before I step off," I said.

"Sure."

I peered over the side—nearly a thousand feet to the bottom.

Grandfather took my hands, held them tight. He'd not done that
before. I thanked him, gripped the rope, and backed off the rim.

"The wind can get real strong down there," Grandfather called.
Then he was out of sight and the canyon wall was in front of me.

I rappelled slowly, allowing the rope to run through my hands. I
was in a good nagual space and was beginning to sense the energy
from the ancestors in the cave four hundred feet below me. After
struggling a hundred feet further down the wall, I was hit by a
strong side wind. I realized I'd have to stabilize. I threw my feet out
and started a catwalk.

"Stay in close," I muttered, "or this wind's going to take you!"

I stabilized, balancing with my feet, and continued down the
wall. Moments later, a gust of wind came off the side of the wall and
blew me out. Another rushed at my back as I swung out, thrusting
me back toward the cliff. The wall came at me much too fast. I threw
up my hands just before impact and hit the wall falling, upside
down. My medicine bundle and my torch fell. I hung upside down,
stunned by the impact, swinging slowly. When I bumped the wall
again, I tried to right myself but couldn't. I was maybe three hundred feet above the cave. I had severe rope burns, blood dripped
from my ribs, and I was in trouble. I knew I had to "slope sling" and
go for it—either that or just hang there and let the buzzards pick my
eyes out.

Slope slinging is tough under any conditions. A strong wind and physical hurts do not help. I had to feed a head-first slide until I got enough fulcrum to swing out and come upright.

"Well, it's a good day to die," I thought and let the rope slide. It fed through faster than I wanted. I couldn't orient myself. The canyon wall was an inverted blur as it passed. I struggled to maintain control. Near the bottom I struggled to right myself, eased the slide, and settled feet first near the cave's opening. I'd made it. I rested.

Before me was the Cave of the Dead, known as "Massacre Cave" to the Navajo. I looked at its entrance, black and foreboding. I was to go in here, enter its labyrinth of tunnels, and find my way out. Nine red-eyed devils would confront me in the darkness. "Those demons are attached to aspects of yourself that love blood and killing," Grandfather had said. "Banish the first eight and kill the ninth. That's the last thing you'll ever kill." That was to be my ceremony.

Kit Carson and the Seventh Cavalry had broken the hearts of the Navajo Nation near here. Colonel Carson, so-called friend to the Navajo, had burned their fields, chopped down their fruit trees, killed their animals, rounded up and shot men, women, and children, then led his triumphant troops out of the canyon.

I walked from the sunlight into the darkness of the Cave of the Dead. As I moved from the cave's entrance into the blackness of the main cavern, I felt the stench of death and gun-powder. I sensed angry spirits, hostile to me because I was half white. Suddenly, wall torches burst into flame. The cavern came alive. Scores of Navajo people fled in my direction. Children screamed. Women covered their children with their bodies. Unarmed men tried futilely to protect the women. Soldiers from the United States Cavalry systematically shot them down. The explosions in the cave were deafening. I held a mortally wounded Navajo child to my chest, helpless. It was more horrible than anything I had experienced in 'Nam. I shouted for the soldiers to stop. "No! . . . No! Don't do this!"

A cavalry officer stepped toward me and aimed his pistol at my chest, point blank. I focused on him with a gaze of power. Then I was alone in the darkness. They were all gone—the spirits, everything. The cavern was quiet and clear of smoke. I was completely alone.

Then I began my exploration of the cavern. I was in a huge upper kiva. I crawled in circles, leaving stones to mark my movement. I increased the circumference of my search. I looked for a wall, a tunnel, a passage out of the kiva. After what seemed like hours, a discomforting thought emerged that I might not find an exit from the kiva, and perhaps I'd wander indefinitely.

I stopped, breathed deeply, and began my "hand sets," exercises to center my psychic energies. First the north sets, then the rest. I also did the Sacred Platforms, an ancient breath and sound meditation taught me by Grandmother Spotted Fawn. At the end of that I felt better. My eyesight was sharp. I could almost see, then realized I was being seen. I turned as a red-eyed demon rushed at me. In the darkness I stumbled, banishing it as I fell. *One*—that was one. Eight to go.

My exploration continued. Eventually I found a tunnel headed away from the kiva. Shall I take it? I wondered. What if there are others? I put one stone at its entrance and continued around the kiva. I soon found a second passageway, where I left two stones. I placed rocks at five more passageways leaving the kiva before I found my first stone. That's it: seven ways out of here.

Then it struck me that none guaranteed exit from the kiva. I decided to examine the entrance to each of them again. I studied air movement and temperature change; I looked for light—anything that might give me a clue. I saw myself groping down each passage futilely.

At the second tunnel, two red-eyed demons appeared, casting a red glow on the wall. I studied them. They watched me. They merged, separated, and flung themselves at me. I banished them, yelling loudly. I'd seen red-eyed demons before, but in the cave they were unnerving. Something was different about them that I did not grasp. Two more came at me fast, went by, and turned at me again. I banished them also. That was four—no five. I ceremonially cut my forearm five times with a sharp rock. (I had to be right for the *ninth* one.) Then I continued examination of the kiva.

I finished my exploration of the seven passageways, wondering why I hadn't checked them more closely the first time around. None seemed more hopeful than the others. Nothing clued me in. I started down the first one. After several hundred yards, it ended. I made my way back, lay stones across its entrance, and went down the second.

By the time I had found my third dead end, I was lost in time. Another demon had visited and been banished.

As I went down the fourth passage, I sensed that this one was right. It *felt* right. Excited, I moved faster. The tunnel sloped downward. I decided I'd found the lower exit. I was elated. In the history of the cave, only two people had come out through the lower level: Grandfather and Gus Grey Mountain. I would claim fame by joining them. I turned a corner in the tunnel and felt a draft of warm air. I stepped forward, hoping to see light. *Boom!* I ran into an ectoplasmic barrier that jolted me like electricity, knocking me backward a dozen yards. I lay on my back, struggling to breathe.

I had no idea what had struck me. I was scared and felt under attack. Another red-eyed demon appeared. Instinctively, I lunged to destroy it. *"Not yet!"* a voice said. I banished it, knowing I was on the edge, struggling between dimensions.

I had to know what waited for me in the passage. I crawled slowly, my hands forward. When I sensed the barrier again, I reached tentatively. *Boom!* . . . I took a lighter dose, but was again knocked backward.

What *is* that? I wondered. I rolled three stones into the darkness. *Nothing*. I threw rocks into it. Not a sound. There was something there I couldn't see, smell, or touch. I tried to reach under it, over it. Two more jolts. I knew then that I could not get beyond it. I gave up and began my return to the kiva. To this day, I don't know what stopped me. I realized I'd found the lower exit from the Cave of the Dead.

Back in the main kiva I sat down. A wave of self-pity washed over me. I sagged into it, wept, immersed myself in it. I was exhausted and hungry. I was filled with despair and shame. I felt beyond hope. I thought I'd die there. I knew that the alchemy of any well-choreographed ceremony would push the participants into the dark side of themselves, their shadow. One must emerge from his or her own darkness to the far side of the ceremony. Yet knowing that was of no use to me.

I considered my life, the path I was on, the endless ceremonies I'd done on this path, Grandfather and his role in my life, everything I'd ever done for him. I felt how little he appreciated me or even saw me. I saw with clarity that he was a madman, that he had tricked me and would destroy me.

Another wave of emotion swept through me. Then I realized Grandfather's frailness. I knew he was near his time. His preciousness filled me. What would I do without him? How could I live without him? My love for him filled me. When my grief subsided, bitterness consumed me. I felt the futility of my life. Why did I want to be a shaman anyhow? I knew that being a shaman would be an ongoing pain in the ass: work that would never let up, little money, minimal appreciation, long hours.

I had not chosen to be a shaman in the first place; it had chosen me. The most I'd ever wanted to do with Indians was to deliver needed supplies from the Mormon Church to the trading post in Tuba City. What was I doing in this impossible cave? If I ever got out, I'd burn my medicine, abandon my pipe! Get with a corporation. Find a life! After a time, I gave it all away, went down the next tunnel, and followed it till it dead-ended.

Two passageways remained. I stood between them and chose the one on the left. "Great Spirit, let my intuition be right!" I prayed. After two hundred yards, the tunnel opened into a large room. I found five exits from the room. I entered the first—a dead end. After three more dead ends I entered the fifth. I prayed again that it was right. The passageway continued on much longer than the other four. I paused and heard sounds, a great whirring. The noise was familiar, but recognition escaped me. I inched closer, feeling vibrations. I put my ear to the earth. I sniffed.

The rattlesnake that had been with me during the Dance of the Snake was suddenly beside me. "It's just us, Little Brother," hissed the snake.

Of course! The whirring sound was rattlesnakes, maybe thousands of them. I thanked my little snake and walked into the sound, singing my snake song. Several hundred snakes slithered around and between my legs. I sang loudly, "I don't want to hurt you; I don't want to step on you; I don't want you to bite me; I'm not afraid of you. Please let me put my feet down and move out of your way."

I was in perhaps the largest rattlesnake den in the world, a cavern three hundred yards across. I stepped through the snakes and slowly picked my way to the other side.

From the far side of the den, I turned to look back as another red-eyed demon came at me. Ducking, I banished it. The ninth demon then rushed at me hard from behind and knocked me forward toward the snakes. I pitched forward knowing I would land on my brothers. I shouted for them to move as I fell. *Poof!* A white flash filled the space. I hung, suspended. Then I was on my feet facing the demon. The snakes cheered and laughed.

Number *nine*! As I stepped toward the demon, it became the killer I had been in Vietnam when I most enjoyed destruction. I reached for my demon, pulled it tight to me, bent into it, and snapped its spine. The demon died simply without a struggle or a sound. It disappeared into the rock. I was stunned at the simplicity of the battle.

"Go on your way!" the snakes called out.

I continued down the corridor. Within ten yards it narrowed. Moments later I was forced to bend, then crawl. The passageway became tiny. I was on my belly like a snake and beginning to fear I might be trapped. Good God, I'll never make it, I thought, pushing myself forward with elbows and ankles. I contemplated a turn-around.

Then I came through into a larger space and sat up. I could make out vague outlines and shadows. I felt danger and realized I was on the edge of a drop-off. Straight down. I tossed a rock over the edge, counted to twenty slowly, and heard nothing. I lobbed another rock into space. Still nothing. I was on a drop-off so deep a stone did not find bottom. Light drifted in from the other side. There was my exit. I threw a stone at the far side. It hit and bounced toward the light. The trail was open. All I had to do was figure out how to cross thirty feet over a bottomless drop into darkness.

I knew I would have to "double"—to teleport my body across the chasm—in order to survive. I'd doubled before, but *never* without the help of Grandfather or Gus Grey Mountain. With them it had been an exercise, a guided activity. This was life threatening, life demolishing. I was alone in the Cave of the Dead now, with a profound understanding of the cave's name. I had to either get across or die. I knew I'd found my only way out; this was my long-sought-after exit.

I began to breathe deeply and started my hand sets, pumping it, pumping. After a time, my body was lighter. I began to project myself and saw my body begin to appear, as in a mirror, on the other side. I continued to breathe, deeper, fuller . . . deeper. I began the "energy nine" hand set, the most powerful of the sets. When I reached the ninth set, I began to shoot my fibers to the far side of the chasm. Slowly, my physical form began to appear on the other side.

There! This is it, I thought. I let go of the consciousness of being here looking there and threw all of it across the hole. I looked back and saw I was across. I wasn't where I had been. I had made it! I cried again, overcome with joy!

I crawled for the light. Again the passage became very tiny for forty or fifty feet. Then I pushed into one of the old storage rooms of the White House ruins.

"I see you made it," said Grandfather.

"Grandfather!" I said. "You are the finest person on the planet!"

"Your friend Gus Grey Mountain just left," he said. "He smoked for you. Says to tell you congratulations."

My body tingled. Every cell danced in happy syncopation. "I have no words for my gratefulness, Grandfather. There has never been a teacher like you—*never*!"

Grandfather smiled his smile that is always with me. "Well," he said, "that makes us a pretty good pair. I never had a student like you! What took you so long?" He had a good laugh.

"Come outside here, SwiftDeer. Some people want to see you. You are the first Irishman to come through the cave."

Grandfather's relatives helped me celebrate. They clapped and cheered when I came out of the ruins with him. They asked to hear my story. "You're gonna be a legend," they said as we feasted. When a cooler of Dr. Pepper soda was presented to honor me, I knew they were sincere.

Later, I climbed into my old Karmann Ghia convertible with the cooler on the seat beside me. I shoved a Doobie Brothers cassette in the tape deck, turned the volume up, uncapped a Dr. Pepper, waved at Grandfather and his relatives, and headed west, knowing I owned the whole world.

GRANDFATHER TWO BEARS' FAMILY

Recorded April 8, 1991

Tom Shiprock Wilson (Two Bears)
Born to Salt Clan (A'ashii)
Born for Bitter Water Clan
Last name of parents:
Mother: Large Whiskers
Father: Shiprock

Grandfather Two Bears was also known as "Hosteen" Man from Black Mesa and "Quarterman."

Grandfather's wife, Zonie
Born to Red Bottom Clan
Born for Nakaidine Clan

Grandfather's children (and their children)

May Hatahlie
Julia	Denny (a roadman)
Arthur	Davis

Nellie Begay
Lorraine	May
Janet	Marlene
Virginia	Mike
Willie	

Tom Klee
Rita	Rosita
Virginia	Mary Ann
Susie	Rochelle
Anselm	Eddison
Thomas	

Sadie Wilson
Rose

Irene Yellow Hair

Mayzie	Elizabeth
Susie	Charlene
Kathleen	Evangeline
Thomas	Dan (a roadman)
Raymond	Marvin

James Jr.

Elsie Wilson

Gloria	Thomasina

Stella Yellow Hair

Sara	Sharlene
Sheryl	Larry
Tommy	Wilfred
Gilfred	Albert

Gilbert Jr.

Annie Yazzie

Marie	Virginia
Mary	Linda
Karina	Franklin
Leonard	Philip

Grandfather Two Bears died May 21, 1980. Hyemeyohsts Storm smoked the Sacred Pipe at his funeral service. Today Grandfather Two Bears and his wife, Zoni, lie next to each other in a tiny cemetery on the Wilson family land on the Navajo reservation in Arizona.

PART 6

HEALING

PART 5

HEALING

THE BATTLE OF
BLOODY HEART

During the fall of 1988, I asked the Deer Tribe for a sweatlodge healing for myself. I was not sleeping, and when I did my sleep was troubled. I recognized the symptoms. Unresolved memories of Vietnam were surfacing. I think it was caused by my opening to these memories in order to tell my story and by the movies I had recently seen about the war, particularly *Born on the Fourth of July*, starring Tom Cruise. I find that each time I go into the depths of what is left in me of the horror of Vietnam, I come out cleansed, able to teach and heal others at deeper levels. I knew what I had to do.

I asked Tim Toohey, one of my apprentices, if he would lead a sweat for me. Because Tim is a Vietnam veteran, he was certain to know what I was after, and I also thought he might get something for himself from the ceremony. Tim brought members of the Deer Tribe together to assist him in the sweat.

The day before the ceremony, I talked with Bill Wahlberg by phone. He asked if I would tape the ceremony. He felt others might benefit from my experience. I told him I had never heard of taping a sweatlodge ceremony, and it was not likely this one would be the first. But during the night something in me moved. The next day I told Tim Toohey to see to it that someone taped the ceremony. He looked at me with his big eyes and said nothing. I was confident he'd get the job done.

The rock splasher in a traditional sweatlodge ceremony typically asks that the door be closed four times during the ceremony. The narration that follows is from the tape, beginning at the start of the "second door." I asked Tim not to run the tape until the sacred powers had been called in, which happened mainly during the first door.

The battle I describe here took place in 1967. I've carried the experience in my psyche much too long. There are thousands of brothers out there who had it just as bad—or worse—and will never have a chance to release its impact on their lives. I pray that God will be with them.

Prior to the ceremony, I had never been able to talk about the "Battle of Bloody Heart." Two hundred seventy United States soldiers engaged the enemy in that battle. Our attack was made by a combined force of marines, navy Seals, and army Special Forces. In addition, a company of South Vietnamese regulars participated. My outfit was assisted by a small but fierce Laotian native group of Montagnards known as the "Mountain People." The Mountain People are the survivors of eight original tribes that were persecuted and killed in Vietnam, Laos, and Cambodia by the Cambodian drug warlords and the Chinese. Several groups of Montagnards volunteered to help United States forces in the fight against communism. Their fierceness in battle is memorable.

For my sweatlodge ceremony, twenty-two members of the Deer Tribe crowded into a traditional dome-shaped structure. In the first door of the ceremony, the participants offered prayers for me and others who served in Vietnam. Tim called for Wakan Tanka, the Great Spirit, the powers of the Four Directions, and other traditional powers, spirits and ancestors, including the spirit of my teacher, Two Bears, to add power to the ceremony. When Tim called for the door to be closed, we were in complete darkness, except for the glow of the rocks.

TIM: Close the flap. Great Spirit, sacred ancestors, sacred grandfathers, and the spirits of all warriors, we thank you for hearing our prayers in the first round of this ceremony. We ask that you be with us in this second door to guide SwiftDeer as he looks into his past. We ask you help him find the strength he needs to go into his heart and mind. Now, Brother SwiftDeer, in the presence of the Sacred Ones summoned here into the lodge and with their help, I ask you to remember the Battle of Bloody Heart. Tell it from the beginning, leaving nothing important unsaid. As you heal, so will we all.

SWIFTDEER: Give me a moment, Tim. OK. It was spring 1967, near the end for me. The night before we went in, we were briefed on an assignment to destroy villages on each side of a bridge, then blow up the bridge. The bridge was the primary target. Our Seals would come down the river, attack the north village, then take the bridge. My platoon was to destroy the south village, the larger one, assisted by Special Forces. Supplies brought across the bridge, a major link to the Ho Chi Minh Trail, were hurting us. The bridge had to go.

Next morning we lifted off from Khe Sanh loaded in our transport choppers, C-119s, and CNC-146s headed the opposite direction from the target for diversion. Bub and I faced each other in the 119. I saw in his eyes what I knew he read in mine: "You and me ain't going down, bro. Or, if we do, that don't matter. Nothing matters. No fucking thing matters! But we won't." Half a dozen Montagnards were jumping with us. This was a first. Their leader was a fierce little man we called Willy Dee. [Long pause.]

TIM: Go ahead.

SWIFTDEER: Yes. I am seeing it, Tim. The jump went OK. Nobody was injured—a good sign because the terrain was rough. We collected ourselves on the ground and made radio contact. We were three clicks from the south village. Willy Dee had told Bub and me he would paint us in our death masks. I called Willy Dee over. "Is now the time?" He said, "No," and went on ahead.

TIM: Open the flap!

SWIFTDEER: Can we talk with the flap shut?

TIM: SwiftDeer, I sense from Grandfather Two Bears that the flap should be open, to talk openly in the light. The story asks to be told that way. The ceremony is about no more pain and suffering for you . . . or me, or any of the 'Nam brothers who suffer.

SWIFTDEER: I just need to be in darkness.

TIM: OK, pull down the flap.

SWIFTDEER: I need my own space. I need the darkness to get to this. It's back in the darkness of my mind.

TIM: Ho!

SWIFTDEER: And if you don't get there, you die!

TIM: Grandfather says the darkness can't hold it. You can be in one and talk from the other.

SWIFTDEER: Well, for once I'm going to do it my way and not his!

TIM: Well, SwiftDeer, that's good.

SWIFTDEER: We approached the south village in four squads, flanked by Special Forces on our right. After the Seals hit the smaller village, they were to cut back across the river and cover our left flank. Recon intelligence reported we'd get resistance from a company of Viet Cong, but not to worry about anything more in the area.

At the edge of the village I asked Willy again, "Is it time?" He laughed. "No, we not ask for death yet. We only flirting."

I heard the fight begin on the other side of the river as planned, then all hell broke loose around us, and four of my men went down. Fast-fire mortar rounds and heavy .50 and .30 caliber machine-gun fire raked our position. Obviously, they had been waiting for us. We scrambled for our lives, pinned down by ridge fire from two canyon walls. It was scary.

One thing was certain: we weren't seeing only a company of VC defending that bridge. Our recon was bullshit! A battalion and a half of Republic of Vietnam regulars were looking at us. The NVA were many times tougher than the VC, better equipped, more disciplined, and pound for pound the toughest fighters in the world. We dug in. I got Captain Rogers of Special Forces on the radio, wanting an air strike called on the NVA. He said he was under heavy attack but hanging on. He reported the ships available for fire support were still at Quan Tri, our diversionary strike. We'd have to hang on three or four hours till they could get refueled and return with covering fire.

Four hours sounded like a long time. Captain Rogers told me to get my men off the ridge, regroup and pull in a perimeter. He'd hold the right flank and let the South Vietnamese cover us at the back door.

"Sir, are you crazy?" I asked. "The South Vietnamese will abandon us with this much shit coming down." There was a pause at the other end, then Captain Rogers yelled at me: "Marine, you do what you are fucking told! Pass the order!" We backed off from the ridge and made do. We came under fire from twenty-five or so snipers while their larger force regrouped, and two more of my men were wounded. I took a sniper scope rifle from a hurt buddy and sited on the NVA snipers. After a few minutes, the sniper fire stopped.

TIM: OK, flap up. Keep it going—I'm just bringing the flap up.

SWIFTDEER: Everything stopped for almost an hour.

TIM: All the way up. Good. Fan a little air in here. SwiftDeer, how're you doing, brother?

SWIFTDEER: Half the South Vietnam outfit had split. Our back door was vulnerable.

TIM: Close the flap. OK. We're with you, brother.

SWIFTDEER: [Long sigh.] Two companies of NVA came at our rear flank. That's the point at which the Battle of Bloody Heart began, I guess, when their first rush came. You can open the door now.

TIM: Lift the flap. Get it up and keep it all the way up.

SWIFTDEER: Our men bunched in so tight we were shooting between them when the RVN swarmed at us. A dozen South Vietnamese soldiers, what was left of our so-called back-door support, broke and fled in my direction. I shot as many of them as I could with my Thompson. A major was leading them. He looked surprised as my bullets ripped through him. I don't regret it. My buddies paid the price for holding the ground beside me, and these soldiers were running through us for safety! I'd do it again.

The fight kaleidoscoped. Everything happened at once. I saw my buddy Vincent surrounded on my right. They were head to head on him. I glanced left at a man coming in on me, and when I looked back for Vincent, those men were down and he was running. Go for it, bro! I thought.

When it looked like they had us dead, they stopped and pulled back. They were teasing. Willy Dee found me and said, "It is time."

"Good," I answered. "Another minute might have been too late."

As he painted me, we heard that the Seals at the other village had also been ambushed and were wiped out. Their radio man and one other wounded would try to get through to us. Then the NVA rushed again. We . . . uh, Tim, I'm having trouble breathing.

TIM: Lay him down!

SWIFTDEER: If someone could hold my head . . . my head's going bad again. I can't get it back!

TIM: Someone hand in a towel!

SWIFTDEER: I can't breathe.

TIM: Do you want ice?

SWIFTDEER: Yeah.

TIM: Hold his head back. Keep it back. Someone fill this with ice and hand it in.

SWIFTDEER: Give me a cloth, and just keep my head back. There, I've got it.

TIM: Here's some ice. Take this towel and put it under his head.

SWIFTDEER: I've got to have something more under my head, man. I can't touch my neck!

TIM: Batty, have you got another towel? Here—here's a towel. Get it under there.

SWIFTDEER: I'm OK now. OK, that's good . . . that's good.

TIM: Close the flap. Now, brother, bring it back.

SWIFTDEER: They rushed in waves. I was locking and loading, letting it all go. We all were. We let everything go at them. They didn't stop falling. They wouldn't stop coming. This part is in memory fragments. Oh, no, please, my head! Don't put water on it! No water! I can't take that!

TIM: Ask for clarity, SwiftDeer.

SWIFTDEER: Captain Rogers was able to get a strike on their position, and they fell back. In the lull, Rogers's men joined us. Willy Dee painted several of my men and also a couple of Captain Rogers's men. I was sitting next to Rogers when I noticed that only a handful of South Vietnamese regular army remained.

"I hope to fuck you are satisfied, Captain. Good men died

because you wanted assholes at our back door. I hope you join them before this is over!"

His face got red, and he called his first lieutenant over to write down what I'd said. While he wrote, crouched on his haunches, a mortar round hit him and he was gone—just disappeared. I remember thinking, OK, Lieutenant, write that down, write that down.

Then they were on us again: a wall of humanity, spread out and coming from everywhere, every direction, screaming. We couldn't hold them back. I yelled at Captain Rogers, "Call it in, man. They're inside our perimeter! Call the air strike on our position. Call it in on us!"

He couldn't do it. He wasn't hit, but he was frozen and out of it. I saw his condition. I grabbed the set from his radio man and called the air strike. I called it in. Within seconds, explosions enveloped our position. Everything blew up in a tremendous earth-shattering roar!

Oh my God, I called it in all right . . . [crying] . . . I saw some good friends die . . . [sobbing] . . . from that strike. I knew we'd catch hell when I called for it, but if I didn't, none of us were coming out. I wanted to survive. I did it because I wanted to live. I knew good men would die from it . . . [sobbing] . . . I didn't care about them. I didn't give a shit! I didn't want to die there, and I didn't want to be captured. I wanted out! . . . [deep sobbing] . . . I killed them. Oh, God! I killed Vincent. Vincent, I never told you—I called in the strike that killed you . . . [deep sobbing—long pause] . . . I've got to get to the Wall.

TIM: Open the flap. I want the light on this man's pain.

SWIFTDEER: OK, but I got to tell the rest.

TIM: Yes, but we'll give it a minute of light.

SWIFTDEER: Sure.

TIM: There. SwiftDeer, do you want the flap open or shut?

SWIFTDEER: Doesn't matter.

TIM: Close it. Go ahead, SwiftDeer.

SWIFTDEER: The NVA pulled back to regroup. We all knew they

were coming again. There weren't many of us left, and I wondered why someone didn't get us out. Where were our evacuation choppers? That is when the Montagnards did their thing. They ran out among the NVA bodies scattered around and cut them up. They took hearts, testicles, tongues, ears, and eyeballs. Dozens of them. They crept up the ridge where the NVA had gathered for their next attack, charged in among them screaming, throwing the body parts at them, stuffing them into the mouths of the NVA they killed.

Only Willy made it back. "Big fight come now," he said. "We stop them."

They hit us so hard I couldn't see uniforms. Dirt, blood, tissue, and guts mixed all together covered us. I was so covered with it, I couldn't see my uniform. We were "sweep firing" at anything that moved. Only God knows how many of our own we hit.

I called a second strike on our position. As the strike exploded on us, I flipped out. I fell to my knees screaming prayers to my maker. "Get me out, God! Get me out! I'll do anything for you. I don't give a fuck for the rest!

"Just get me out! I'll serve you for life!" I meant it. I couldn't stand the horror anymore!

Then I got a better idea and prayed I'd die, begged for my death. I was hysterical, a marine combat sergeant gone berserk!

I looked up, and Bub and Willy were staring at me. "Don't fuck with me!" I yelled.

"Nobody is going to fuck with you, old buddy," said Bub. "I am God, and I am giving you your request." He aimed his .45 at me and cocked it. Something in his eyes snapped me out of it. "Good," he said. "Now let's get ready for the party."

The NVA came again—their hardest rush. The fight became a blur. I picked up whatever I could shoot: fire left, right, front, rear. Bub was screaming. I was getting high. I hit everything I shot. I couldn't miss. I was shooting faster than I thought possible. I was high. "Come on!" I screamed . . . [pause] . . . Please, open the flap. I can't breathe.

TIM: Get the flap up! What do you need, Swift?

SWIFTDEER: Air, some air . . . [gasping] . . . uh, I'm suffocating.

TIM: Are you OK?

SWIFTDEER: I, uh . . . yes. Let me finish this.

TIM: Yes. Keep the flap up.

SWIFTDEER: I was high on the fight and getting higher—like a drug high. Bodies were everywhere: ours and theirs, piled grotesquely, sometimes wrapped around each other. We shot into them. *Thunk!* Ever so often one of them screamed. I felt invincible! Everything happened fast-forward in slow motion. I was hit in the hip, arm, and knee, and felt no pain. I was exhilarated—totally off on it!

Just as it seemed it would never end, in a mad, surrealistic crescendo it was over. The NVA pulled back and out. Everything stopped. Quiet. I got up and wandered, slowly comprehending that they weren't coming back. It was over.

As my high receded, it was replaced by a great sadness as I looked at the carnage around me. I found Willy where he lay on his back staring at the sky, hurt and exhausted. Tears streamed down my face. "They had us, Willy. Why didn't they finish us?"

He looked at me from a faraway place. "They break your heart, sergeant, but we break their spirit," he whispered. Our choppers came in over the tree line to get us out.

TIM: Bring seven rocks . . . seven red hot. Then close the flap. I'm going to pray again for this brother while I splash the rocks and for . . . [crying] . . . for all the brothers who didn't make it back from Vietnam. Great Spirit, please hear this prayer for SwiftDeer and for me and all the bros who fell over there and also for their families:

> Great Spirit, may we walk in beauty!
> May beauty be above us,
> So that we might receive beauty.
> Great Spirit, may we walk in beauty.
>
> May beauty be in front of us,
> That we might perceive beauty.
> Great Spirit, may we walk in beauty.
>
> May beauty be to the left of us,
> So that we might know woman's beauty.
> Great Spirit, may we walk in beauty.

May beauty be to the right of us,
So that we might see man's beauty.
Great Spirit, may we walk in beauty.

May beauty be behind us,
So all who are behind us know we walk in beauty.
Great Spirit, may we walk in beauty.

May we touch ourselves and others with beauty.
Great Spirit, may we walk away from Vietnam in beauty.
May all we have from that be beauty.
For this is the Blessed Beauty Way.

This is what I ask.

Open the flap. Fire People, assist these people as they leave the Lodge. Mitakuye Oyasin.

The official name of the Battle of Bloody Heart was Operation Raincoat. The ferocity of the engagement led to a much larger operation called Operation Phoenix. Seventeen Americans survived the fight. Three Congressional Medals of Honor were awarded, two posthumously. One Legion of Merit was given, and five marines were presented with the Silver Star. The other survivors were given bronze stars. For his part in the fight, SwiftDeer was awarded the Silver Star the third highest honor given by the United States military. Willy Dee, the only Mountain People survivor, was given rice and fish.

MY FIVE SONS

It is a statistic of the Vietnam War that an unusually high percentage of the children of the veterans of that war have found difficulty in their own adjustment to society in the post-Vietnam era in the United States. Often they mirror the inner world of their parents. Many are angry and lost. Love and happiness come slow. The dreams SwiftDeer had for happiness with his own sons have long been abandoned.

When I look at my life, the only regret I have, other than the pain of the war in Vietnam, is the tragedy of my sons, and I suppose much of that is a result of Vietnam.

At the time of this writing, my oldest son, Steve—Sawaikee SunWarrior—lives in Austria, an expatriate. He works for the United Nations and is a musician in Vienna. His life is together. I'm proud of Steve. I know he felt it necessary to move far away from his family, even his country. I understand this and accept it. We don't talk much. I have seen him only twice in the past eight years.

My second son, Jeffrey—Nidokie Painter of Visions—is in prison in Canyon City near Colorado Springs, Colorado. He has been incarcerated nearly fifteen of his thirty years, and I think he's been stoned, high, drunk, or trying to get that way for a dozen of those years. Jeffrey's had a difficult time in prison. Any chance for parole is finished. We talk clear and straight to each other now, father to son. He tells me he loves me, and I tell him the same. That feels good. But I can't turn back the clock. The good days of companionship and laughter are gone, and I don't know for certain he wouldn't break into my home and steal again if the opportunity were his; in the past he has taken the most valuable of my medicine items to sell or trade for drugs. I don't judge him now. I miss what might have been.

Todd—Nocosie Big Bear—is my third son. He lives at Rosewood, a halfway home in San Pedro, California. Todd has permanent brain damage caused by excessive use of PCP and other street substances. He is a diagnosed schizophrenic. It is suggested that he will remain

213

sedated, a ward of the state, the rest of his life. I picked him up at
Rosewood a while back and brought him to my home to visit. We
both tried hard to connect. It was a difficult weekend. He asked to be
taken back to Rosewood before his time at my house was finished.
He feels safe at Rosewood. He knows the routine. All that damage in
just three short years.

I think about my son Todd every time I sit down to do a healing.
I try not to, but it runs through the back of my consciousness every
time I smoke the pipe to heal someone else. I say, "Son, this one's for
you." Inside, my tears begin to flow. I wish to God I could do it for
him. I think Todd will visit again. We have to keep trying.

David—Chokie Little Crow—my fourth born, lives in California
not far from me. He is a computer analyst and is doing well finan-
cially. His wife, Jill, was a member of the Deer Tribe years ago. She
insists that their only child, a son—and my only grandchild—died in
a miscarriage because a Navajo skinwalker threw medicine arrows
meant for me. She blames me. Can you grasp the enormity of that?

David avoided me for years—not a word. Jill wants it that way.
The other night, David knocked at my door at 2 a.m. and asked if he
could come in. He wanted to talk. We did—for hours. I pray for rec-
onciliation. He says he will return. He is curious about who I am.

Raven—Osaqua Bird of the Night, my youngest—is twenty-four.
He is serving a thirteen-year sentence in Buena Vista State Correctional Facility in Colorado for burglary and related charges. He tells
me he expects to die violently in prison. His brothers led him into the
drug culture. I didn't think my heart could bear another breaking.

The worst memories of my life come from the period following
my return to the family after Vietnam. The first years included
throwing my sons against a wall while I was in a violent rage. If the
boys got in my way or couldn't move fast enough, I'd have my hands
on them, smashing them across the room. I couldn't check my anger.
When it rushed through me, I vented it on them.

My violence horrified me. Can you picture it? I loved them all so
much. I would have died for any of them. Still, I beat them. I was
unpredictable: I would be loving and supportive, then explosive and
violent. It happened more times than I care to remember.

My anger wasn't at them. They were precious to me. I wanted to smash something inside myself I detested, something that left me exhausted and confused. I sense now that in those days, in some bizarre way, I saw them as extensions of myself that I needed to smash. I see that they also mirrored my guilt. I wasn't the father I wanted to be. But they didn't mirror enough guilt to account for that much violence. The Vietnam War was trying to work its way out of my system. I thought I should have felt good about myself—what I did for my country. I'd done my best over there. At times I did far more than my best. I was truly willing to die for my country in Vietnam. But when I came home, I felt dirty and confused.

In those days I struck violently at anything that upset me. If my sons reacted rebelliously to me, I felt justified in hitting them. I dealt with them like my dad had disciplined me when he was angry: with his fists.

At times I have considered that perhaps my dad was, in his way, a casualty of *his* war. Fourteen straight major battles in the Pacific, almost without a break! Perhaps his own unresolved war found its way into fists that landed on me. I do not judge him. In his time, there was no fancy diagnosis like post-traumatic stress disorder.

I wasn't always mad at my boys. There was plenty of joy and fun when they were little and lots of hugs and kisses. We especially enjoyed life when we played sports together, or went scouting, or did the medicine work. All five of my sons were exceptionally fine athletes and also good at martial arts. All had natural abilities in snake medicine, the study of sorcery.

Each excelled in scouting for a time. But except for Steve, after they advanced so far, they dropped out. When scouting was new and exciting, they liked it. As their advancement became more difficult and required internal discipline and time, their interest faded. Everything had to be intense, fast moving, and exciting, or they would quit. They were unable to finish things. Jeffrey, Todd, and Raven dropped out of school. David finally did graduate. The other three still do not have high school diplomas and probably never will. Diplomas have not been important to them.

I realize that their academic failures are partially my fault because I shaped their school attitudes. I didn't want the schools to mark my sons. I'd forgotten the importance of high school in my life, and I didn't have the vision to see how profoundly my attitudes affected them. I was repulsed by our American school system. I saw *everything* wrong with it. I'd participated in one of the bloodiest and ugliest wars this country has ever experienced. I was bitter and angry at the powers that had created it.

I hated the mentality that had choreographed Vietnam, and I wanted something better for my sons. I loved the Marine Corps, but I was furious with the government. To me, the schools and teachers of America were part of the system that was responsible for that war. I decided that one way to assure my sons something better than the offerings of public schools was to point out the weaknesses of the schools so my boys would not be duped. While ridiculing the schools they attended, I endeavored to train them as independent, thinking warriors. I immersed them in Native American medicine, sorcery, stalking, scouting, athletics, and the overwhelming force of my personality. I introduced them to power plants, the sacred psychotropic herbs, as part of their experience.

It was my aim to develop a different tradition for them within the system, free of the weakness I saw in it. I ridiculed their teachers, suggesting that they were shallow, ignorant, and stupid. I told the boys the schools were useless. I led my sons to believe they were unique and superior to others around them. Without realizing it, I pushed them away from the opportunity to find *their* way to adjust to the system and its structure, rules, and laws.

"That classroom stuff is just a fucking game," I'd say. "It's not the real world. Learn the rules and get your diploma, but know what they teach you sucks. It is useless."

I taught my sons the skills I thought they needed while openly scorning the schools they attended. They didn't have the maturity to integrate my efforts toward their education. How could they? On the one hand, they idolized me; on the other, they were terrified of me. Eventually they rejected school, authority, and all structure—with nothing to replace them. Then they discovered street drugs. Predictably, they failed in school, dropped out, or were expelled.

I truly thought my approach to their education was realistic at the time and would be helpful for them. Even now I think my idea was a good one, though it never really had a chance, given my own personality difficulties and inconsistencies with them. I never dreamed that my fathering would contribute to the disaster of their lives. I failed them. It all went wrong. They didn't get what a boy should get from his dad: protection, understanding, love, and support for *his* life issues—and *consistency*. A boy needs encouragement to find his own path. I insisted they walk my path. I pushed my will on them.

My boys became lost, and except for Steve, they have stayed that way. I wanted each of them to be the best, the strongest, and the smartest, and I felt I knew how to make that happen. Certainly I didn't want them to be corrupted by the weaknesses of the public school system. Unknowingly, I corrupted them myself. I encouraged them to skip important developmental steps. I was too much into their space, too strong in their circle.

When I introduced power plants to my sons, I did it to help them develop their gifts of insight and power. I've come to regret that, and I believe it was a mistake. They couldn't handle the experience. Today, three of my sons are still drug dependent. Would that have happened had I not brought power plants into their lives? I wish I did not have that question to consider.

I used to blame my wife for the problems that developed. I was working full time, going to school, and studying the medicine with Grandfather. I expected her to anticipate what the boys needed and care for them. She did fine when they were little. As they grew older, she had no chance. Without awareness, I undermined her attempts to help them with a normal school and social life. They were male, *my* sons. I was a man, and I was determined they would be the men I wanted.

It all went wrong . . . and has stayed that way. I love my boys deeply. I tried to father them while a jungle war raged within me. I don't feel guilty anymore. With the help of the Tunkashila and many sweatlodge ceremonies, I no longer have space in my circle for guilt about anything I have done in my life. My sons live with their own karma. They know this. But I do love them and miss them, and sometimes I wonder what it would be like to be a father surrounded by five strong sons.

THE WOMEN IN MY LIFE

Four main women have impacted my life since I left my childhood home. Each one came into my circle when I needed her most. Each gave to me fully, completely, as only a woman can and then moved on. Only NightBird remains.

A woman is a mirror for a man. From her he learns about his hidden self, both his shadow and his beauty. I would not be the man I am today without these four women. I pray that I gave something worthwhile to them. They gave so much to me.

Nicki was my high school sweetheart and the mother of our five sons. We were married in 1959. That the marriage lasted eighteen years is a tribute to Nicki's tenacity, courage, and her dream of a home for our sons. We were together during the formative years, the hard times, the years that forged the emergence of my present character. The relationship was tested beyond its strength and did not survive. As our children became older, the dream faded. Nicki was drawn to the Mormon Church; I studied shamanism. Our choices were not compatible. We separated. During our early years, Nicki filled my need for a relationship and family; she loved me and was loyal, and our sexual relationship was amazing. Neither of us knew how to parent our sons.

Near the end of my time with Nicki, I found Mary Mac. She became a great love in my life. Mac came into my life when I most needed what she had to give. She helped me melt the ugliness I felt inside myself. She taught me how to love. I learned to love again, something I could not do after 'Nam. She saw past my darkness into something no one else saw, including myself. From the beginning, she believed in me. She sensed my dream and mirrored it for me until I integrated it for myself.

Mac saw beauty in everything around her. Her delight with the world helped me open my eyes. She taught me how to feel again.

She did this simply by loving me. Mac showed me that a relationship can be beautiful. I healed with her. Though she was with me less than three years, I found my heart again after four tours "in country" as a killer.

Mary ShyDeer came into my life as Mac went out. Like Mac, she was younger than I. Obviously, both women brought youth and hope to me, the cynical and battered warrior. They rekindled the trust and innocence I had known in my pre-Vietnam youth. Shy-Deer's strongest influence with me was her infectious "never-say-die—go-for-broke!" attitude.

When we met, I was a part timer in numerous activities. With ShyDeer's support and enthusiasm, I integrated and founded the Deer Tribe: A Shamanic Lodge for Ceremonial Medicine. ShyDeer's natural enthusiasm and spirit helped me jump into my dream and make a commitment as a full-time shaman, teacher, and Sweet Medicine sundancer. We began to travel—teaching, healing, building sweatlodges, and doing ceremonies around the United States, Africa, and Europe. I was becoming well known. Large crowds attended my seminars.

"Hon', how'd you know we could make it?" I asked her happily one night following a huge gathering in Switzerland.

"It's in your teachings," she answered.

"What?"

"It's what you've been teaching. Do you ever listen to what you are saying?"

She laughed and punched me in the ribs. I chased her around the room. That's the way she was!

When ShyDeer left me, my grief was beyond anything I'd ever known. Sadness for everything I had ever lost poured through me. I sobbed deeply. I also was very angry. I blamed everyone possible. I felt that my personal loss and the loss to the Deer Tribe were irreparable. I worked listlessly. I grieved for weeks and thought I would never be over her.

One night as I sat in the sweatlodge, sweat pouring from my body, lost in sadness and remorse, I felt something different in my tears. I no longer sobbed for ShyDeer. I wept for the men I'd lost in Vietnam, buddies I could not cry for over there, for their wives and families. I was deeply moved. When I considered this, I knew I had turned the corner and could finally live without ShyDeer.

The Deer Tribe grew stronger after ShyDeer left, something I could not have foreseen. The Great Spirit always knows things we cannot have foreseen. Strong people filled ShyDeer's place, and my heart opened more deeply to NightBird.

Dianne NightBird represents the stable, mature relationship. She is my equal counterpart in our love affair. Each year she is stronger, more deeply rooted in her strength as a woman. She brings consistency and reliability to me and to the Deer Tribe. NightBird has become my teacher, as well as my apprentice on the Medicine Path. NightBird has become the "woman to the nagual." NightBird endures and prevails. She is the nagual woman needed in my mature years.

Grandfather Two Bears bonded me with NightBird because he knew she was the nagual woman. He saw her greatness, her stability and loyalty, her leadership—he saw those qualities in her before I did. That's why he would not bond me with ShyDeer. He knew she would leave. He had forbearance and vision; I didn't. He saw that NightBird would become my counterpart, my equal reflective mirror, and have the maturity and depth to be there no matter what happens.

Every year NightBird is like a new woman. She brings strength and steadiness, reliability and truth to the Deer Tribe. She is wise. She is an inspiring and moving ceremonialist. She has an uncanny sixth sense about handling relationships between me and members of the Deer Tribe, and I rely on her judgment. She has replaced all the energies, all the mirrors, of the other three women in my life.

NightBird, my dear mature love, I pray we continue to grow and love for a lifetime.

THE VIETNAM MEMORIAL

On April 25, 1989, I visited the memorial to United States casualties of the Vietnam War in Washington, D.C. Veterans commonly refer to it as the "Wall." Emotionally, visiting the Wall had not previously seemed possible for me. Accompanied by my wife, NightBird, I faced the black wall on the mall at midnight.

It had been a nice, sunny day. That night we wore overcoats to warm us from the chill that had settled in. We delayed going to the Wall until midnight to give us quietness and privacy. Tim Toohey and his wife, Ina, accompanied us to D.C. Tim had been to the Wall before. He and Ina separated from us as we came close; we had different places to visit.

Approaching the Wall was difficult that night. The names are engraved on each quadrant according to the date of death. The experience was powerful beyond words. I was tremendously impressed. The creators of the memorial had a magnificent vision, setting it up so the brothers could easily be found.

I sensed NightBird's feelings. I am sure even had she been alone she would have been deeply touched. She told me later that being with Tim and me intensified everything. The many rows of names on that black wall opened her heart to all those men and their families. When we stopped in front of it, she burst into tears. I was overwhelmed. I have seen nothing like it in my life.

Numerous mood changes during the day indicated a strong resistance to remembering what I had suppressed for twenty-one years. I was terrified of the flood of memories waiting for me. I felt they would be too much. I knew NightBird was trying to support me without getting in my way.

Eleven names were written on the piece of paper I held in my hand—men I wanted to find at the Wall. NightBird walked with me. After I dropped the list a second time I handed it to her. "Dianne, will you find the names for me?" Because the Wall is lit at night, it should not be difficult to find a name unless one's eyes are filled with tears.

As NightBird found the names, she'd say, "Here he is, Swift-Deer." She'd read the man's name. I then talked to my Marine Corps brother.

At the first name, I turned suddenly back to NightBird. "Dianne, I've got to do something!"

"Well," she said, "you have a cigarette in your hand. Leave it like a prayer stick."

So I did that. Imagine, I couldn't remember something that simple until she told me. I was not aware I was smoking. I placed a "prayer cigarette" at each place, my giveaway. I stayed a long time with each man. Dianne stood at my right and slightly behind me. I would tell her my buddy's story, how he was hurt or killed, the way it happened. I cried and said good-bye. I felt the depth of my love for each man, our deep level of brotherhood.

Though my heart ached, I felt something else at the Wall, too. I felt a sadness beyond what Dianne and I experienced personally. We were surrounded by layers of it. Sadness extended far beyond us. Standing at the Wall with her, I told NightBird what my buddies and I did together in 'Nam when we went on R and R . . . how we'd prepare for combat and what I could remember of what it was like to make it one more time back out of the combat zone. We'd cut loose and party, knowing pretty well that the next day, or the day after next, or whenever we were going right back into the CZ and do it again.

I talked about the ones who died because they were real fuck-ups and the ones who should never have died because they lived and fought so impeccably. It was just obvious that some of the brothers had written it that way. They bought it because it was their time.

It was strange seeing a bro's full name. I knew their first and last names and serial numbers and often a nickname. I laughed with NightBird at some funny middle names—one was Percival.

There was laughter in 'Nam, too, because that's the way it was with all those brothers. We shared all the good as well as all the hell and bullshit and horror. Part of my saying good-bye was needing to talk with them about what I had experienced with them. I didn't want just to say good-bye; I wanted to remember them the way they were. I needed to remember how they died, and I needed to say what I didn't get a chance to say. There were some real good times.

I was angry when I saw the movie *Platoon*. That's not what my guys were like, indifferent and estranged. That's not my unit. I hated the implication that all outfits over there were like that. *Platoon* didn't show any of the love or the caring. The only good time it showed was when the guys got stoned out of their minds. Sure, there was some of that in our unit, or getting drunk. Hell, there was a lot of getting drunk. With my outfit, though, there was also a deep brotherhood, a caring and knowing and understanding.

I'll share a story about what we did when we went on liberty after my buddy lost his woman back home. She'd found someone else and sent a "Dear John" letter. He was blown away by it. He took it hard. He was slipping into that place where a lot of the brothers went after rejection letters. He felt abandoned. We knew that if he stayed in that emotional space, he was gone. So we tried to pull him out of it. We worked our butts off talking at him—kidding and poking fun at him, trying to see if we could force him out of the bad place.

It more or less worked, but I could see he wasn't getting clear. So we took him on R and R, and all five of us got him a woman. This probably sounds silly now—I don't even know if NightBird understands it—but we all made love to her from our place of caring for him. We each went in and made love to her for him. It was our way to try to express our feelings of brotherhood and support for him, to help him see there could be other women.

It was a futile attempt. He died the next month feeling abandoned and betrayed by his woman. He said she was the only thread that had given his life meaning.

I don't believe that the story of the beauty in a marine outfit has yet been told—the humor and integrity, the loyalty and caring between the brothers. It's waiting to be written. Maybe it hasn't been told because it's just too precious to tell or share with anyone. There's also a part of me that doesn't think anyone will understand anyway. Unless you've lived it, you can't.

I've tried to create this kind of love between the brothers in the medicine lodge, but it never seems to develop to that level. There's something wrong and sick in society when the only time you can have that kind of tight brotherhood is when you are at war. Maybe that's what it takes. Maybe when you live constantly that close to the edge of death, you feel the love and loyalty at a deeper level. In the kind of unit I was in, life was precious, and so was death.

In some units you survive because you do your best to not get close to anyone. That's kind of what they tried to show in *Platoon* with the typical line grunts. But that's not the way it is in a specialist unit. There you stay alive because you know your buddies so well you tune into each other for survival. You live another day because your buddy sensed danger on your flank, and you did the same for him. You care and you stay close. And yet you can't acknowledge to yourself just how much you do care. If you do, your buddy's dying keeps you from doing your job.

I needed to go to the Wall because it gave me a chance to say good-bye without it getting me killed the next day. I couldn't say good-bye in 'Nam, because if I really felt how much I cared I wasn't going to get my own job done. That's what my visit to the Wall meant for me. It was a way to recall the good times and remember it all—to know I am alive because of them, particularly two of them.

At times it just shouldn't have happened. Once we were trying to get back to the helicopter. I was carrying one wounded marine, and my buddy was carrying another. We got them both on board and were ready to lift when we saw another marine carrying a wounded man. Ten yards from the chopper he got hit and they both went down. The helicopter was off the ground about three feet, and my buddy jumped down to help them, the same way he'd saved my life on another mission.

Fire was coming in and the gunner was yelling, "We got to pull!" I was yelling just to hold on, because he's going to make it! Then the two brothers he went after got hit again—raked—and he had to turn around and come back. He reached the helicopter and was crawling in just as we started to pull away.

"C'mon, Bro!" I shouted, as I yanked him toward me. Then he got it in the back of the head, and his brains blew all over me. . . . It just shouldn't happen that way. I mean, we were almost clear.

Those times hurt, but I guess when it's got your name on it, it's your name and it's your death. That's the way we came to see it, and that's the way it is. But it is hard when you're left holding your best friend.

I felt the presence of some of my buddies at the Wall. Several spirits were present. I prayed to Tunkashila. I prayed to the ancestor spirit world. I felt that most of my buddies were there. I saw three of them—two of the three I wanted to say good-bye to the most. I saw Raoul Guzman. I felt good about that. That was a healing for me. And Vincent.

It's obvious I need to go back to the Wall. I'm not clear of my pain even now. I doubt if it's ever gone. I don't know if you can ever clear it. You can smooth out the edges so it doesn't hurt the same, but it still comes to you, and when it does, you cry. I read that some of the brothers have actually gone back to Vietnam, to where they fought. I wonder what that would be like.

All of those men are part of me. I took their light when they went down. The eleven I said good-bye to had been in my platoon, in my squad. I was in 'Nam for four different tours, so I had to go to different places on the Wall. They are spread far apart because of the different years. It took a little hunting to find them all. God, it was good to connect with Raoul. I felt so grateful.

After I finished talking with a brother, NightBird would come forward and thank the man for fighting for something he believed in, for his country. "Dianne, he was fighting for you, hon'," I said. "And for me." Then she thanked the bro for that too.

One of the hardest things for me was knowing I was the only survivor from our original unit. There was one brother who lived, but he was killed in Central America recently. Of all the men in my personal squads for four tours of duty, I'm the only one who is still alive. I've wondered about that.

After we spoke with the eleven men, we crossed over to look at the sculpture of the three servicemen near the Wall. Dianne walked slightly behind me on my right. It was the way we had walked over there: she was flanking me, protecting me. She was beautiful. She did that from instinct. I felt so much love for her. Then we met Tim and

Ina and walked over to the Lincoln Memorial and sat on the steps.

I had previously been to the Lincoln Memorial. I like what that man had to say about America—the greatness of this country and what can cause its fall. I am moved by Lincoln, his words, and what he stood for. He was a man who walked his talk. I went to Lincoln to speak with him and pray with him. Then I walked down below and sat quietly on the steps with Tim. A motorcycle officer in boots and helmet approached me. I held a can of Dr. Pepper, which he must have thought was beer.

He said harshly, "Get rid of that alcohol, mister. Trash it!"

I looked at him calmly. "This is a Dr. Pepper, not a beer, officer," I said. "I've just been to the Wall and want to be alone. I have come up here with my buddy to talk with Mr. Lincoln and do some healing. You aren't part of that and never will be, so leave me alone."

The officer looked at me closely. He must have sensed something, because he apologized, then asked politely if I would put the can in a receptacle when I finished. He saw the situation and left.

Tim and I both laughed about it when the officer was gone. You know, you go all the way over there to 'Nam and go through all that shit, and then you still have to come back to that mentality. The world doesn't seem much changed as a result of any of it.

As I sat under Lincoln, I realized how much I had changed since Vietnam. I came back on such a fine edge, with so much pain and anger inside. There was as much anger as sadness—probably more so, because I was young and really believed in our cause. I felt betrayed later. Much of what brings the sadness and heartache from the loss of a loved one is the absurdity of it, the uselessness. I had as much anger as sadness and grief back then. It has taken many years to find an inner harmony.

I had no anger at the Wall that night. I felt only sadness and beauty and love. I felt Ed Parker and Grandfather Ding Poan and Grandfather Two Bears and Grandmother Spotted Fawn and all the great people who believed in me and gave to me. Time, the teachings of my people, and understanding from all the people of the Deer Tribe and others around the world have helped me make a separate peace.

❈❈❈ EPILOGUE ❈❈❈

CONTROVERSY WITH TRADITIONALISTS

There is no question about my tendency to create controversy with Native American traditionalists. I have been confronted, challenged, and threatened numerous times by various factions, individuals, and groups claiming to be guardians of traditional Native American customs. My problems with these people emerge because I speak openly about my beliefs and teachings, well aware that my words will bring criticism and anger from purists in Native American circles. People ask me, "Is nothing sacred to you, SwiftDeer?"

To me, only truth and knowledge are sacred. I do not respect a tradition that suppresses knowledge. I will confront any system, rule, or law that I believe squelches individual, autonomous freedom. I am consistent in my support of two sacred laws: "Everything is born of woman" and "Nothing shall be done to hurt the children." When I find traditional Native American customs ignoring these two laws, I part with tradition.

Though I did not know it at the time, my problems with Native American traditionalist medicine people started when I began my apprenticeship with Grandfather Two Bears Wilson in 1966. Like many Twisted Hairs, Grandfather lived a double life. In one aspect of his personality, he was a well-known Navajo elder and president of the Native American Church in the Navajo Nation. He worked hard for his people and was highly respected.

He was influential in the introduction of the medicine man training program at Rough Rock, Arizona. He saw the importance of training Navajos for this role so vital for his people. Grandfather Wilson knew that if the Navajo lost their singers, an important aspect of their culture would be gone forever. At the Rough Rock school, established singers were hired to train younger Navajos as medicine men, thereby ensuring that the Navajo ceremonies would not be lost when the old singers died. Younger men were subsidized by the United States government to take the training.

Grandfather also worked twelve years for the adoption of a policy ensuring that Navajo singers would be paid for the work they did in Southwest hospitals. Today, hospitals paying traditional Navajo singers for healing ceremonies inside U.S. medical institutions is a reality. This provides an invaluable blend of the "old" with modern medical procedures. In 1973, *Human Behavior* magazine featured Grandfather Tom Wilson's healing work in an article entitled "Medicine Man: The Wave of the Future."

This was the traditional and known part of Grandfather Tom Wilson. There was also the Tom Wilson called Two Bears, who was a Twisted Hair and a member of the Sundance Council of Elders. Other than his wives, his family did not know he was a Twisted Hair until the last three years of his life. They knew he was doing something in medicine but had no idea of the specifics. No one pressed to find out. Navajo people have an inherent suspicion of anyone "doing medicine." Their fear is that a skinwalker might turn on them from the dark side of sorcery.

I studied with Grandfather Two Bears for six years before I learned that he was also Tom Wilson, a family man who lived a hundred miles from our usual meeting place. I thought his home was the hogan we worked in near Tuba City, Arizona. I had no idea of his other identity. When he introduced me to his wife, Zoni, and his family six years after I began my apprenticeship, the conflict within the family flared. Most Wilson family members accepted me as a half-breed studying with Grandfather, but when he later adopted me into the family, I was resented because Grandfather taught me Navajo medicine. Some were particularly bitter when Grandfather passed some of his medicine bundles on to me.

I have stayed connected to members of the Wilson family for twenty-five years, since Grandfather presented me to them. They are mainly Tom and Zoni, when they were alive, and their six daughters, Irene, May, Sadie, Stella, Annie, Nellie, and Elsie. In the beginning, Grandfather's son, Tom Jr., was cool to me, but time and deeds have softened our relationship. Irene's husband, Tom Yellow Hair, is now supportive of me. The grandchildren and great-grandchildren are happy to receive us when we visit. We always bring gifts for the kids.

Annually, the Deer Tribe donates dozens of blankets from the Deer Tribe Sundance to the Wilson family. The blankets and foodstuffs are presented at our annual family reunion near Rough Rock, Arizona, where Grandfather and Zoni are buried. The immediate family distributes the blankets to other family members. It is a festive time, a day of feasting and remembering. In 1991, members of the Wilson family attended our Deer Tribe Sundance.

So my Navajo family became the first source of conflict with Native American people. Though time has healed the family tensions, I am still very attuned to the possibilities of misunderstandings and resentments that can develop within a family when an outsider is adopted into the clan.

I have also experienced conflict with some Navajo skinwalkers who have penetrated my circle and hurt me. I believe Navajo skinwalkers have the strongest medicine, black or white, in Native American sorcery. It has been near impossible to avoid all the arrows thrown at me. Because my lungs are vulnerable, I've been hit there.

Billy Turtle was at my place once when I was ill. After examining me, he concluded I'd been hit by a sorcerer's arrow. He went to work on me. Eventually, he sucked a tiny arrow from my chest. Spitting it into his hand, he studied it. "Looks like the work of a Navajo skinwalker."

Lifting it between thumb and forefinger, he handed it to NightBird.

"Is this what made the problem?" she asked

"He's gotta cut out Jakarta cigarettes, NightBird," said Billy Turtle. "Causes chest problem." He smiled.

NightBird held the little arrow in her hand wondering what to do with it. She looked very scared. Billy and I cracked up laughing.

Billy Turtle is a "roadman," a leader of the Native American Church. He is a southern Cheyenne respected by his people. In addition to his earthy humor, he has strong medicine. Three heart attacks have only made him stronger. Billy Turtle was with us that day to lead a Native American Church ceremony for the Deer Tribe.

It is ironic, yet understandable, that one source of criticism coming to me is from the Navajo family that adopted me. I'm also criticized because I teach medicine ways to non-full-bloods, or *metis* people. It is my sacred dream to do this.

It is noteworthy, and perhaps typical, that some of the people who are angry because I teach non-Indians do not live traditional medicine lives themselves and could not know what I am teaching. I respect a brother or sister who is living a traditional medicine life. I hear their criticism of me and understand it. Whites took everything they could from Native Americans in ruthless and unscrupulous ways. They still do, when it's possible. Nothing I have ever heard of is more ruthless or calculating than the ongoing murder, genocide, and heartless discrimination against Native Americans in every state of the Union. Too many white people in the Americas are driven by greed, ignorance, self-centered religious piousness, and the continuation of something called "manifest destiny," a concept developed by whites to justify the decimation of other cultures. These are historical and current realities.

I respect people insisting that their circles be exclusively Native American if they live their lives according to their traditions. I walk my talk as best I can and respect any person who does the same. I do not respect the persons criticizing me unless they live their lives with the integrity of their people's customs.

I believe we must share our medicine teachings with good-hearted mixed-blood people. The prophecy of the Red Road suggests that one day people of all colors will come together and pray together to determine how all people can be helped. These are the Rainbow People. Earth Mother has been hurt badly and needs everyone's help. She particularly needs the healing power of Native American ceremony.

A third criticism comes from within academia, the so-called scholars. This group includes anthropologists who say the Sweet Medicine Sundance Teachings do not originate with Native American Twisted Hairs because anthropological research has not verified it. This confrontation is similar to criticisms of authors Carlos Castaneda and Lynn Andrews, who as non-Native Americans have been attacked by traditionalist elements in academia. However, as with Castaneda and Andrews, the source of the teachings is chal-

lenged, leading to questions about my credibility, but the power of
my teachings seems to be accepted.

Several anthropologists in the United States have utilized Sweet
Medicine Sundance medicine wheels in their teachings. Anthropologist Joan Halifax does a brilliant merging of wheels from Turtle
Island with her extensive knowledge of and experience in Bud-
dhism. Joan is one of the top visionaries in America at what she
does. She brings world-class minds together from around the world
for interaction about planetary concerns.

Anthropologist Francis Huxley, an eminent member of the distinguished Huxley family, noted in the Western world for its scientific
and literary contributions, spoke to me one day. He had accompanied his wife, Adele Getty, when she traveled with me on a medicine
journey to Tangalunda, Mexico, in 1987. I liked him very much and
admired his brilliance and wit.

"SwiftDeer," he said, "these teachings are excellent, top-notch!
I like them!" Then he looked at me with his penetrating gaze and
asked, "Why don't you drop this Twisted Hairs Council thing and
give yourself the credit you deserve and become famous?"

I understood his meaning and laughed. Wouldn't I like to, I
thought, but that would make big trouble with the council. I looked
at him for a moment, thinking.

"Francis," I said. "You and I have different roles in life. You and
your family are the guardians of this time, of the *now*. In a sense,
your family has been doing that for generations. As a shaman, my
role is different. My teachings come from storytellers from another
dimension. I speak for many times."

Francis looked at me fiercely. "Hmmph," he said and smiled.

I can't do what Francis suggested, of course, because the teachings do *not* originate with me. They come from twelve teaching
shields gradually being released by the elders of the Twisted Hairs
Council. I am not the source of the teachings.

Recently, at the request of the Deer Tribe, I prepared the sources
of all of my teachings, in addition to those received from the council.
I included Grandfather Two Bears, Grandmother Spotted Fawn,
Martha Spins Fire Eagle, the Grandmothers' Council, Hyemeyohsts
Storm, who passed me the Star Maiden's Circle, and others.

The Twisted Hairs Council of Elders exists. The council has its origin in the Canis Major constellation, specifically from the planets within the reaches of the star Sirius. The original council met around a sacred configuration composed of twelve full-sized quartz-crystal skulls and one amethyst skull known as the Arc of the Wise. This is according to a legend taught me by Grandfather Two Bears, as it was to his teacher before him.

Anthropologists who are familiar with the Cherokee Nation know the legends of the Arc of the Wise. Anna Mitchell-Hedges of Ontario, Canada, is presently a keeper of one of these skulls. For many anthropologists, the legend of the arc is an "interesting story," a myth of the "natives." For me, it is the history of my people.

I meet members of the Twisted Hairs Council in the fifth dimension to receive Sweet Medicine Sundance Teachings. If you do not believe in the fifth dimension or a dreamscape, you will have a problem with the history of my people. If you do not believe human beings are descended from the stars, you may have a problem with the history of many cultures. Even Christian mythology relies on the guidance of a star for wise men, kings, and shepherds to locate the stable in Bethlehem where Christ was born. The Twisted Hairs Council also meets regularly in the third dimension and is scheduled to meet on this plane for its twelfth-year medicine conference in August of 1994.

The harshest criticism of me comes from Native American traditionalists who are upset because I permit and encourage women on their moon cycles to enter my sweatlodge ceremonies, to dance in Deer Tribe Sundances, and to work with medicine tools. It is said that I do not honor the Sacred Pipe because I do these things.

I am not against all the old ways, but I have discovered through experience that some ceremonies have been more complete simply because women on their moon have added power to the ceremony. A woman in harmony with her menstrual flow can be an important resource to a ceremony, as the menstrual cycle is attuned to the major cycles in nature. Alignment and harmony with the cycles of nature are important to the alchemy of all healing ceremonies.

Traditionalists insist we should covet the dogmas of the past. They suppress and shun new knowledge primarily to protect the old

ways. I am convinced that one of the reasons my teachings are
ignored by traditionalists is because acknowledging them means
change for some of the old ways. Old dogma would have to die. In
this sense, I bring death. I am the Death Bringer. Understandably, I
am a threat.

I agree that most of the old ways must not change. They must be
kept for the ancestors and the identity of our people. I suggest, however, we do not have to hold to *all* the traditional ways.

I am puzzled that traditionalists do not confront me directly.
They do not face me personally across the pipe, which is the true
Indian way, the way of my people. Instead, I hear criticism indirectly.
A Chumash elder I admired broke our relationship without a word
to me while I was away on a medicine journey. I hear his criticism
from others, but he says nothing to me. I am told my use of New Age
terminology offends his elders, and because I call my apprentice
Batty ThunderBear and my wife, NightBird, sweatlodge chiefs, his
elders requested that he "break the blanket" with me.

The truth is, Batty ThunderBear and Dianne NightBird *are* sweatlodge chiefs. They are both full medicine people in the Deer Tribe.
They have more than two thousand hours of intensive training in
ceremonial work and have choreographed and led hundreds of healing sweats in the United States and Europe. They are both impeccable medicine healers. In addition, Batty ThunderBear is a lodge chief
in Europe.

One Native American medicine man did bring his personal criticism to me. In May of 1984, Wallace Black Elk, a Sioux lineage carrier,
spoke with me in Ojai, California. "SwiftDeer," he said, "I do not
understand what you are doing. By everything I've heard, you don't
follow the sacred teachings of my people. It is said you ignore old
and proven ways, basic to what we believe in. I acknowledge that
what you do works for you. That you have strong medicine is appar-
ent. However, I cannot support you, because in your medicine you
turn away from the traditional ways of my people." Wallace is the
only elder who has ever spoken to me personally. I respect him for
approaching me directly. Wallace Black Elk is a good and great man.

A few years ago, Wallace himself came under attack from Lakota
purists because his path is to share traditional customs with people

of good heart from any race. It is a tribute to this great man's integrity that he continues his role as Lakota Sundance chief each year for persons of any skin color, if they prepare themselves with good heart.

Wallace's Sundance is impeccable, of the highest discipline and integrity. The dance is traditional Lakota. I know of no Native American who walks his talk for his people more impeccably than Wallace. His life is committed to his people. But because his personal vision for his people does not coincide with that of *all* traditional Lakota medicine people, he is criticized. Every year two or three people dance in both Wallace's Sundance and the Deer Tribe Sundance.

I believe most Native American traditionalists do not understand the true purpose of tradition. When undertaken properly, tradition is a practice from the past to guide people in the present for balance. It exists to help people understand truths for living in harmony and order, with purposeful direction for tomorrow. Yet few Native American traditionalists dare to view tradition this way.

Tradition changes as soon as you pick up a gourd. When the gourd or drum is lifted for ceremony, tradition becomes alive. Anything alive must change. That is a law of life. The moment you pick up a gourd for ceremony, something is going to change. This will come quickly or slowly, but in the end, it is going to change. Change is the law of the universe. It must meet the needs of the people in the present, or it is valueless as a guide for the future. It must be alive and attuned with current times. Wallace Black Elk keeps tradition alive and vibrant with people of good heart, even though they may not be Native Americans.

Historically, Native American people have been caretakers for Grandmother Earth. For hundreds of years, we lived in harmony and balance with the resources of the Earth. Today, we are no longer good environmentalists. Native Americans sometimes betray Grandmother Earth, exploiting her for profit and greed just like whites.

Grandfather Two Bears wept about this. He battled the Peabody Mines Corporation his entire adult life. Peabody employs many Navajo Indians. They are hired to exploit the planet and because of tribal poverty seem to have little choice. Today, millions of gallons of Arizona desert water transport Peabody coal to distribution plants in the Southwest.

My heart is aligned with Native American people, and I am saddened by the changes I see in our values. I love the Native American culture. Its basic values offer the only hope I see for the future of the planet. I have deep compassion for my people. We have been raped continually for more than two hundred years—physically, emotionally, and spiritually. Still we survive and prevail.

My love for Native American culture lives in everything I teach and say. I am a Sundancer in every aspect of my life. However, I relate strongly to Chippewa teacher Sun Bear's statement that he was interested in a philosophy only if it grows corn to feed the children! It is critical to our times that traditionalism be practical and able to "grow corn."

Making Sweet Medicine Sundance Teachings available to metis people is critical for the planet. Many people are needed to undo the damage already done to the Earth. I teach the use of "moon cycle" power to my followers for one reason: the knowledge I give them is needed to help heal and nurture the planet. I allow women on their moon to sundance because I know they increase the power of the dance. And that helps the planet. Women can be awesomely powerful! I invite those who disagree to join me across the pipe to talk in the old way. I know that my teachings are aligned with cosmic and universal laws and demonstrate the proper use of energy.

Traditional Native American leaders have deep, powerful, and needed leadership resources for the planet. But they must give up tribal mythologies that hurt the planet in order for their leadership and vision to be released to help everyone.

I realize that some changes are happening. History shows their own ancestors changed Native American tradition to align with the times. I am not invested in being accepted personally, but I do ask that my teachings be acknowledged. I request that traditionalists who criticize me look at the Sweet Medicine Sundance Teachings for themselves and decide whether they offer help for Grandmother Earth.

There are no native people with more integrity and knowledge than my mother's ancestors, the Tsalagi Aniyunwiya, or Cherokee. There is depth in their teachings. The power in my medicine comes when I merge with them and they live in me. They are my people. I am rich with my roots. I *am* my people. I also love the Irish in me as much as I love the Native American.

However, I am more than the sum of my heritage. I am a two-legged human being with responsibilities to the planet. My concern for the well-being of Grandmother Earth is more important than my appreciation of my roots. If being true to my Cherokee heritage meant stepping back in time two hundred years, ignoring the threat to Grandmother Earth today, I would choose to let go of my tradition and heritage as a Cherokee. This may seem harsh, but for me, it is a reality. Many people do not comprehend the gravity of our planet's condition.

I see a tremendous waste of planetary resources because traditional Turtle Island people quarrel with each other. If representatives of all native peoples would learn the many ways to combine our knowledge of medicine harmoniously, the planet would receive a tremendous boost. There is power available in Native American integrity and cosmology beyond anything we have experienced. If Native Americans are unable to unify and integrate, they are not different from Catholics, Protestants, Muslims, and Jews who squabble over the "true way" while resources for planetary leadership are diluted.

Too many traditional spokespeople say they have the "true way." It is impossible for any tribe to have the one true way. The ways of the universe are myriad, and all of them have beauty. We won't heal this planet until we agree about this and stop the warring.

The universe is a great wheel. It has many spokes—many paths, many ways, and many truths. All of them lead to the center. Each person must find a starting direction he calls his truth and point himself on his path to the center of the Wheel of Life. The light of the children's fire burns at the center of the wheel. The moment people make the commitment to walk toward the light, speaking and sharing their truth, *their* path becomes their way. This is why there cannot be only *one* way.

Some traditionalists malign whites endlessly for events of the past. Many prefer complaining to doing. I call this the "poor me" Indian syndrome. It is the nature of some people to blame, whine, and avoid the focus necessary for change. The "poor me" syndrome will never truly help even one Native American.

The destruction, demoralization, and decimation of Indians and Indian culture by whites is well documented. Education, legislation, and action to block its continuation today is necessary. However, ongoing bitterness and lamentation about the past becomes useless and self-destructive. It is poor use of energy. Knowledge of the past is necessary for consciousness and action in the present and the future, but the energy invested in the past is waste.

My great-grandmother and her mother suffered on the Trail of Tears. Yet I never saw Grandmother angry about it. She stayed aware of what helped her family in the present. Anger about history was not important. I'm sure that if she thought anger would help her people, she'd have been very angry. That was her way. She wept and let it go, though she never forgot. How could she? Her clan, the Cherokee Raper family, owned thousands of acres of land in North Carolina before the Trail of Tears. Only four thousand of twenty-two thousand Cherokee people survived the forced relocation. That's a real horror story. Grandmother said simply, "We can't change what happened."

I don't really give a good rat's ass if my great-grandfather and your great-grandfather killed each other in some great raid, ambush, or siege a hundred and fifty years ago. So what? To me what matters in the 1990s is that you and I are brothers and sisters and care for each other. I can't change any of that tragedy from all those past years. I see the injustices of the past, and I am not insensitive to the pain. I am not callous to suffering and destruction. However, misfortunes and mistreatment hit people everywhere they gather on the planet, not just Native American people!

Today I feel a strong urgency that Native American spiritual leaders get their separate acts together and walk their talk in harmony with each other. We must work together to help the planet and quit the warring and separation. If we don't, we may not have a planet.

A Sundance that excludes people working for Grandmother Earth because of skin color is not a true Sundance. Until our spiritual leaders unite on behalf of *all* people, I will not concern myself with their criticism of me. I'm going to do what I have vowed to do. I will continue to get the knowledge of the Sundance teachings out to all of the people of the planet I am able to reach—to the Rainbow people of all colors and creeds who quest after knowledge to make better tomorrows for themselves and the Earth.

That is my pipe. It is my vision. It is the heart of my sacred dream and my Sundance vow. To my dying day, I'll talk and walk behind that vow. In this way, I have spoken.

Awinesticah. Ho!

It is reported that on July 16, 1992, in the underground city of Olmectican in the sacred kivas of the Twisted Hairs Metis Medicine Society Council of Elders, Harley SwiftDeer Reagan was sealed and locked down as an elder in the thirteenth gateway as a full member of the Council of Elders. He was coronated as the heyoehkah war chief of the Council and Circle of Law of the Elders. His official status as of spring 1993 with the council is as the eighteenth dreamers' nagual of the Eighteenth Feathered Winged Serpent Wheel of Turtle Island.

✦✦✦ APPENDIX A ✦✦✦
THE SECRET LODGES

Traditionally, all secret apprenticeship lodges are designed to increase the initiate's self-responsibility as he or she moves toward personal enlightenment. Personal enlightenment lodges are known to have existed for more than three thousand years. The lodges I will now describe are as they were given to me by Grandfather Two Bears. He says their form was developed in Palenque, Mexico, around A.D. 1150 and has been passed on by many generations of Twisted Hairs.

The rattlesnake, a traditional depiction of Grandfather Sun in physical form, was chosen as the symbol for these lodges because the snake physically embodies the process of enlightenment. The snake erases personal history by shedding its skin on a yearly basis. It adds a year of maturity to its tail with each shedding. In a sense, it carries its gateway movement in its patterns. The diamond pattern on the rattlesnake's back contains all major architectural symbols: the circle, the parallelogram, and double triangles. One might say that metaphorically, we can see our transformational path in the snake's patterns, beginning at its tail and moving toward the head, or temple, as symbolized by the diamond pattern.

Within the Deer Tribe we identify six "apprentice lodges." Each lodge provides a structure and theme for the Deer Tribe apprentice to develop knowledge on the path to enlightenment.

THE GREEN LODGE

The *intent* of the Green Lodge is to provide informational meetings about the Deer Tribe and the gateway ceremonial experience. It includes basic introductory workshops and elemental exposure to the numerous keys and wheels that come from twelve ancient shields of knowledge.

PRE–RED LODGE

The *intent* in the Pre–Red Lodge is to wake up, to help you find your heart, to become a "one-hearted person." At this level, you begin to take responsibility for your circle. Your words and deeds begin to become congruent.

The *process* at the Pre–Red Lodge level is threefold: (1) The basic teachings are examined so that you, as an initiate student, can find your "Path of Heart." (2) The Pre–Red Lodge provides the prerequisite knowledge, an overview, of the gateway ceremonial steps. (3) You are given help to find the way to your own commitment and discipline.

The *end result* sought in the Pre–Red Lodge is autonomy. You find your own unique ways of connecting with your medicine tools and your peers. You learn to understand your agreements with them. This is when the magick of the path begins, for with true autonomy, whatever you integrate into the luminous aspect of your being becomes an extension of yourself. When you have established a heart connection and understand your agreements, you integrate other luminosities and expand within sacred law. This is the moment you know that the teachings become the "path of heart." It's like coming home.

THE RED LODGE

This lodge is referred to as the "Truth School." Its *intent* is to gain awareness of your own individuality and uniqueness and to realize at a deep level that the price of knowledge is commitment. Often in this lodge the student learns through pain, because he or she often does not yet understand that "not understanding" or "not keeping agreements" hurts the personality.

The *process* of the Red Lodge is applying the elemental teachings and learning the alchemy of the first and second gateway ceremonies. Here you begin to understand your *shideh*, or shadow self. You begin to see that all blocks to emotional integration bring discord. This is an internal awareness.

The *end result* sought in the Red Lodge is entrance into the "Portal of Truth." As a student, you learn how much you don't know. You also learn that your physical body must deal with the heart connections you have made. With this awareness, you are ready to enter the Black Lodge.

THE BLACK LODGE

The Black Lodge is also referred to as the "Mystery School." Its *intent* is for the student to learn to understand the mystery of the truth that *the body is inside the mind.* Our physical abilities can expand only when we stop thinking "my body knows" and realize that our body knows only what our mind tells it.

The *process* of the Black Lodge is experiencing the third gateway ceremonies and the warrior task assignments. These help the student experience death. Students begin to challenge the illusion that physical substance is total reality.

The *end result* sought in the Black Lodge is physical mastery and the beginning application of the teachings of magic and alchemy: allowing the body to experience itself stretching past the mind's limits so one can truly learn about the cycles of death, life, change, and rebirth. The student is learning to learn through pleasure and discovering how to change a personal identity based on pain. In this phase, you are building your personal and inner "Sundance Lodge."

THE WHITE LODGE

The White Lodge is also known as the "Memory School." Its *intent* is threefold: (1) to deepen your heart connections and be able to verbalize your agreements with the Four Worlds, your medicine items, and your teachers; (2) to step into sobriety and leadership on your path; and (3) to empower your own individuality, autonomy, and free will. All this requires opening the "portal of memory," learning to coordinate clarity and change patterns through perfect timing. These concepts are presented both cognitively and experientially in the White Lodge.

The *process* of the White Lodge is the participation in the fourth and fifth gateways experience. Students at this level are full "road people," taking the knowledge out to their own areas and teaching by example. The process of this lodge includes establishing your agreements with your medicine tools and deciding what you want the tool, as an extension of your energy, to do. At this level, you can demand that your medicine tools do certain things because they are an integral part of your matrix. The creation of your "soul bundle" is also a significant part of the process in the White Lodge.

The *end result* of this lodge includes the understanding that *organization empowers freedom*. One learns to implement the awareness. Nature is the best teacher of organization. The soul bundle, the Twenty Count, and the Star Maiden Circle are primary tools to facilitate ways of organizing freedom. From the teaching of the Twenty Count, one learns that everything in the universe has order. From the Star Maiden Circle, cycles and patterns of the two-leggeds are understood. For the student, organization means placing things in a hierarchy or pattern. By changing the pattern to fit the needs of a given moment—for example, opening the portal of memory—one gains freedom.

THE GOLD LODGE

The Gold Lodge is also called the "Mirror School." Its *intent* is to gain the sobriety needed to do sorcery and shamanism. The *process* of this lodge is the mastery of all your medicine tools. It means working in the sixth and seventh gateways, experiencing the "shamanic deaths" that miror the deepest levels of the self.

The *end result* sought in the Gold Lodge is learning to access, feel, and understand the source of the life force and to experience your connection to it. Everything is everything. In other words, each thing is connected to everything else. In the Gold Lodge, you recognize that your power is related to your creative energy and that a creative act connects you to all things in nature. Mental images can then be brought to form because power is always present—it only seeks a force. Your sense of power bonds with you if you recognize it and can hold its image in the movment of all things.

THE PAINTED ARROW LODGE

The *intent* of this lodge is to know the "lodge of freedom," to shatter the "mirror of self-reflection." It is the freedom to choose with power, to know your destiny and be able to walk your path. The *process* is experiencing your transformation through the challenge of the eighth through tenth ceremonial gateways of the lodge.

Movement through the various lodges is always accompanied by levels of consciousness. Those in the Red Lodge have consciousness of neither fate nor destiny. Students living a Black Lodge reality know they have a fate, but don't know what it is. Those who live a White Lodge reality know their fate but won't accept responsibility for it. Those living in a Gold Lodge reality accept their fate and recognize their destiny but fight it. Those who reach a Painted Arrow Lodge reality recognize their fate, accept it, and try to walk their path of destiny.

In the overall context of movement within the lodges, the Red Lodge symbolizes enlightenment at the lowest level, wherein the student learns to crawl. In the Black Lodge, one learns to walk. In the White Lodge, the student runs. In the Gold Lodge, one learns to fly like the feathered winged serpent. Finally, in the Painted Arrow Lodge, one attains enlightenment and wisdom and is no longer considered a student of the lodge structure.

~~~ APPENDIX B ~~~
GENITAL SENSE
OF SELF

Masters in all secret lodges know that any path to enlightenment must include experiences and teachings that free the life force in the personality of the student. The limiting belief systems of the initiate must be challenged and dissolved. Though it has not always been true, most personalities in Western culture today are attitudinally blocked and armored in their "genital sense of self." Today's image makers—the parents and family, the church, the schools, and the government—enforce numerous sexual rules and laws, do's and don'ts, that are repressive to the life force. Sexuality is encoded and equated with pain, punishment, sin, and fear. In fact, sexuality is the primary target for the three most known suppressive energies to the life force of human beings: guilt, blame, and shame.

All paths to enlightenment include sexual teachings designed to help students gain knowledge and experience that will reencode *positively* all attitudes and beliefs that are repressive to the life force. The genital sense of self must be free of repressive and negative molding and armoring for the student to advance on the path to enlightenment.

The genital sense of self holds our awareness of being alive. It is our aliveness, our vitality, and our primal sense of being. It controls our pleasure response. It is the foundation of our "temple of self." It is, of course, also the place of our greatest wounding. Repression of sexual energy, the *prana*, the *ki*, or the *orgone*, is the dominant and recurring cause of all ill health, depression, disease, and death.

Traditionally, most native people knew this intuitively and consciously. They included puberty ceremonies and rituals in the upbringing of their young people that precluded the possibility that guilt, blame, and shame would repress the vital life force. Sexual vitality was a source of pleasure and renewal with them. They regarded it as one of their sacred resources, a gift from the Great Spirit, and passed this attitude on to their children.

Grandmother Spotted Fawn was aware of the importance of what she was doing with me when she took me to Martha Spins Fire Eagle for a sexual education that would encode beauty and pleasure in my genital sense of self. Grandmother had seen the effects of sexual repression with her people. She had experienced their loss of spirit and vitality. I'm sure with me she hoped to keep a spark of the old ways alive. She was right. The sexual teachings Martha Spins Fire Eagle passed to me are the nucleus of our lodge teachings about sexuality. Our *chuluaqui quodoushka* spiritual sexuality classes are designed to help our students develop a genital sense of self that includes freedom, pleasure, creativity, and personal integrity. We strive to help our students live free of guilt, blame, and shame.

Because it is our genital sense of self that is most severely affected by our conditioning, we move slowly in our spiritual sexuality classes. Initially, people tell their stories. The stories of pain and sexual suffering and abuse must be told; you can't reencode sexual attitudes from pain to pleasure when people feel guilt and shame. We bond with each other. We build trust. We share. Gradually we reshape the genital sense of self so its identity is aligned with pleasure and vitality, excitement and freedom.

Susan's story is typical. She came to our sexual spirituality class to be "healed sexually." Her marriage had failed. She was seeing "monsters" who insisted she was to blame. She had never been orgasmic in her life. She reported she never had any idea how to be a sexual being. As a child, she was left numerous times with an aunt and uncle who took her to bed with them and abused her sexually. She knew something very bad was happening to her, yet she was seldom touched or shown affection at any other time in her life. A conflict developed in her child psyche. She enjoyed being touched sexually, yet she sensed that the experience was something evil.

Susan, of course, felt she could not tell her parents about her experiences with her mother's favorite sister. "They wouldn't have believed me. I'd have been told I was making it up. If they had believed me, they would have punished me for causing an embarrassment in the family. I began to withdraw. That's when the voices started. 'You are bad,' they said."

In time, Susan's aunt and uncle introduced her to their teenage son, who invited his friends to have sex with her. Her nightmare continued for several years. Susan felt dirty. She was ashamed. "It must have been my fault," she said after telling her story.

"How could it be your fault?" I asked. "You were six years old—a child. Your aunt and uncle were your parents' age, and their son was a teenager."

"I don't know," she said. "It doesn't make sense. But I feel responsible. It's because I liked it. It felt good. That's why I'm responsible. God punished me—still does—because I liked what I knew was evil. It's really crazy. I knew I was too little to stop what they did, but I felt it happened because God was punishing me for liking what was evil."

Susan is bright. She has a master's degree in special education. But she can't work in her field. She's unable to sleep. She has nightmares. Tight bands of muscular armor protect her from feeling. During the weekend of the quodoushka class, she cried for the first time in her memory. Afterward, she was given follow-up support and specific ceremonies to help her let go of guilt, shame, and self-blame. She will attend more classes. Her healing will be slow.

We help our students understand the importance of a full orgasm to the health of the personality. They learn the importance and characteristics of four levels of orgasm. Students learn that as early as the seventh to ninth month in the womb, we began to experience orgasm. As spirits that have taken on physical form, our personalities are aware of their physical substance through their own genital touch and orgasmic responses. Genital stimulation brings us alive. In the womb, we need it to help us turn around for our birthing. In most instances, an infant is born with a positive, flowing, vibratory genital sense of the self.

In his book *The Function of the Orgasm*, Wilhelm Reich suggests that the orgasm is essential to our health and evolution. He is correct. The "primitive" people's rites of passage expressed a knowing about this long before Reich. Much early ceremony and ritual in a young person's development was empowered by the elders' knowledge of the importance of the gift of sexual vitality.

All our students know that the image makers punish and repress us severely in our genital sense of self. They are drawn to the healing energies of our spiritual sexuality workshops. The severity of their sexual repression leads to armoring and plates of amnesia and anesthesia, which shut off the level of pleasure they could and deserve to experience.

The armoring of the genital sense of self is primarily focused on the first four chakras. Attention must be given to help the student regain chakra vitality. "Pain tapes" become locked in the buttocks, thighs, legs, and diaphragm. This armoring takes place during the first eight years of life. We are trained to diminish our breath. Our workshops introduce the "fire breath" and other powerful deep-breathing practices to repattern the shallow breathing that often accompanies sexual repression.

During our formative years, our bodies take on particular characteristics to ensure survival based on how we react to our social molding, sculpting, and armoring. Our bodily and muscular reactions can be called the stance or posture of our character structure. Body armoring shuts down our artistic, receptive, and creative energies. Armoring limits our freedom of expression, of adventuring forth into the world with pure energy in motion. Our creative potentials are dumped into the shadow as our bodies are numbed by armoring.

The armoring also affects the balance of success or failure of the personality, our sense of beauty or ugliness. The armoring affects what we will decide to be, our sacred dream. It determines the beauty of our giveaway and influences the product of our "medicine." It contains our interconnectedness to all forms of all things.

Our genital sense of self defines our relationship to all that exists. It contains our life force potentiality. It shapes our rate of aging and dominates our attitudes about old age and death. Our genital sense of self contains our experience of pleasure.

I believe that all young people should be taught that the Great Spirit's design of our genitals ensures an experience of pleasure through our capacity to have orgasm. It is brilliant and logical from the Great Spirit's point of view that what brings us genital pleasure also contributes to our physical well-being. The Great Spirit designed us with a mons gland, or clitoris, for the sole purpose of pleasure and a full orgasmic regeneration of life-force energy.

Through sensation, intuition, thinking and feeling, as channeled through our genital sense of self in supportive teachings, we find a new identity. We give primary attention to teaching the "eight lovers masks" in the sexual spirituality classes, for these masks enable us to let go of past pain and reencode the beauty, vitality, pleasure, and joy that are naturally intended to accompany the adventure of living.

≋ APPENDIX C ≋
CHULUAQUI QUODOUSHKA: SPIRITUAL SEXUALITY

Some of the most important of all the Sweet Medicine Sundance Teachings are about *chuluaqui quodoushka*. These teachings are presented in three-day intensive workshops in spiritual sexuality sponsored and organized by healing professionals and other interested individuals throughout the United States and Europe. Based on traditional Native American sexual-initiation ceremonies that, according to Mayan scholar Hunbatz Men, were introduced in North America by the Maya, these workshops are designed to help participants identify early sexual "pain tapes" and develop a positive sense of the "genital self." Knowledge about sexuality and lovemaking and learning to integrate the powerful sexual energies all two-leggeds are born with is the theme of the workshops.

These spiritual sexual teachings stress a harmonious balance with all aspects of the self. We do not see any relationships sustaining themselves with excitement and richness if personalities are not balanced within themselves. We teach and encourage people to relate to others from the center of their being. When two people dance in each other's hearts, the relationship is honored by the Great Spirit. When they dance in each other's hearts, they breathe together, they implode and explode in union, and together they create something greater than their separateness. They have union with the "Higher Self," and they dance with the energies of the chuluaqui quodoushka. They are sexual with themselves, each other, and the universe.

Chuluaqui is the Cherokee word for "energy" in all forms of all things. It is experienced as pure light, as image, as spirit, and as substance. Some consider it the Tao, but it is much more than that. It is the everything that is nothing, and it is the nothing that is in all things. It is prana and chi and orende and orgone combined. The chuluaqui is that energy that allows all things to manifest from spirit into substance and back into spirit.

Quodoushka means that any time two equal chuluaqui energies come together and merge and exchange and intermingle, something will emerge from their union that is greater than the sum of the parts. This kind of exchange in form is both implosive and explosive, and in humans it is experienced most commonly through breath. When we breathe together, we merge. In our merging as we breathe, we implode and we explode together in an ever-extending and expanding energy of movement. That movement gives birth to something new. At the very minimum, what is birthed are knowledge and pleasure—or this can be experienced as pleasure in knowledge.

A seed of corn planted in the earth may grow, bearing ears of corn that feed the people. Through a natural quodoushka process of implosion and explosion, one seed becomes many, although the ears of corn have come from one seed. Similarly, when an apple falls to the ground and rots, many trees may grow bearing apples. Clearly, the apples come from many trees. Yet they have their source in one. That is the metaphor of quodoushka. It means the spiritual and sexual energy of the universe merging, imploding, exploding, and becoming greater than the sum of the initial parts. That is chuluaqui quodoushka. Chuluaqui is the energy that gives life to all things. Quodoushka means the sacred marriage, the sacred union of the energies. Our quodoushka classes help us learn to understand the sacred marriage, the sacred union of the energies.

In our medicine-wheel view of two-leggeds, we see emotions as water, the body as earth, the mind as wind, the spirit or personality as fire, and the void as our soul. The soul is the catalyst for these four aspects. It enables the human to find harmony in emotions, body, mind, and spirit. Within the soul lives our sexuality. This means that if the human is spiritual, he or she is also sexual. Sexuality and spirituality in the human are synonymous. One cannot be spiritual without being sexual, nor can one be sexual and not spiritual. This concept, the chuluaqui quodoushka view of sexuality in the universe, should be experienced as a natural flow in our life activities, contributing to our health and happiness. However, most of us have

experienced powerful sexual repressive institutions in our upbringing, led primarily by religions that suggest spirituality and sexuality
are opposing aspects of our being.

I have seen much harm done to human beings by church man-
dates stating that one seeking the highest level of spiritual development must abstain from sexual activity. Such a position is
suppressive to our natural creative energies. According to many
church leaders, sex is evil or bad, except in a sanctioned context.
We are told not to make love except to procreate.

I find these edicts contrary to the way the Great Spirit made us.
Certainly they are in opposition to nature and the law of quodoushka, which is the one to the many and the many to the one—an axiom
of magickal law. Any organization advocating abstinence from sexuality is contrary to the natural movement of all forms of energy.

The Great Spirit gave us free will and orgasm, a significant
delineation from the other worlds of the mineral, plant, animal, and
ancestors. If we deny our catalyst energy, our sexuality, we invite our
water, earth, fire, and wind to implode and explode out of propor-
tion. Without sexuality, we go out of alignment. We also go out of
harmony and balance and become prone to disease.

All religions seem to agree that we are here to seek enlightenment. The various churches teach and guide us more or less from the
principle of "As above, so below." We are taught that the "Above" is
perfection and is our source. We are encouraged to seek harmony
with the Above. To repress sexual activity is a denial of the true
nature of the Above, which is in constant, never-ending union and
ebb and flow of orgasmic quodoushka energy. If we truly are going
to live the "As above, so below," we must not deny the true way the
Great Spirit created us as beings. As humans we must increasingly
learn the ways to allow orgasmic energy to help us come into alignment. Physiological orgasm is an important gift from the Great Spirit
to help keep our bodies aligned and healthy.

I know that the greatest damage done emotionally, spiritually,
physically, and sexually to human beings comes from religious
dogma suppressing human sexuality. Much of the good the church
does is eradicated by its sexual teachings. Repression of human sexuality has caused more illness, disease, and ignorance than any other

single influence. Our teaching on the medicine path is that the degree to which you are nonorgasmic and nonexpressive of your sexuality will demonstrate itself in your lack of health and the amount of disease and sickness you will have in your body.

The value of quodoushka teachings is that they offer people a way to break the old sexual myths surrounding them. Participants are given the knowledge to challenge the ignorance and superstitions, the moral, ethical, and religious rules and laws with which we are raised. People are asked to not *believe* anything that is taught to them. Rather, they are encouraged to take what is presented and weigh it with other sexual teachings they have received and find out what is true for themselves. It is important that they come to *know* rather than believe.

On the medicine path we acknowledge only two truths in our belief system: "Everything is born of woman" and "Nothing shall be done to hurt the children." To be considered sacred, all laws and rules must come from these two truths. We do not consider repression of sexuality for any reason as coming from either of these two sacred beliefs. And so with our quodoushka teachings, we help our students find their own enlightenment. Each person's way to God must come through him or herself. In the words of one of my teachers, "We are not all here for the same reasons, nor have we come here for the same lessons. We do not all ask the same questions, nor will the same answers provide solutions for everyone."

For me, the quodoushka teachings are at the heart of learning to find our own "path of heart." All human beings must find their own path of heart to become fully human. That is an extremely important and challenging thing for humans to do. And of course it is something people find difficult to do. For example, if two individuals feel that it is their path of heart to come together and exchange sexual energy, make love, and even live together without the official sanction of the church, they will be criticized by the church and by those who follow the church doctrines.

I would personally support a church recognition of the beauty of two people coming together to make love if they dance in each other's hearts, whether for a "quickie" or an extended relationship.

Their heart space is of primary importance. From my viewpoint, a marriage exists when two people come together with one heart. That is the old way, the way of personal beauty. Lovemaking is the consummation of love. The sacramentalization of the physical is love. There is no clergy involved. Love is fulfilled in marriage, and marriage is the consummation of love.

APPENDIX D
HEART PLEASURING

One of the most valuable things Martha Spins Fire Eagle taught me during my time with her was the chuluaqui "heart pleasuring exercise." At the time, I couldn't see why she stressed my learning to self-pleasure in this special way, when she was there to make love with me. Today I understand. Martha Spins Fire Eagle knew that the quality of my orgasm would be a key to my creativity. How well one actualizes one's personal dream is related to the level of one's orgasm. Third- and fourth-level orgasms, those of the highest and most intense levels, are desirable resources for the health and well-being of all aspects of the personality.

Heart pleasuring is an important key to the third- or fourth-level orgasm. You can make love every day, but if your orgasm is only at the first level, you might do better having a fourth-level orgasm alone once a week or even once a month. Self-pleasuring increases the level of the orgasm, which is a key to self-actualization in all aspects of one's life. One's sexual *orende*, or sexual vitality, determines the vitality of the entire personality, because it is in the first chakra. If the energy does not move there, how can it move to the rest of the chakras? The first chakra is the fire, the starting place. If that chakra is not open, the others are not going to move as well as they could.

Many people feel they are deprived of the opportunity for a high sexual orende if they are not in a sexual relationship—and sometimes they make bad choices about partners for this reason. Martha Spins Fire Eagle taught me that through heart pleasuring one can have a high sexual orende by making love with the self. It is part of my pledge to her to teach people to heart pleasure. I am not talking about emotional orende, though one can literally feel a connection with the universe and the Great Spirit through expanded heart pleasuring.

Many people believe that celibacy means abstinence. In reality, celibacy means to celebrate. In essence, when one does the *chuluaqui* heart exercise, the self-pleasuring exercise of *quodoushka*, the activity is an act of self-celebration. One celebrates the gift of life given by the Great Spirit. Self-pleasuring is an honoring of the Great Spirit. *Chuluaqui* is the energy that gives life to all things. *Quodoushka* means "sacred marriage" and is the sacred union of chuluaqui energies.

It is important and perhaps necessary that the heart pleasuring exercise be done a minimum of three times a week in a seven-day cycle for three months in order to change the body's coded pain tapes about sex. Every human being has coded memory tapes built in from childhood that determine his or her sexual vitality. With heart pleasuring we reencode body memory for three months, which is nature's cycle for change in the seasons.

Heart pleasuring is the most natural of things. Babies in the womb self-pleasure. They begin to stimulate themselves sexually in order to get turned head downward for a proper birth. The memory of this pleasurable experience is encoded somewhere in each of us. One way to find the memory of this early pleasure is to do the heart pleasuring exercise.

This exercise has little to do with how much you are making love in a sexual relationship. It is your own personal, separate celebration of the self. It is what enables you to come to your relationship with high sexual vitality, facilitating a merging of you and your partner in third- and fourth-level orgasms.

In our culture nearly everyone is locked up sexually. Our sexuality holds our fears, angers, and frustrations. These are the emotions we bring to our sexual partners if we have not freed ourselves with new sexual tapes. From the moment each child comes into the world, it will stimulate itself sexually if permitted. When you take a baby's clothes off, it will reach for its genitals—naturally and intuitively. Each time a parent slaps the baby's hand touching its genitalia, plates of "armor" encode over the body, and the baby's creativity, sensitivity, and actual spiritual power begin to be repressed.

Martha Spins Fire Eagle helped me reencode all this negative sexual coding during the time I was with her. I did everything she told me, religiously. She emphasized the heart pleasuring exercise.

"Humans are intended to be orgasmic," she said to me. "It's what the Great Spirit gave us, along with free will, to separate us from the animals. Animals walk naturally in beauty—in harmony and balance. The Great Spirit intended us to use our free will and orgasmicness to learn to walk in beauty. It's our precious gift. You must be aware of the preciousness and power of that gift. The heart pleasuring exercise will keep this in your memory and honor the giver of the gift. The orgasm will help you walk in beauty. Abstinence is against natural law. Celibacy is not. In celibacy you pleasure yourself and celebrate yourself. In abstinence you deny yourself and the gift of the Great One."

Quodoushka students learn there is a special way to calculate their sexual orende. I tell them to notice how often they have an orgasmic release without emotional or physical contact with another person. The response will fall into one of four cycles: (1) A person having an orgasmic release without contact with another person during a period of twenty-four to forty-eight hours is considered to have a sexual orende of five. (2) If the time period is two to five days, we consider the sexual orende to be four. (3) Five to fourteen days means the sexual orende is three. (4) Fourteen to twenty-eight days suggests the orende is two. My basic belief is this: If you are alive, you are orgasmic. Within a month you will have a first-level orgasm through a wet dream, an ejaculation, or other natural orgasm. I have known people to report an orgasmic response when they sneeze!

The orgasm comes to us because the Great Spirit gave it to us for our health. He knew we were going to put obstacles in our growth, so he gave us the orgasm to help us realign. The physical orgasm has one function: to stabilize the body, tune it, and keep it in alignment. That is the reason we were given the orgasm. Of all the other creatures, only the dolphin is able to have it.

Following is the heart pleasuring exercise, as Martha Spins Fire Eagle taught it to me:

First create your environment and your space in a sensual and spiritual way. Do this in a manner that brings pleasure to you. Use candles, incense, music—whatever you like. Do it in a bubble bath or any other place that suits you. The setting should be pleasing and stimulating. You are going to turn yourself on. You can use visual stimulation if you like. Then begin pleasuring yourself. This means with fingers, hands, water, pillows, vibrators—any object—or with fantasy. As you stimulate yourself, you will want to put your mental focus, your emotional feelings, your physical arousal, and your spiritual fire in the first chakra and continue to stimulate yourself with pleasure. Begin to breathe deeply. Really enjoy. This is an experience between you and the Great Spirit.

The breathing is basically like the waves of an ocean, like the wave in and then the underpull and the lull. You are pulling the energy from the first chakra up to the second. Pull it like a wave, pulling with your breath and muscles, then let it recede and flow back down to the first chakra. You are bringing it in and letting the wave go over, bringing it up and letting the wave go over. Do this at whatever speed suits you. You can do it slowly, you can do it quickly, or you can vary the pace.

As the arousal increases, let your breathing start rising so you bring the energy up from the first chakra. Be sure to stay connected to the first chakra. Push your breath down there. All your breath is going to the first chakra.

When the first chakra is lit, you begin to bring all the focus—emotionally, physically, mentally, and spiritually—to the third chakra and then down to the first. Now the wave is longer. Your breathing goes there and the heat starts rising. When the third is fired, do the same to the fourth, which is the heart chakra. At the fourth you are breathing deeply, the waves are longer. Probably your breath is accompanied by sounds of pleasure. Take yourself right to the edge of orgasm, so close that if you stimulate yourself five seconds more you will go into orgasm. Get as close to the edge as possible.

Hold on to the fourth-level images with full concentration of all your energies, but stop the stimulation and let the energy subside naturally. Stop only for a brief time. Let the energy drop only to the third or second chakra; you do not want it back in the first chakra at this time. Then start the self-pleasure again.

You have done what is called the "first rise of power." Continue as before. Bring the breath up to the heart again, almost reach orgasm, then let it subside. This is the second rise of power. Stimulate yourself again and bring up the third rise of power. Each time you should breathe in a higher level of intensity. Let the third rise of power subside.

The fourth time you bring the power up you are going to go for a complete orgasm. Draw all the energy into the heart chakra and let it burst up through your crown. The minute you hit that orgasmic peak, take a breath—

breathe deeply. You want to let the feelings leave your heart. Don't hold them there. Let your eyes roll back, let your body go into its natural arch, and let that wave of orgasm and sound take you out of your body. Ride that wave as long as you can stay in it.

That is the chuluaqui heart pleasuring exercise. If done regularly, it will increase your sexual orende, replace old pain tapes, regulate premature ejaculation, and generally increase your sense of well-being. When you have developed it, you can heart pleasure with your partner—which for me is about as close as I ever hope to get to Heaven.

◈◈◈ ABOUT THE AUTHOR ◈◈◈

Bill Wahlberg was born in Clifton, Colorado, in 1929, at the base of the western slopes of the Rocky Mountains. He reports that after ascertaining the presence of kindly parents who would look after him, he went to sleep until 1946, when he sensed correctly the importance of waking himself to face a ferocious opponent for the city wrestling championship at West Denver High. Following the match, he went promptly back to sleep. In 1952, a troop ship on which he dozed anchored in Inchon Harbor, Korea. Surrounded by explosions, burning oil drums, scary rifle fire, and the drama of war, Bill was deposited on the outskirts of Inchon City. He awakened. He suggests he has been more or less awake since that day.

In 1960, Bill organized a creative writing class at Fordson High in Dearborn, Michigan. He studied the material he taught his students and learned to write. In 1967, he was appointed to the counseling staff at Henry Ford Community College in Dearborn. For eighteen years he studied the human spirit on the campus. In 1985, he co-founded The Rainbow Bridge, Inc., an organization that helps people discover the best of their inner resources, and left "higher education" to find his way as a psychotherapist.

Currently, Bill is busy leading three ongoing weekly psychotherapy groups, consulting, sponsoring workshops, and seeing individual clients. In addition, one weekend a month, ten months a year, he and his wife, Judy, facilitate a dynamic and intensive group called Community 15. Fortified by a belief that mature love is the strongest healing power on Earth, they combine modern psychological principles with vision questing and ancient ceremonial traditions to help Community members heal from traumatic experiences of their childhood. During Community weekends, participants rediscover the importance of heartfelt communication between family and clan members.

Bill and his wife Judy are presently working on a book narrating the significance for the culture when family members feel that they are seen, heard, and respected by each other. *Community: The Magical Journey* describes their inspirational and magical experiences leading Community 15.

BOOKS OF RELATED INTEREST
BY BEAR & COMPANY

ANCIENT VOICES, CURRENT AFFAIRS
The Legend of the Rainbow Warriors
by Steven McFadden

CRYING FOR A DREAM
The World Through Native American Eyes
by Richard Erdoes

GIFT OF POWER
The Life and Teachings of a Lakota Medicine Man
by Archie Fire Lame Deer and Richard Erdoes

JOURNEY TO THE FOUR DIRECTIONS
Book One of Teachings of the Feathered Serpent
by Jim Berenholtz

MEDICINE CARDS
The Discovery of Power Through the Ways of Animals
by Jamie Sams & David Carson

PROFILES IN WISDOM
Native Elders Speak about the Earth
by Steven McFadden

SEXUAL PEACE
Beyond the Dominator Virus
by Michael Sky

Contact your local bookseller or write to:

BEAR & COMPANY
P.O. BOX 2860
Santa Fe, NM 87504-2860